IMAGES
of America

AROUND FARMERSVILLE

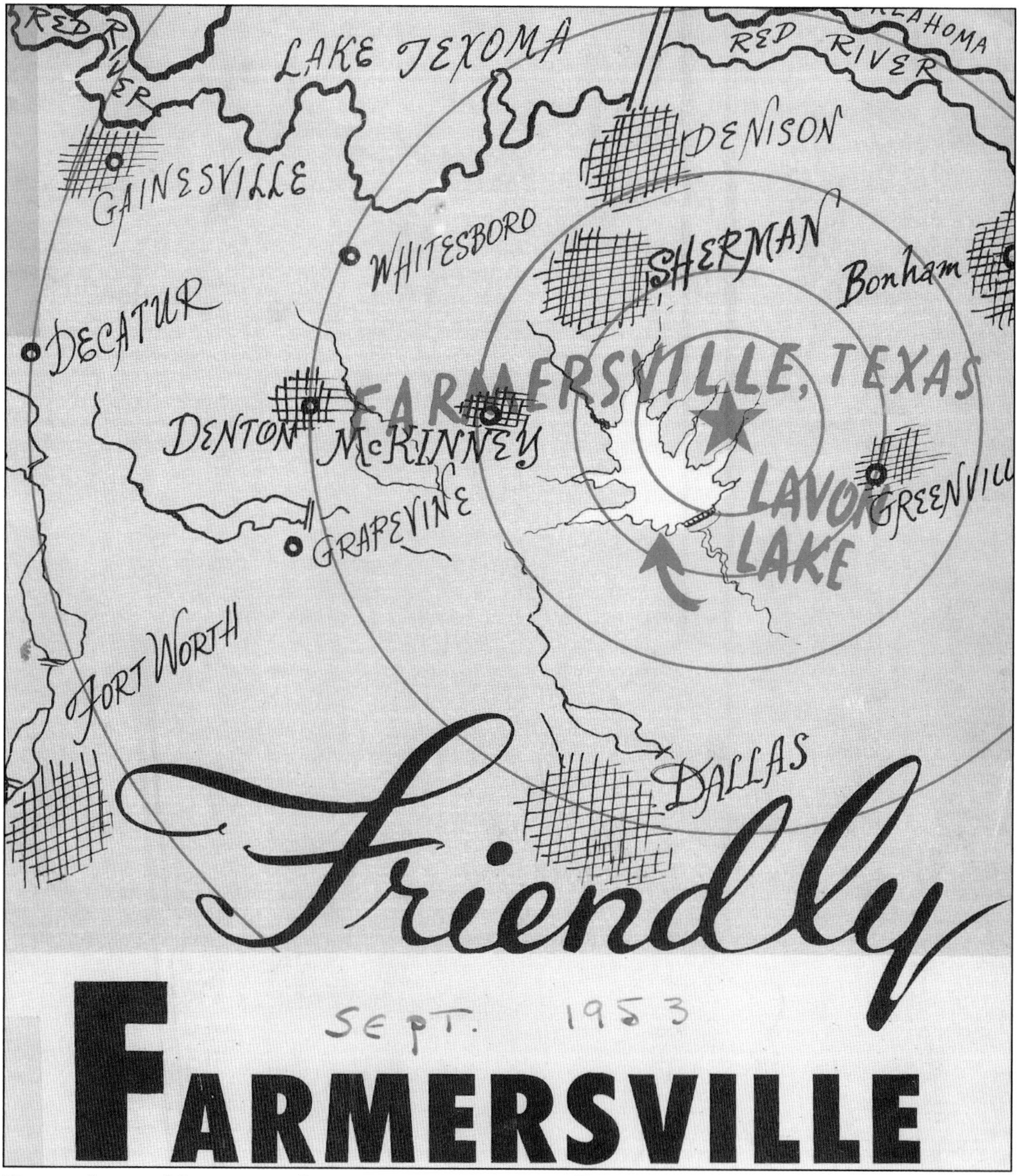

Due to the need for more and more water in many small towns scattered around the area, a large supply of water became necessary in order to meet those needs. Taking in many acres of land surrounding it, construction of Lake Lavon began in 1948. The North Texas Municipal Water District was created in 1951, with construction of the lake completed in 1954. Farmersville was the first city to receive water from the new lake, even before construction was complete. Lake Lavon is within three miles of Farmersville city limits, and, fortunately, has an 80-mile shorefront. It supplies approximately 40 surrounding cities with water.

ON THE COVER: Onions became a very important part of the economy in Farmersville in the 1920s and 1930s. Charles Rike, a local druggist and self-made historian, made this display for the first onion festival in 1935, arranging it in the window of his drugstore. His aim was to show many of the ways the lowly onion could be used in medicine, cosmetics, and the arts.

IMAGES
of America

AROUND FARMERSVILLE

Pansy Hundley

ARCADIA
PUBLISHING

ISBN 978-0-7385-7971-9

Published by Arcadia Publishing
Charleston, South Carolina

Printed in the United States of America

Library of Congress Control Number: 2010938465

For all general information, please contact Arcadia Publishing:
Telephone 843-853-2070
Fax 843-853-0044
E-mail sales@arcadiapublishing.com
For customer service and orders:
Toll-Free 1-888-313-2665

Visit us on the Internet at www.arcadiapublishing.com

I feel that because of his untiring, continuous preservation of any historical information that came into his hands, Charles Rike should be remembered. This book is dedicated to him for his foresight in that preservation.

CONTENTS

ACKNOWLEDGMENTS

The majority of the images in this book are from the collection of historical photographs that Charles Rike kept over the many years that he was a pharmacist and a citizen of Farmersville. Much of the history in written form was from newspaper clippings that he made into scrapbooks. During my 28 years with the library, which is named after Charlie, when I would put another piece of history in a file or make a new file, I would say to him in my mind, "Okay, I'm helping you here, Charlie." And I felt that I was. He was so conscientious in preserving so much, that I felt it was part of my job to continue to preserve that history. There are about five or six large photograph albums in the library that I've filled with pictures that Charlie had kept through the years. I felt that those pictures, that history, should be made available for anyone interested to look through. And many people did look. Sometimes a couple had bought an older house in town and came looking for the history or pictures of the original house. There were men that had bought an old building on the square, looking for that same information. Charlie's collecting, and the good he did in preserving so much, will continue for many years.

The Farmersville Historical Society has been so cooperative with anything they could do to help. Rita Roose, Glenda Hart, Ann Rose, and Wynelle Mitchell all have helped with this book of memories. Rita Roose was kin to everybody in the old town, so she was talking about her ancestors.

Jerry Hart has been a fount of information. He has lived here all of his life. He's one of those boys who went to look in the door of the jail to see who was there.

Thanks to all of these and more. My daughter Suzanne has helped immeasurably with that confounded new computer. Trisha Dowell has given much help and support. If I've missed anyone, just know that your help, in whatever way, was so appreciated.

INTRODUCTION

The history of Farmersville begins with a family named Yeary. Walter Yeary, a native of Tennessee, along with seven other families, came to Texas in 1839. They originally settled in Honey Grove, a small town in Fannin County. Due to an Indian attack in the early days and other hardships, Yeary and his father-in-law, Moses Jones, along with John Haven and Hugh Gotcher (other members of the Honey Grove settlement) moved to Collin County in 1845. In that same year, Yeary's wife gave birth to a son, John, the first child born here.

Yeary set up a frontier store about three miles from the present location of Farmersville, which people called "Yeary's Place." This small store handled such stock items as sugar, flour, coffee, whiskey, lead, powder, and the like. Most of these were hauled from Jefferson, which was then a very busy entry to Texas. On one trip to secure needed supplies, sugar came in before other items. For several days, all Yeary had to sell was sugar. Through this, "Yeary's Place" suddenly became "Sugar Hill." It's not hard to imagine the teasing that brought about this change of name, by all the settlers needing supplies to cook with while only sugar was available.

Sugar Hill consisted of one or two stores and a saloon. In 1854, on Christmas Eve, with whiskey flowing freely in the saloon, an argument ensued and a brawl began. Capt. John Yeary, acting as peacemaker, was shot. Innocent bystanders John H. Glass and Samuel Glass—who were brothers, ages 19 and 22—were also killed.

Captain Yeary had fought in the War of 1812 and participated in the Battle of New Orleans. He was the father of Walter Yeary. His death and the other useless killings seemed to begin an exodus to a nearby settlement, at one time called White Hall, which had several stores and had been there since 1850.

That small settlement eventually became Farmersville. It was given that name around 1857. Several citizens, in casting about for a name, settled on the name suggested by Johnny Hendrex, since that was the occupation of most of the people in the area.

William Gotcher, related to an original settler, gave the land for a square. He laid off the square on March 4, 1859, and deeded the square from Washington Street to McKinney Street and North Main to South Main Streets, selling lots around the square to businessmen. A handwritten copy of the original deed, notarized by Moses Jones, is in the possession of Farmersville. Farmersville is located on a portion of the W. Williams survey, a land grant given by Anson Jones, president of the Republic of Texas. The original patent was dated November 16, 1845.

The original site of the square was marked by a round metal marker in the street. Until the square was paved, there was a bois d'arc post with three nails in it marking the spot. Brick pavement was laid down in the mid 1920s. The town was incorporated in June 1873. There was a slow but steady growth in population and businesses.

In 1885, Pendleton, Yeary, and Rike opened the first drugstore. From that time forward, until 1965, when ill health forced Charles Rike to retire, there had been a Rike working in a drugstore in Farmersville.

The *Farmersville Times* printed its first issue on March 23, 1885, and is still in business in 2011. The *Farmersville Times* is the oldest newspaper in Collin County.

Farmersville has suffered three disastrous fires, the first being in 1886. The south side of the square was destroyed after a jovial customer in the Tidal Wave Saloon evidently dropped an oil lamp. In 1890, half of the north side of the square was swept by fire around 1:30 a.m. All wooden structures burned, equaling about 15 businesses. Plans were then made to replace the wood with brick or rock buildings.

In 1906, fire struck yet again. The east side of the square was destroyed. Farmersville had a new fire wagon, but new hoses would not fit the newly installed hydrants. McKinney and Greenville, neighboring towns, came to help, to no avail. The fire burned from the Aston Building, made of rock, to the Masonic Temple, also made of rock. These are the only two original buildings still standing to the present day. At least nine buildings, including the First National Bank, were destroyed. Friendly Farmersville came back again, however. Within weeks, the ruins were cleared and new buildings were being constructed.

In the early 1900s, cotton became king in many areas of Collin County. Farmersville was one of the centers of the cotton-producing areas for the next several years, shipping 12,000 cotton bales in 1900. Then, during the 1920s and 1930s, onions were being planted in many of those cotton fields as the crop took over the economy in Farmersville. Until the late 1930s, more than 1,000 cars of onions were shipped yearly by rail. The first Onion Festival was held in Farmersville in 1935, and continued for several years. However, the festival was suspended during World War II.

Farmersville survived the Depression years and, even though most farming has ceased, the town has thrived. New stores have opened, including antique stores and restaurants. New industries have moved to the area and are flourishing. Land has been purchased for a branch of the Collin County Community College to build there in the future.

There are four Farmersville schools now in existence. Tatum Elementary School begins the children's education. Since the N. O. Wright Gymnasium and Field House were damaged by a tornado, they were demolished. A larger middle school was erected, replacing the one that had been there for several years. The new high school was built on Highway 78, near the old building. That previous high school is now the junior high school.

Highway 380, the road that leads to Greenville and McKinney—and the road so many will travel when the college is built—is being widened at this time. Even though the construction is annoying, when finished, it will greatly enhance Farmersville.

New housing developments have been built in the past few years, and new schools have been enlarged and updated. With those additions to the town, it is felt that as the community college is built in the next few years, Farmersville will change and grow in many ways.

One

A Small Town Is Established

Farmersville was built on part of the land grant given in the W. Williams survey for service in the fight for Texas independence from Mexico.

More and more land was homesteaded. Collin County was included in "Peters Colony," which was a Texas land grant totaling 16,000 square miles, given in 1841 to "introduce" into Texas a colony of 600 families within three years.

According to descriptions made by Joshua Gotcher, an early settler of the area, at the beginning of the settlement the land was a vast prairie, cut here and there by timber, which marked the course of some little streams. There was game everywhere—bear, wolves, wild cats, turkey, and other animals roamed the area. Deer traveled in great herds. Wild horses were plentiful. The few Indians who visited the area were friendly.

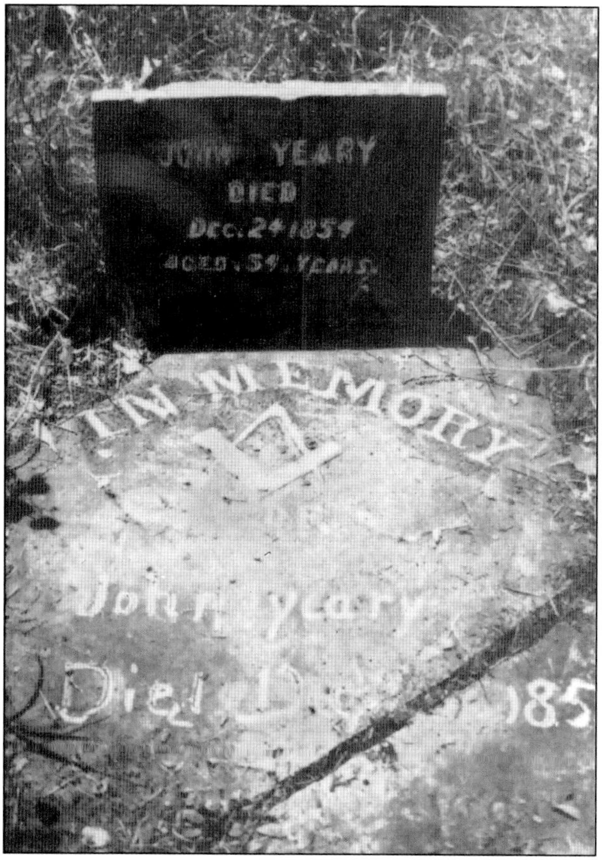

Capt. John Yeary was killed while acting as peacemaker in the saloon brawl at Sugar Hill on December 24, 1854. Some of the saloon-goers, having imbibed rather too freely, were involved in the shooting in which Yeary, along with the two Glass brothers, were killed. Yeary is buried in the Jones-Yeary Cemetery located northeast of Farmersville.

Brothers John H. Glass and Samuel Glass, ages 19 and 22, were killed in the saloon brawl at Sugar Hill on December 24, 1854. They were innocent bystanders. The two brothers were buried in a double grave in the Glass-Chapman Cemetery west of Farmersville. Their marker reads, "Sacred Memory of John H. Glass, Died December 24, 1854. 22 years old. Samuel M. Glass, Died December 24, 1854, 19 years old. These deaths were due to trouble at old Sugar Hill."

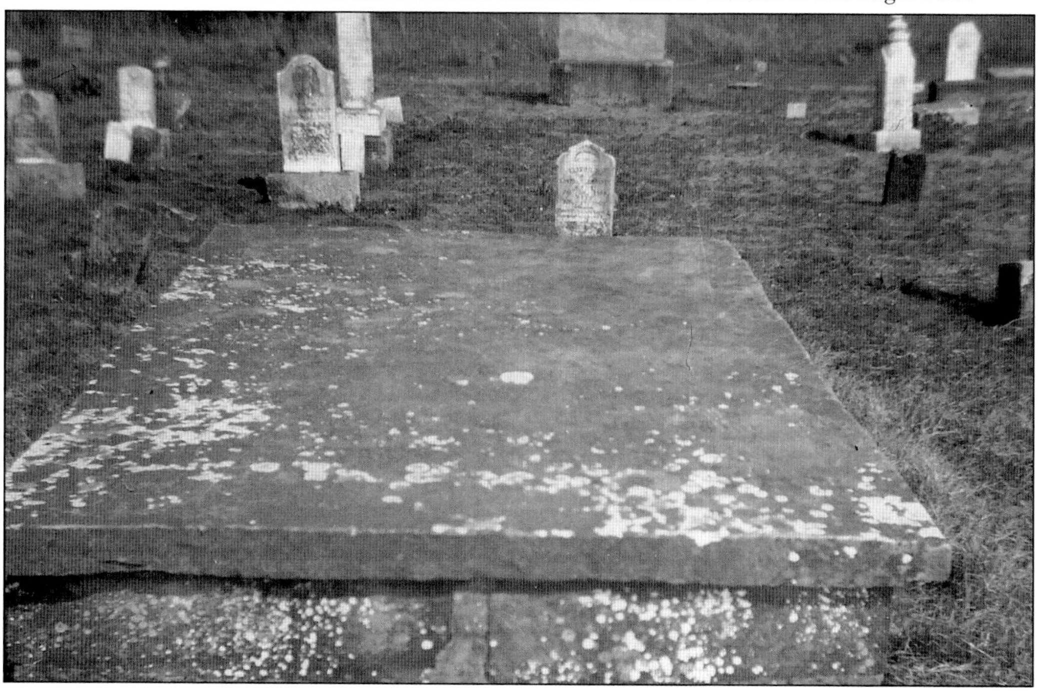

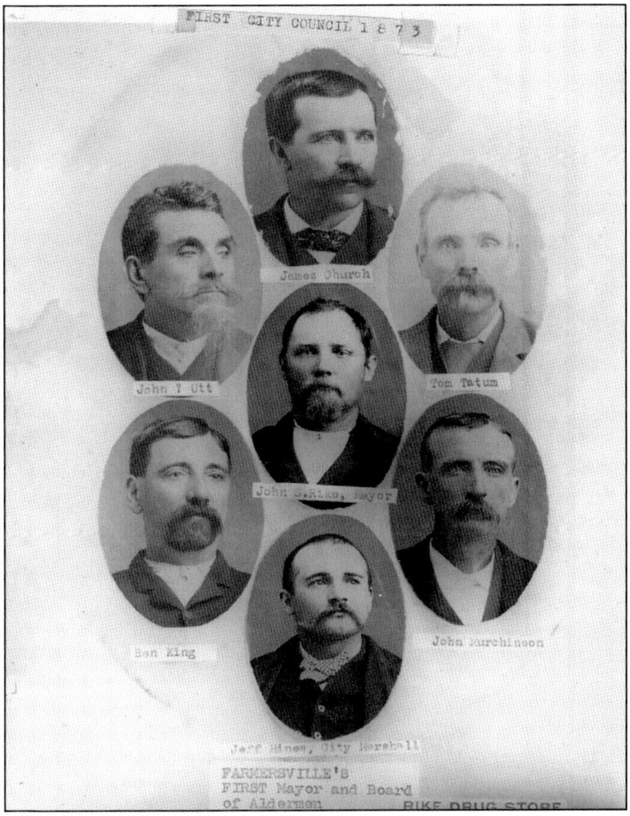

This is the first city council, or "First Mayor and Board of Alderman" as the text reads, for the newly incorporated city of Farmersville in 1873. The town had been in existence for nearly 20 years prior to the incorporation. Pictured in the center is the first city mayor, John S. Rike. Aldermen, reading clockwise from the top, are James Church, Tom Tatum, John Murchison, Jeff Hines (city marshall), Ben King, and John Utt.

Pictured is the building on South Main Street that now houses city hall. This was the location of the volunteer fire department until it moved in later years. Remodeling was done, making this the present city hall, with city council chambers located at the far end of the building. That section, with the three large windows, is where the generators were located back in the 1930s.

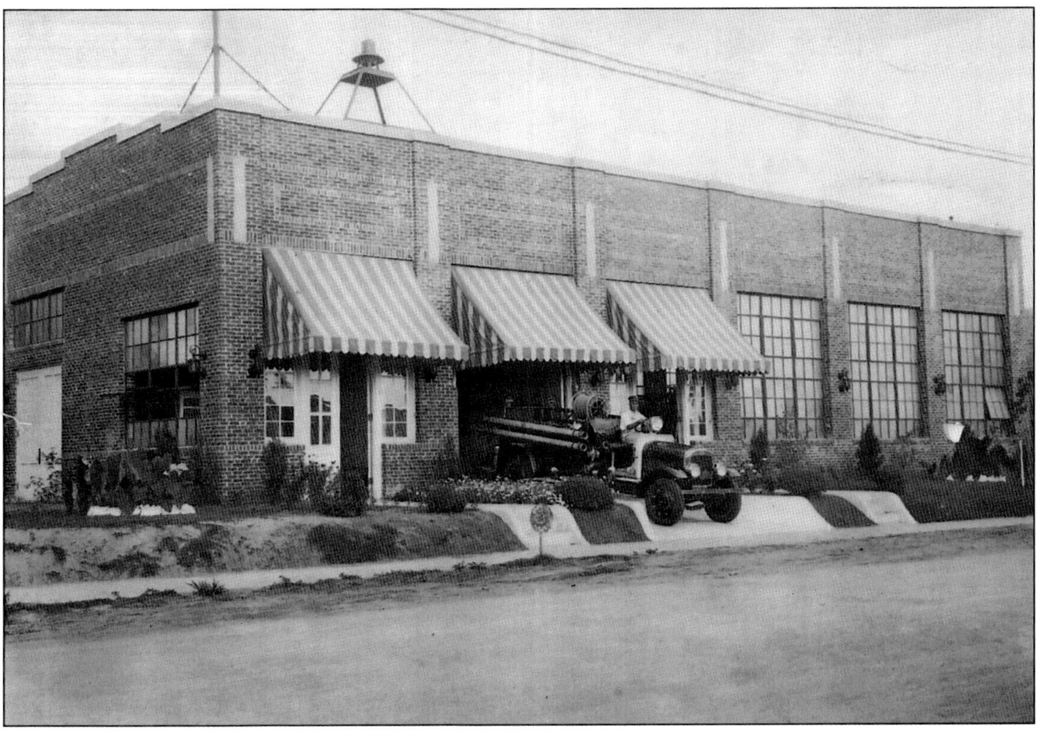

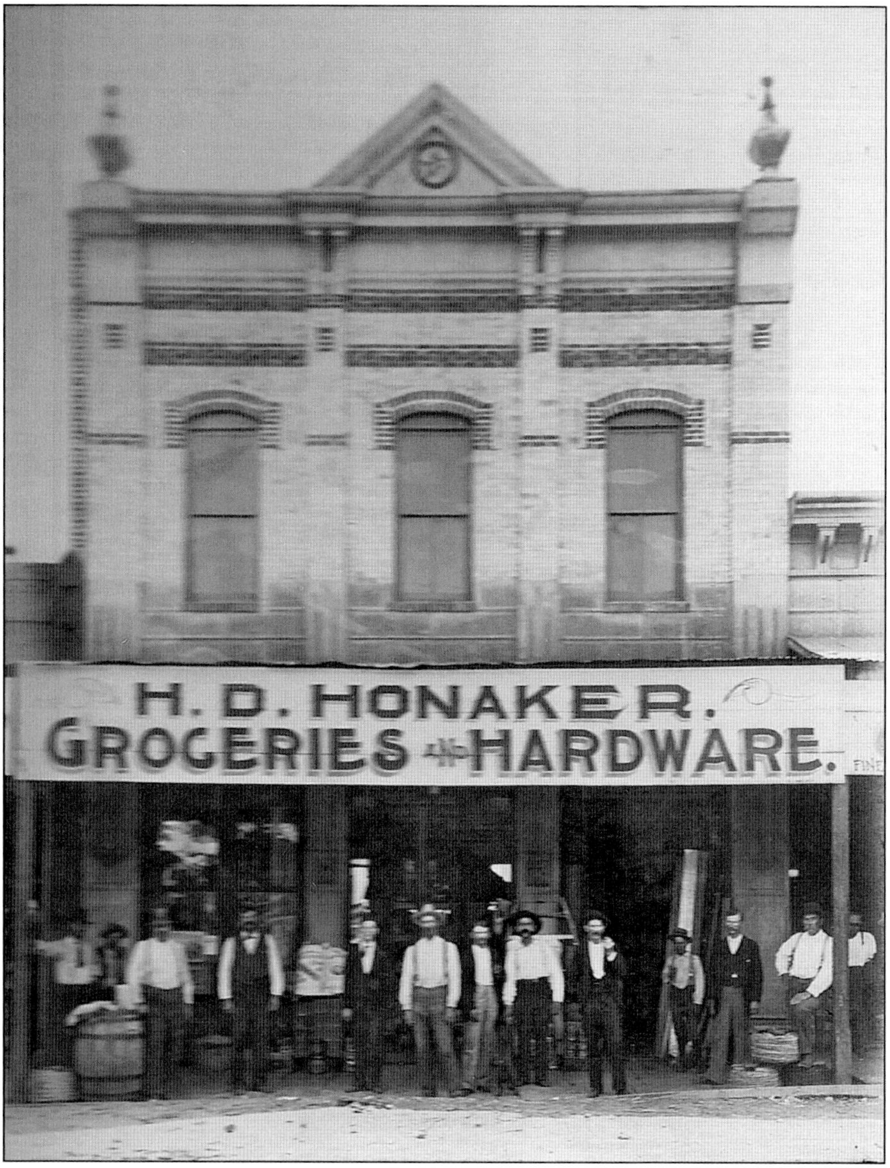

The Aston Building was originally built in 1888 by J. A. Aston and his brother, using local rock and stone that was quarried from the rock pit of R. A. Rike. The front-facing stones were hand cut, and chisel marks are still visible on many of them. Over the years, several businesses have occupied the building. Standing vacant for many years, the building had deteriorated to the point that only the front and walls remained standing. Purchased and restored by Bob Heath in 2007, the building now greets visitors to shining wood and wrought iron. Wood from the original building rafters were used to build the stairs, estimated to be 120 years old. An entry step was uncovered, revealing these words: "J. A. Aston and brother." It is believed to be in remembrance of J. A. Aston by his brother, W. S., since he died before the building was completed originally. The Aston Building is currently on the National Register of Historic Places. The image above, taken around 1895, shows that at that time, H. D. Honaker Groceries and Hardware did business there. Standing, from left to right, are two unidentified, H. D. Honaker, unidentified, Milburn Honaker, five unidentified, Johnny Honaker, and two unidentified.

In 1900, Farmersville was the wealthiest town of its size in Texas and third in the United States. The population was 1,856, according to the U.S. census, a gain of more than 600 during the past decade. There was much discussion over naming the town. At a meeting of citizens, Johnny Hendrex suggested, since this was a community of farmers, that the town be called Farmersville. And it was so.

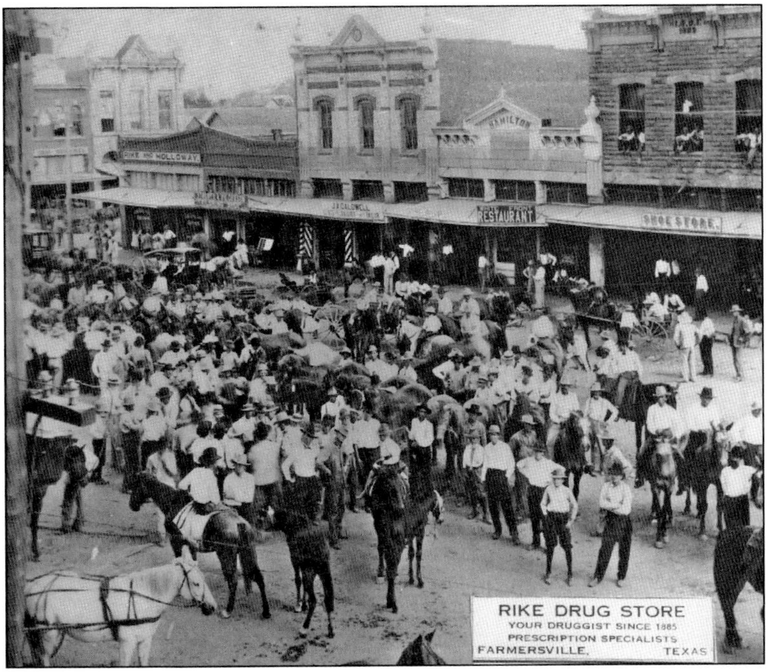

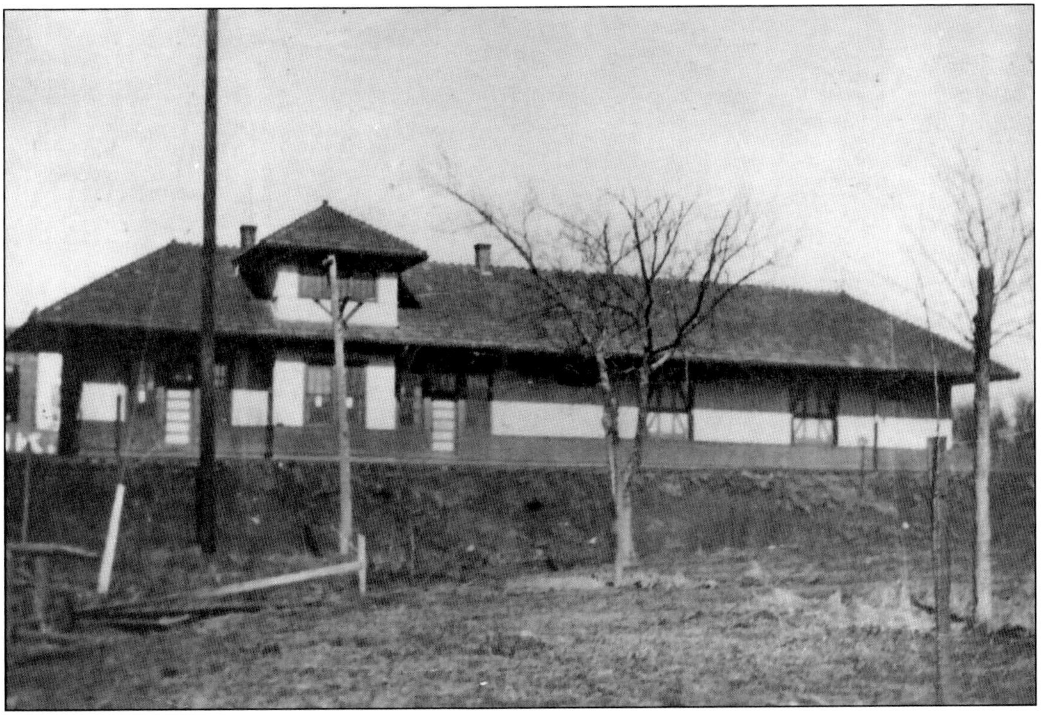

This photograph was taken around 1920 when two passenger trains made two round-trips to McKinney and Greenville daily. The first railroad to reach Farmersville and McKinney was in 1886. In 1956, the last regular passenger train ran from Farmersville on the Santa Fe Railroad. When the railroads came to town in 1883 and 1887, Farmersville boomed. Many trains were met by horses or carriages, for a return to their home or next destination.

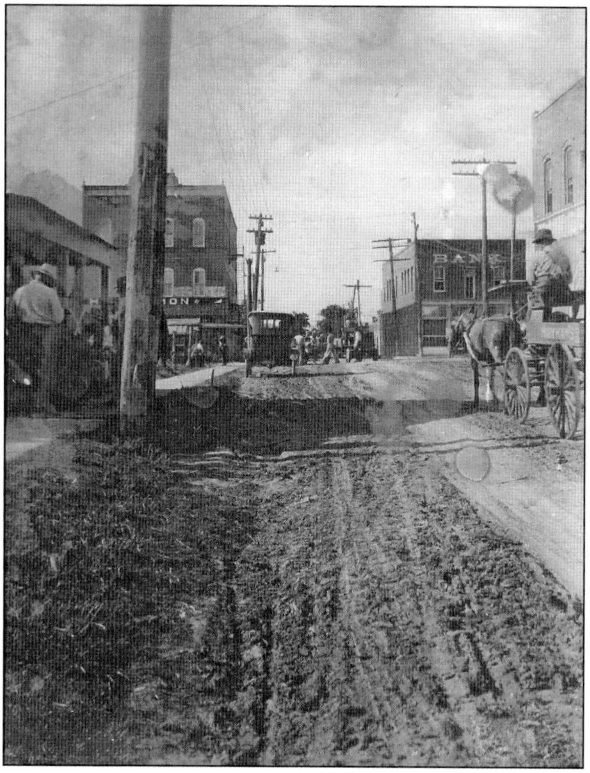

This is South Washington Street in May 1922, looking north from the Baptist church. The building with "Bank" written on it is now Farmersville Auto Supply. The large building on the left is known as the Merle Norman Building and is home to a business on the bottom floor. The store to the right, by the side of the horse and wagon, is now Dyer Drug. There is concrete on that street now, replacing the mud.

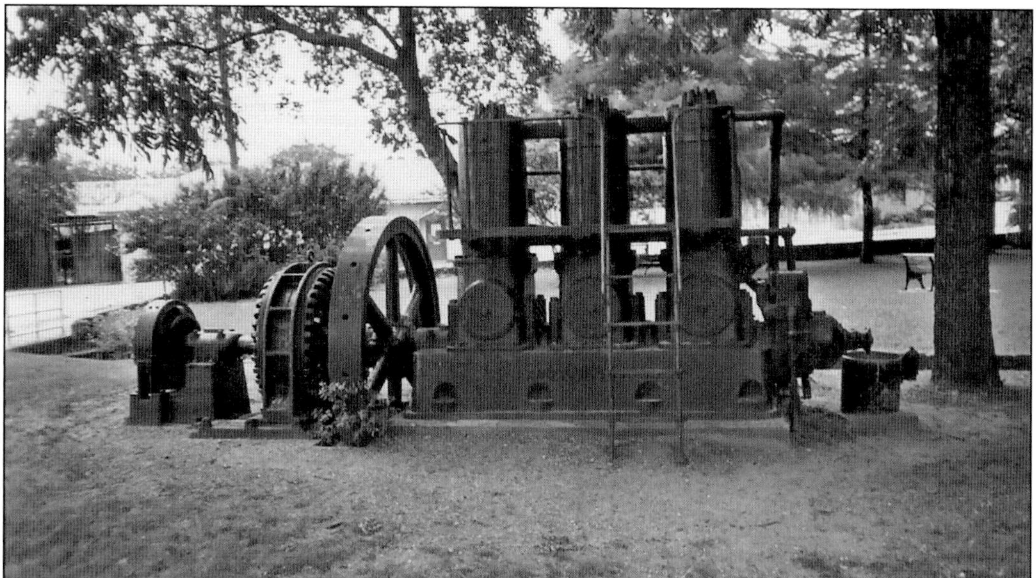

The municipal lights were turned on for the first time in 1930. Farmersville was the first municipality in Collin County to own its own electric facilities. This picture shows one of the generators that were used to generate the power. Waldo Spain, Bill McElyer, and Jimmy Morrow worked three eight-hour shifts to upkeep the generators that made the electricity in good running order. When no longer used, this generator was placed in the park for children to investigate. (Courtesy of Jerry Hart.)

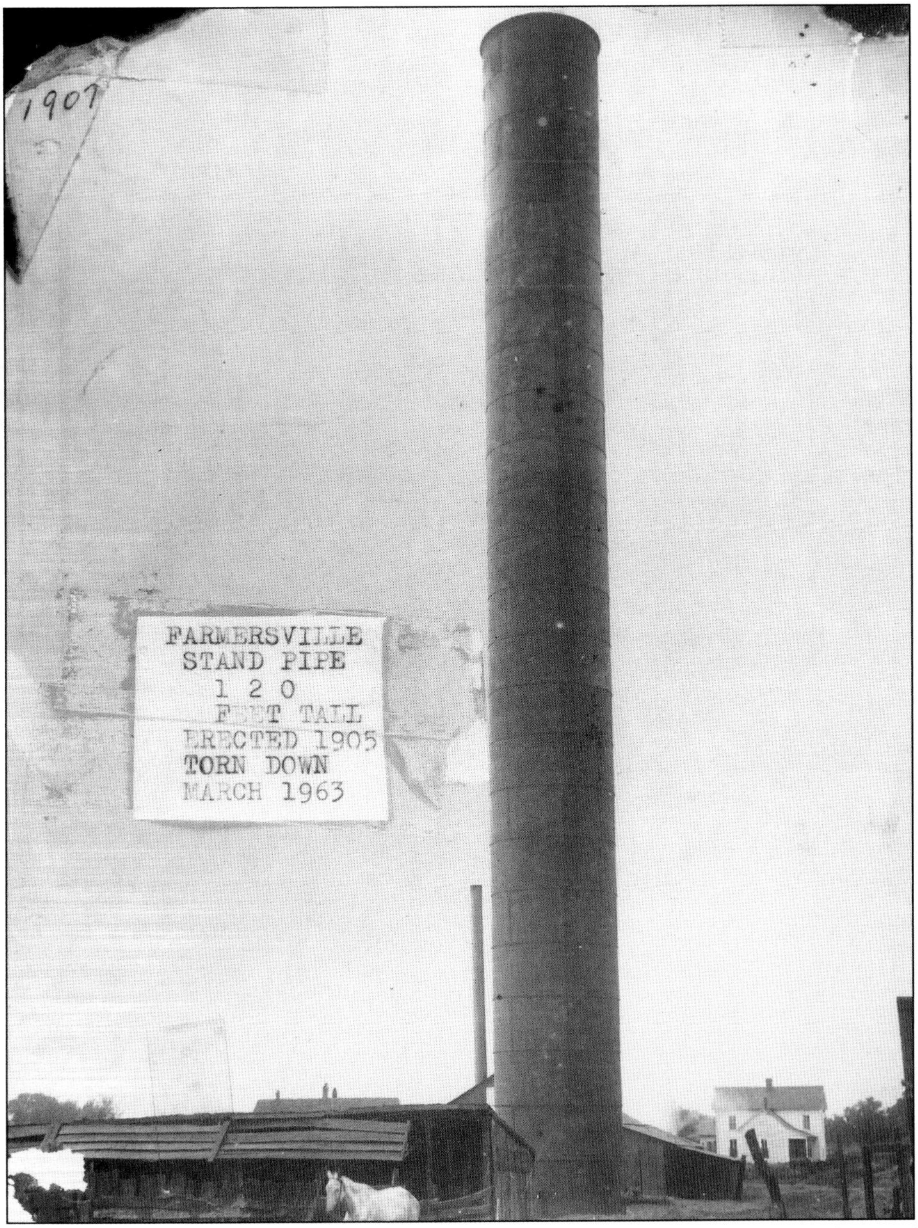

With the need for a larger water supply, city council made a contract around 1901 for a well that it hoped would supply artesian water. Drilling was started in 1902, and a 120-foot standpipe was erected with a capacity of 101,000 gallons. The well was completed in 1905, drilled to approximately 1,700 feet. The water contained an enormous amount of salt and other minerals and could not be used for drinking. In 1918, the well was deepened to 2,500 feet with no improvement in the quality of water. In 1921, the city constructed a lake covering 42 acres, one mile southeast of town, which gave an ample amount of water for several years. However, by 1934, as more and more water was needed, a second lake was built that covered 57 acres and was located 1,400 feet south of the first lake. Construction of Lake Lavon began in 1948, and the city contracted to receive water from it before completion. The standpipe was torn down in March 1963, and the well was filled in.

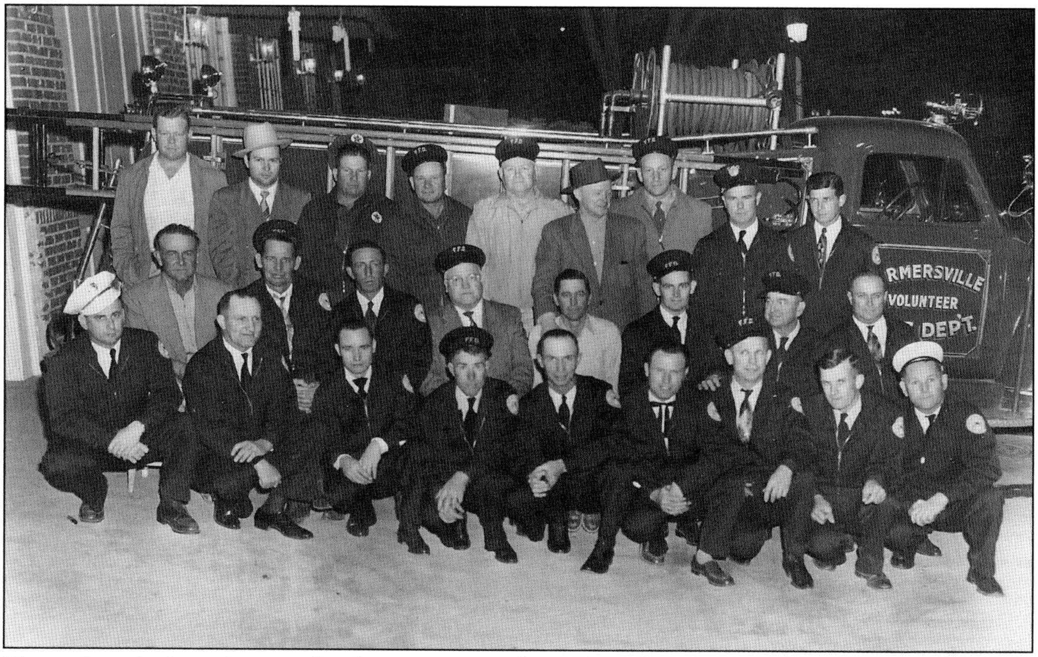

Shown here is the volunteer fire department in the early 1950s. Farmersville is fortunate to have an excellent fire department. There have been 23 fire chiefs since the 1950s. The fire department consists mainly of volunteers to this day.

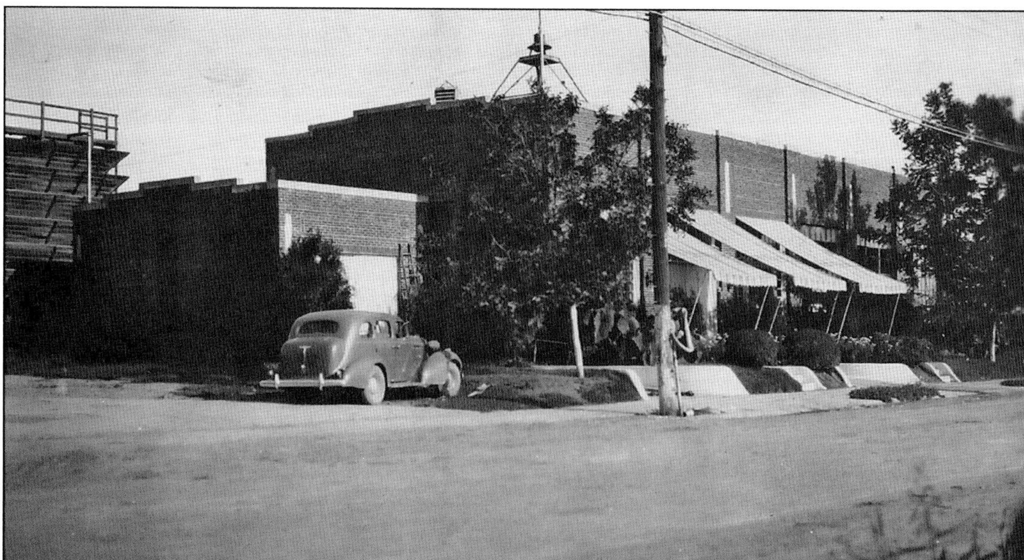

This photograph shows the old fire department building. At one time, this structure housed the police station. The lone jail cell was located at the back of the building with a wooden door opening to the outside. Immediately inside was the cell with a metal door. During the summer, the wooden door would be left open for ventilation. The story goes that the boys in town could go down to the jail to see who had landed there overnight.

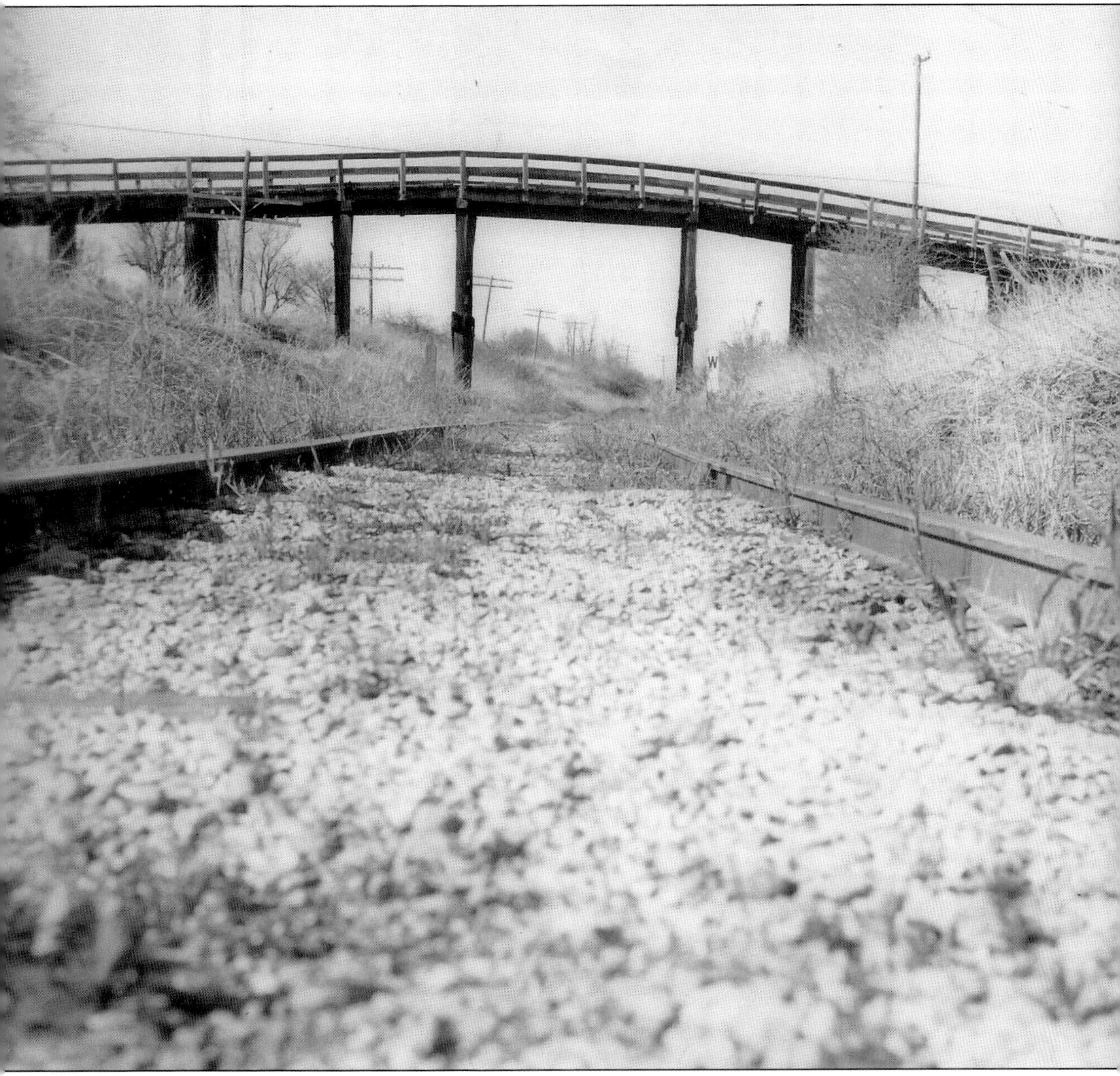

This unique, one-way overhead bridge, built in 1884–1885, was destroyed in 1970. The bridge sat on piers that were made of bois d'arc, a native wood that rots very little. The piers were milled at a local sawmill, operated by Sam Carver. That mill felled hundreds of bois d'arc trees for pilings used by the Santa Fe Railroad in building bridges on the line between Dallas and Paris, Texas. The bridge rose 25 feet over the Atchison, Topeka, and Santa Fe Railroad right-of-way and was 200-feet long, including its ramps. Many in Farmersville felt the bridge was a landmark and should be kept intact. Many adults speak of daring feats accomplished on that bridge in their younger days. On a dare, one young man turned his Model A Ford around in the center of the bridge, which was 12 to 15 feet wide. Another daring soul walked across the rails that spanned the top of the bridge.

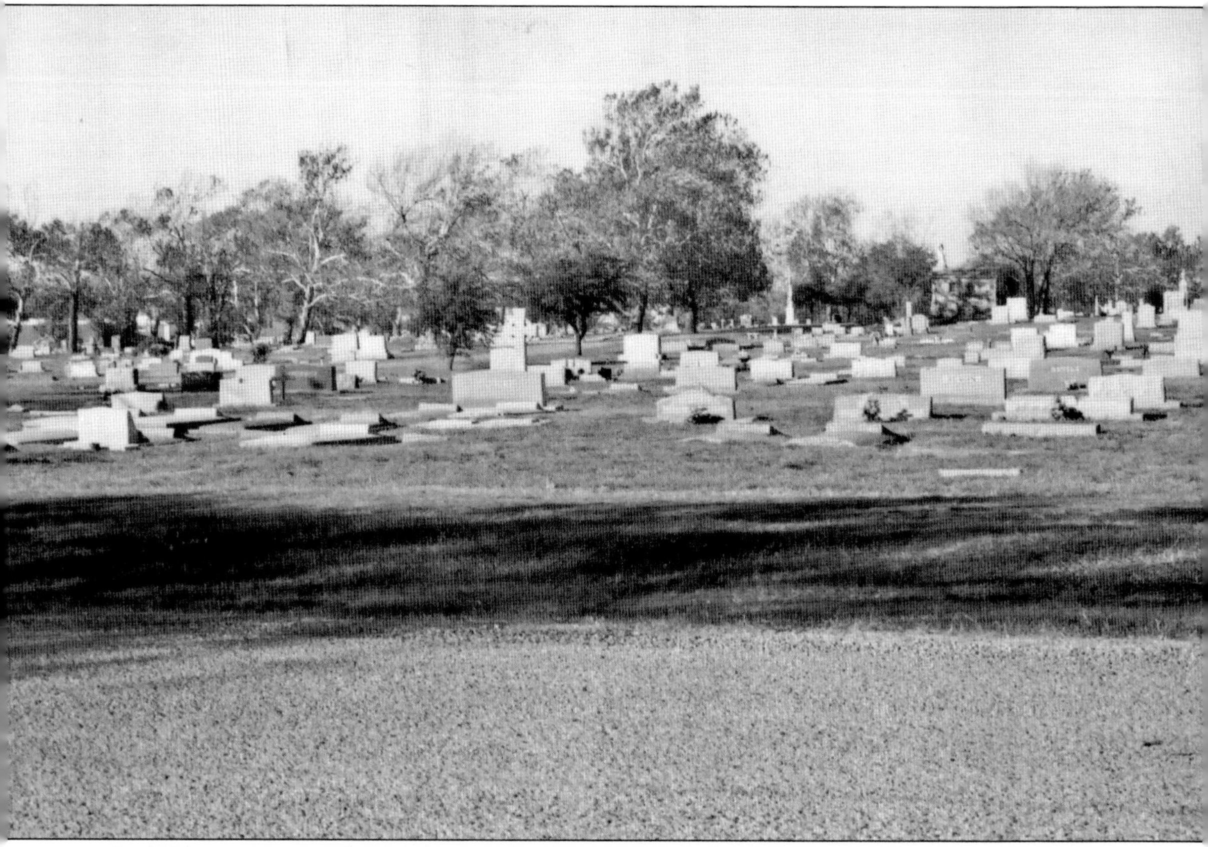

In 1899, citizens saw the need for a cemetery nearer to town. They chose 20 acres of land about one mile north of the square. The first burial was that of Mrs. Sid Hicks (Mattie Robinson). Many bodies were brought from outlying rural cemeteries and private graveyards and were interred in the new cemetery. There are numerous small cemeteries located around Farmersville. Many families have, in years past, buried their loved ones on land they owned. As the families have all passed on, there are instances where just one or two graves are in the middle of land that someone else has bought. Many times, these isolated graves are unreachable for descendants, and the land is even posted. The cemetery is referred to as "IOOF," short for Independent Order of Odd Fellows. It has expanded immensely, but burial lots are still available.

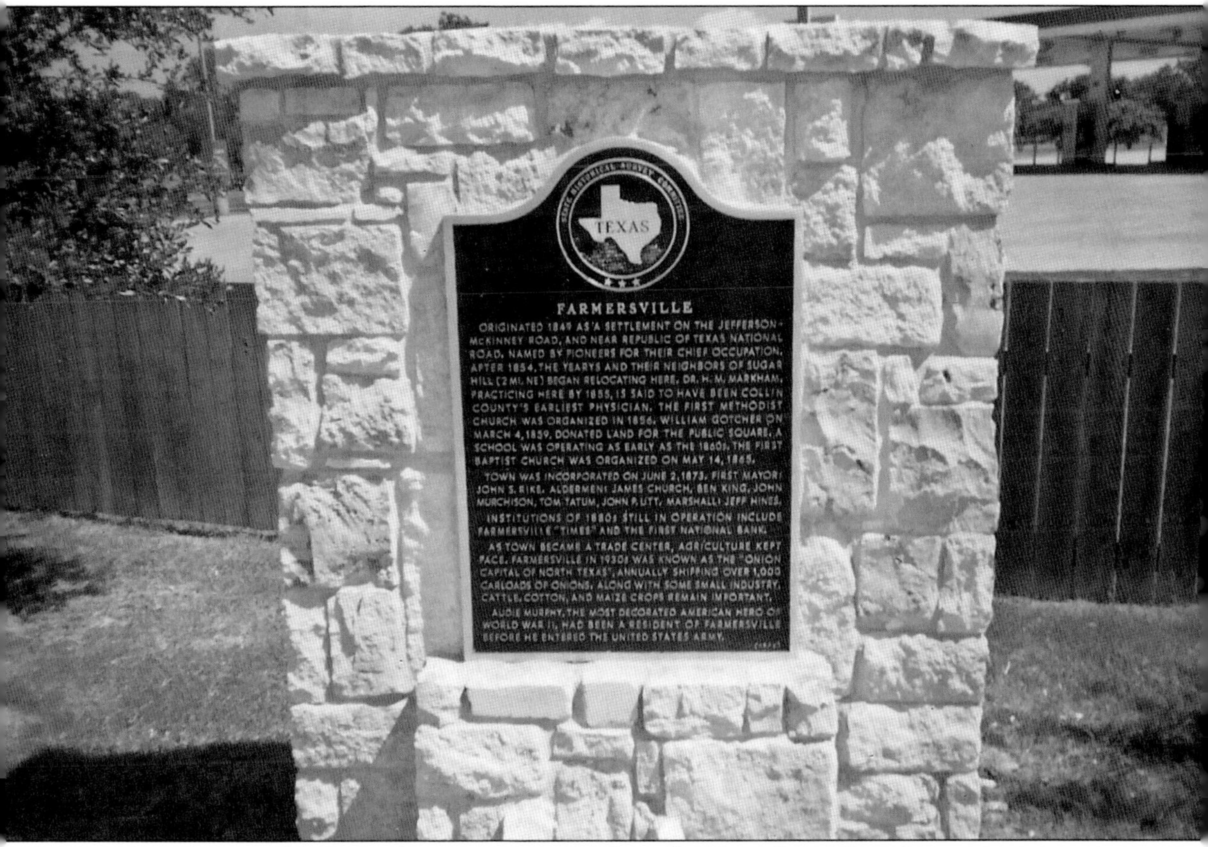

In 1996, Farmersville received a Texas Historical Marker. It is located at the intersection of Farmersville Parkway and Highway 78. A short rock wall was constructed to hold the marker.

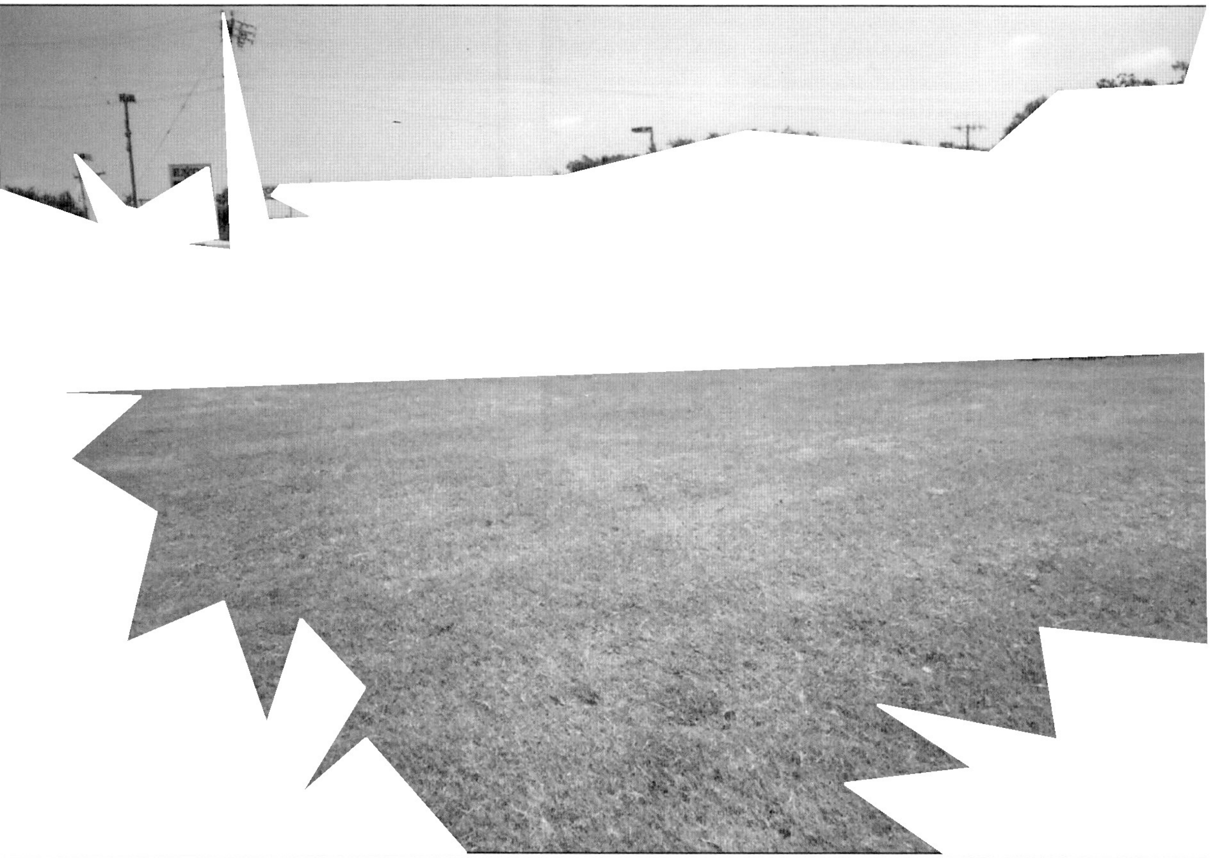

A long wall, constructed of the same rock as the marker in the previous photograph, inscribed with the name of the town, was built at the marker location and surrounded by planted shrubbery, making a small park of its location. Farmersville was named a Main Street City in 2000. There has been a downtown revitalization through historic preservation, with $9.9 million invested in downtown since 2000. Farmersville is one of 91 Texas Main Street Cities.

Two

Remembering the Ancestors

So many of the ancestors who came in the early years of Farmersville stayed when they settled here. Many of them had moved about to other locations over the years. But this area seemed to have what they were looking for, and they built a good life. There are still those same names two or there generations later.

There are streets with the names of most all of those earlier settlers. That speaks well for the area. They came and they stayed and they made a mark on the area.

The Charles Rike Library has a huge collection of many books of some of these families. It has other genealogical information that has been collected or bought over the years. There is historical information on Collin County, as well as microfilm for the county, and a large collection of obituaries that have been kept over the years. The library collection also has books showing the location of graves in the cemetery in town, and books about burials in many of the small cemeteries located about the area.

1850 CENSUS OF SUGAR HILL

STULLER, D. H. and wife, Mary C.

DEWUSE, Wm. G. and wife, Mary and 2 children

DUPREY, M. D. and wife, Mary, 3 children and 1 slave

PATTERSON, Robert, 3 children and 4 slaves

GOTCHER, Joshua and wife

GOTCHER, William and wife, Mary and 7 children

HAVENS, John and wife, 6 children and Mary Gotcher

GOTCHER, Hugh and wife and 5 children

*YEARY, John and wife, Mary E., 4 children and 2 slaves

**YEARY, Walter and wife, Margaret and 2 children

YEARY, David and wife and 1 child

YEARY, J. W. and wife and 1 child

JONES, Rev. Moses and wife and 5 children

HARVICK, Martin and wife, Malvinia, 4 children and 1 slave (In later years, Malvinia's name appears as: Malvina; apparently either is correct, and one and the same)

*JOHN YEARY was our Great Grandfather.

**WALTER YEARY was our Grandfather; David and J(ames) W. were his brothers

Martin Harvick was son-in-law of John Yeary; his wife, Malvinia, the red-haired girl whom the Indians wished to capture in the 1841 raid, was John Yeary's oldest daughter.

14

This 1850 census shows the population of Sugar Hill that year. It lists the family names of those that first settled Sugar Hill and the location of the fatal shooting of Capt. John Yeary and the two Glass brothers in the local saloon.

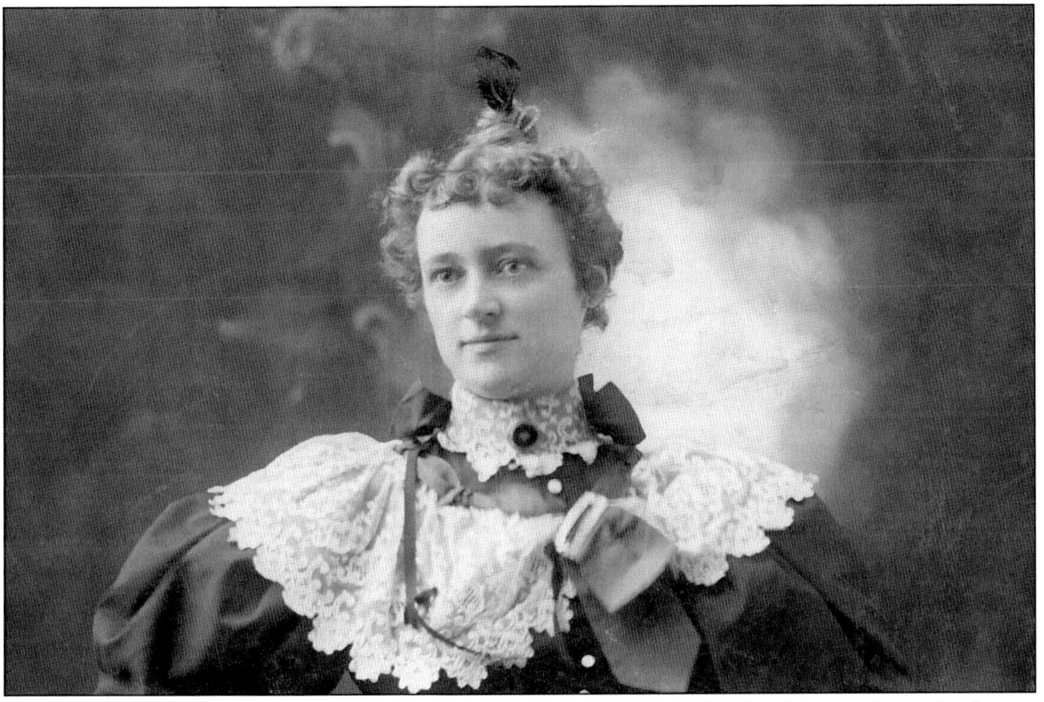

Ida Sharp is pictured here in 1880 wearing an elaborate dress of the day. Notice the wide sleeves and variety of lace she is adorned with.

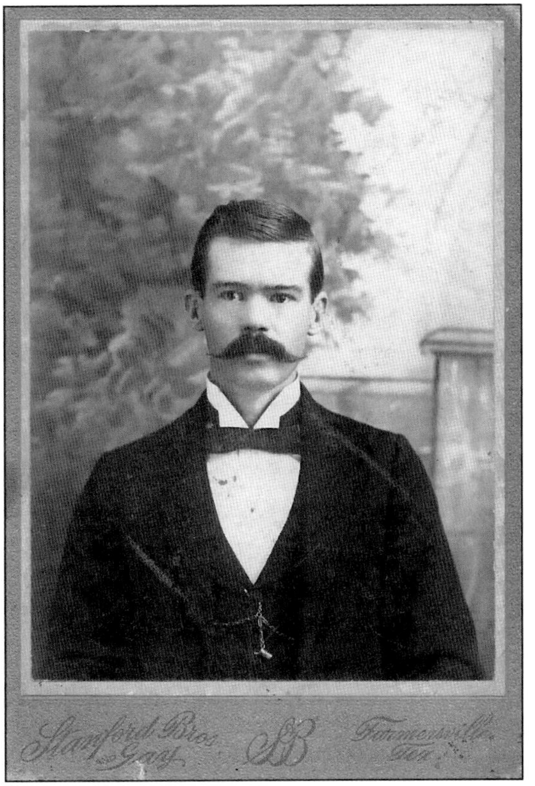

This young man is Joe Clements. Note the photographer's name. Stanford Brothers operated their studio for many years in Farmersville.

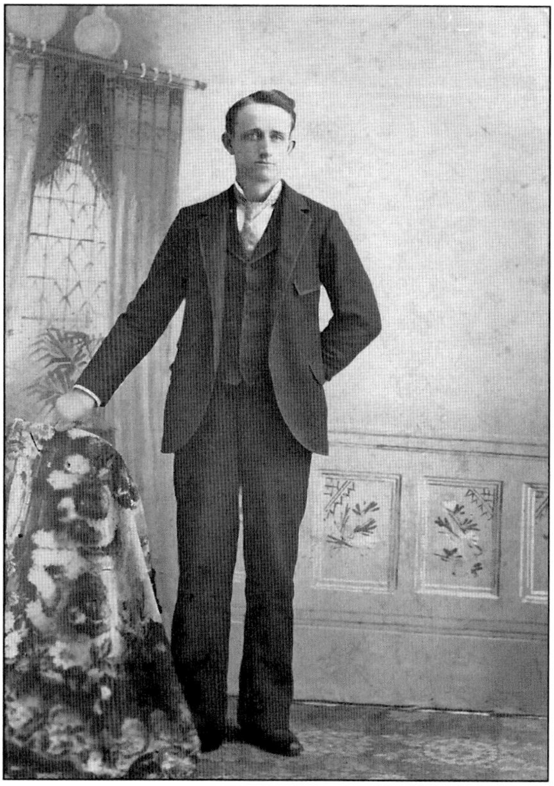

Allen Murchison is one of many with this name who settled in the town in early years. There is a street with that surname.

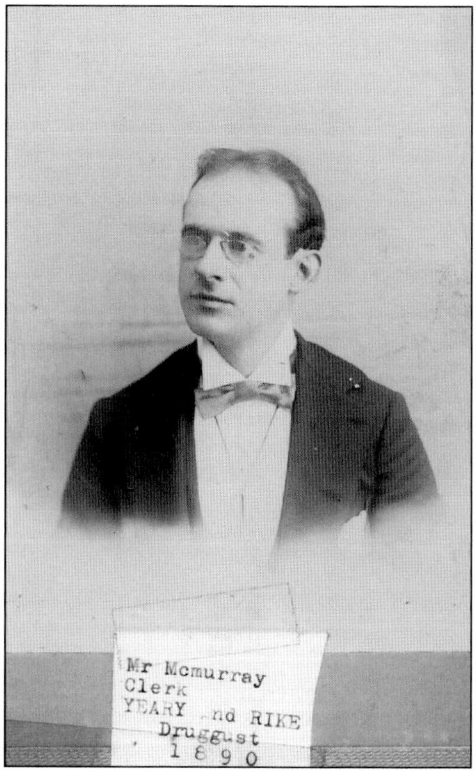

Doug McMurray was a clerk at the Rike and Yeary Drug Store from 1898 to 1900.

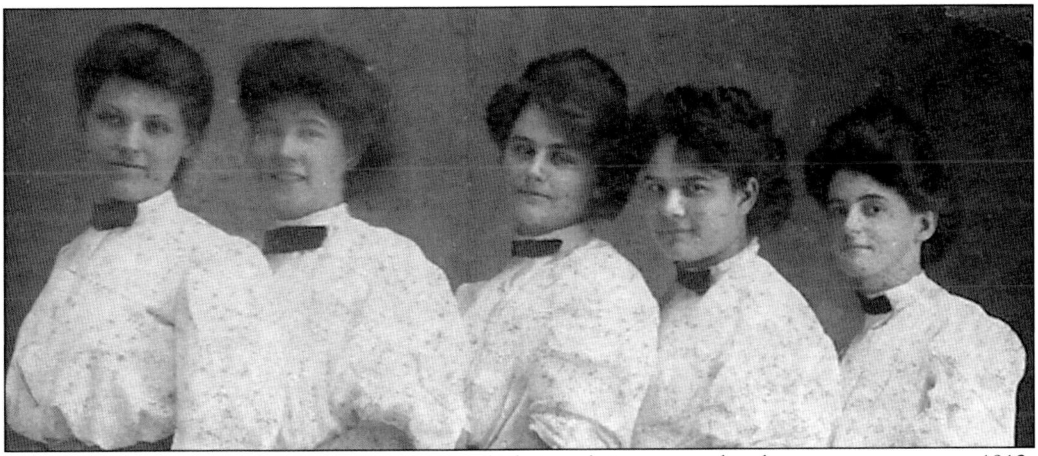

These five young ladies, identified as the "Melody Maids," were evidently a singing group in 1912. From left to right are Mamie Coffey, Annie Sears (Johnson), Gaynell Wade (Rike), Vera Leverett (Hale), and Addie Chapman.

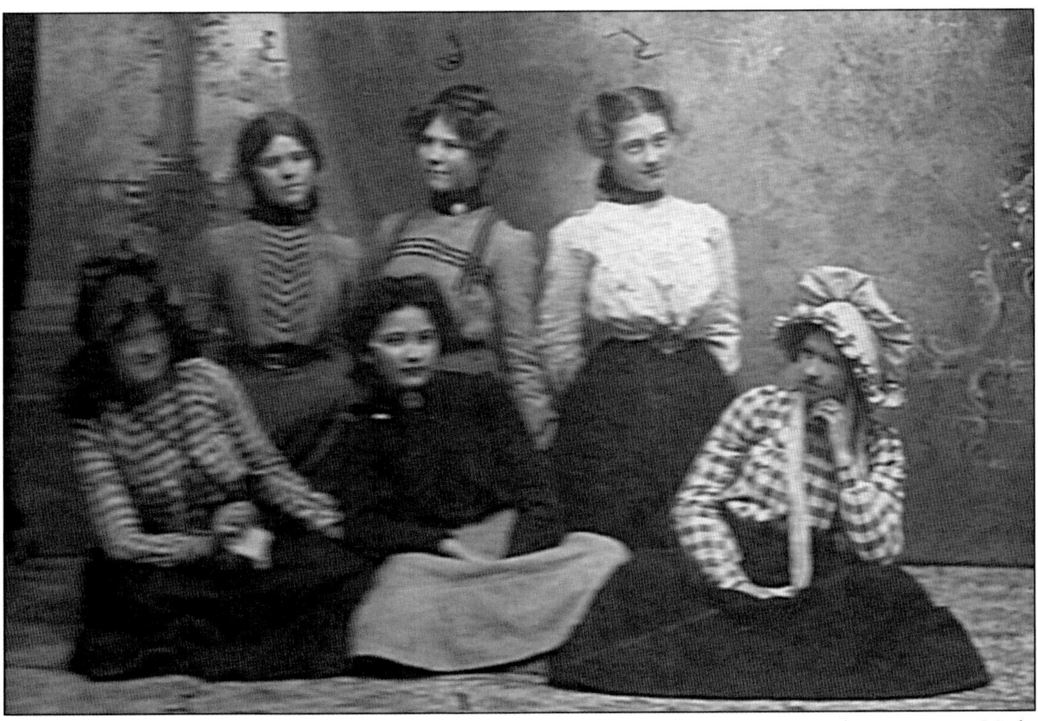

Pictured in 1900, this group of young ladies includes Cardie Horn, Rosamond Simington, Vada Holt, and Desda Coffey.

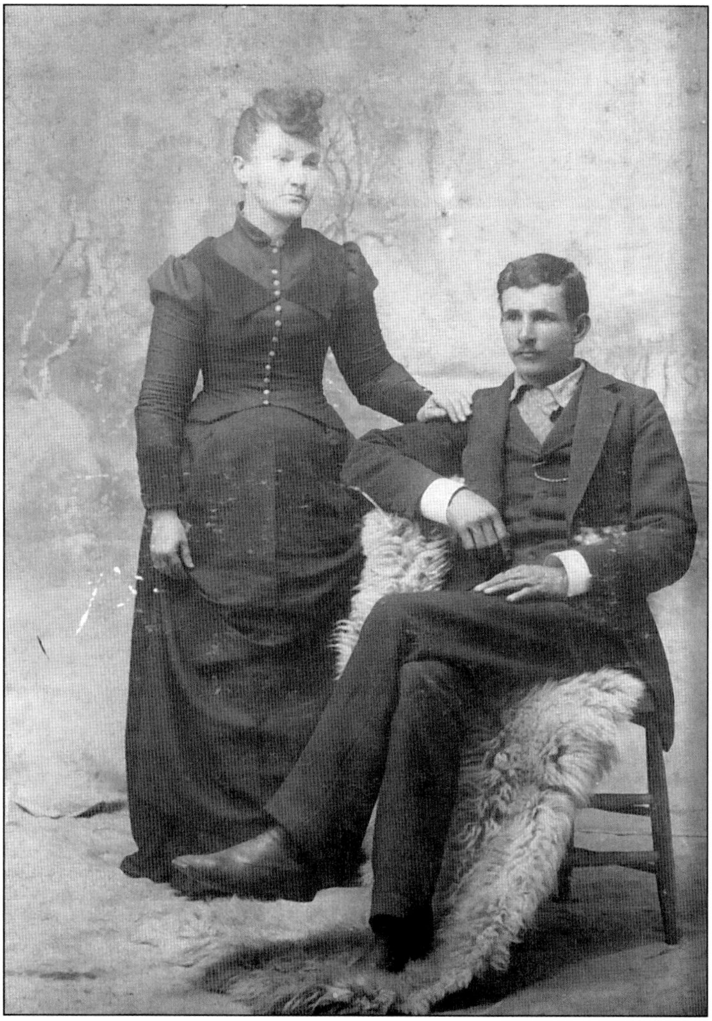

Joe Brice and his wife were early settlers of Farmersville.

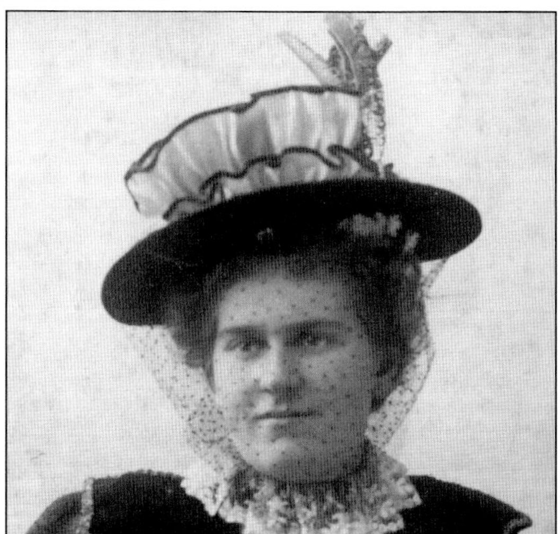

In 1894, two years before this photograph of Nell King was taken, a second newspaper, the *Sentinel*, was established in Farmersville. The weekly paper was published for about 20 years. Display advertisements in the *Sentinel* in 1895–1896 showed professional cards for Dr. John Stark, dentist; Jay Woodall, tonsorial parlor; Charles Forsker, blacksmith; W. M. Hildreth, the Palace Saloon; J. Rothstein and Company Liquors; and the Central Saloon. Saloons were voted out of Farmersville in 1898.

Another Rike descendant, Ida Rike Phillips, is pictured here. Her ancestors arrived in the area as some of the first settlers. Records show that R. A. Rike arrived in 1847, only two years after Moses Jones and the Yearys came, originally settling only a few miles from the present town of Farmersville.

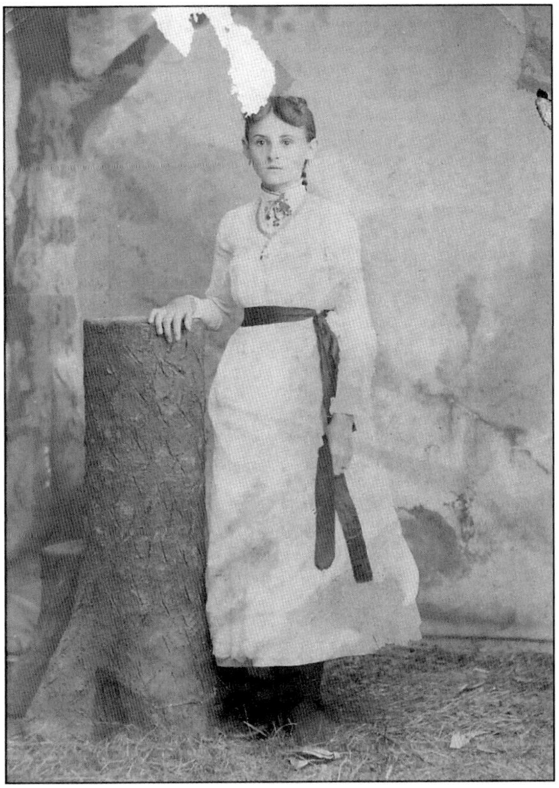

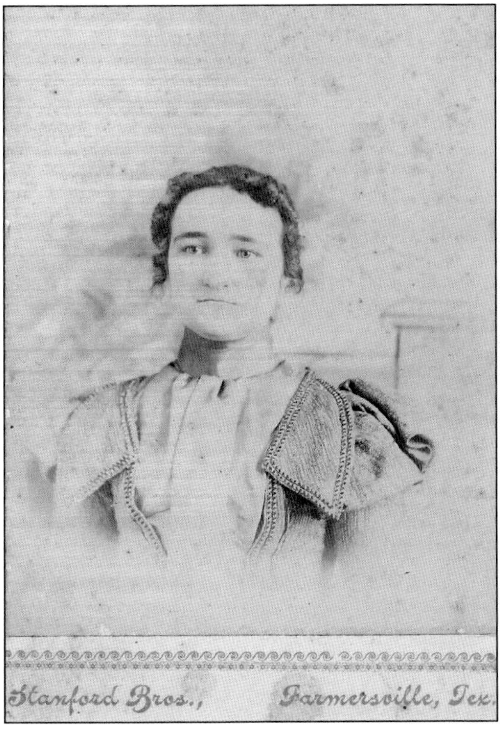

Pictured here is a niece of Billie and Lou Cox of Farmersville and the Red Oak Community. The Cox family was settled early in this area. This photograph was taken at the Stanford Brothers studio in Farmersville. For many years, these brothers operated the studio located on South Washington Street.

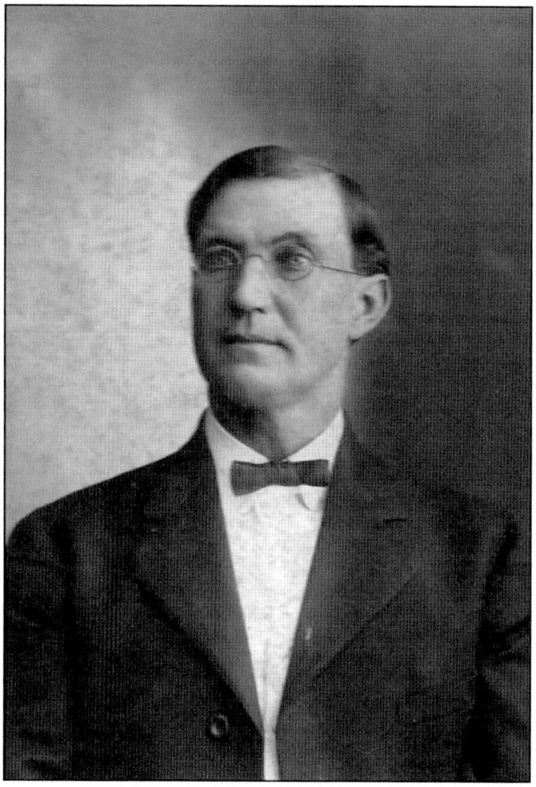

In 1887, Dr. Jack S. Welch (pictured) was listed among customers of the Yeary and Rike Drug Store. The first doctor to come to Farmersville, in 1855, was Dr. Harvey M. Markham. There is a good possibility that he was also the first doctor in Collin County.

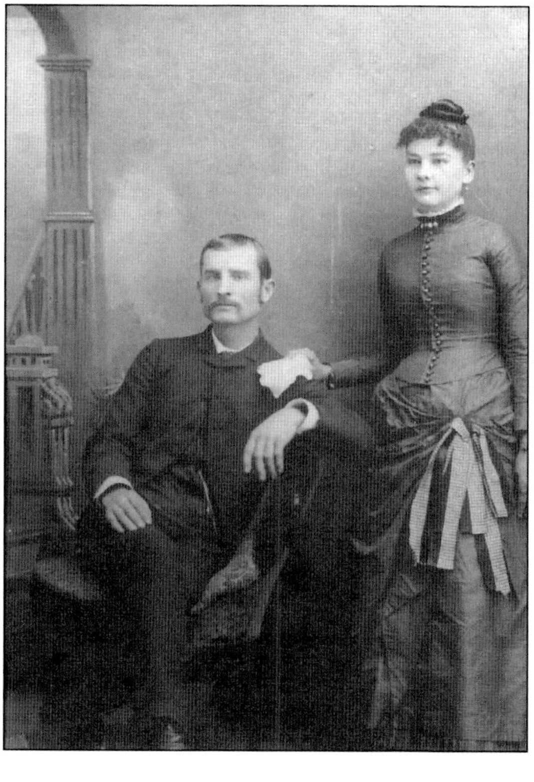

This 1885 photograph shows Mr. and Mrs. George A. Rike. The name George was passed down from generation to generation in the Rike family, as was the case with George W. Rike and George A. Rike. George W. Rike was the father of Charles Rike, for whom the library was named. G. W. Odom, the father of Mrs. George A. Rike, in 1862 was a member of Company F, 51st Regiment, Georgia Volunteers, with Robert E. Lee's army in Virginia. He was injured and captured three days before the South surrendered.

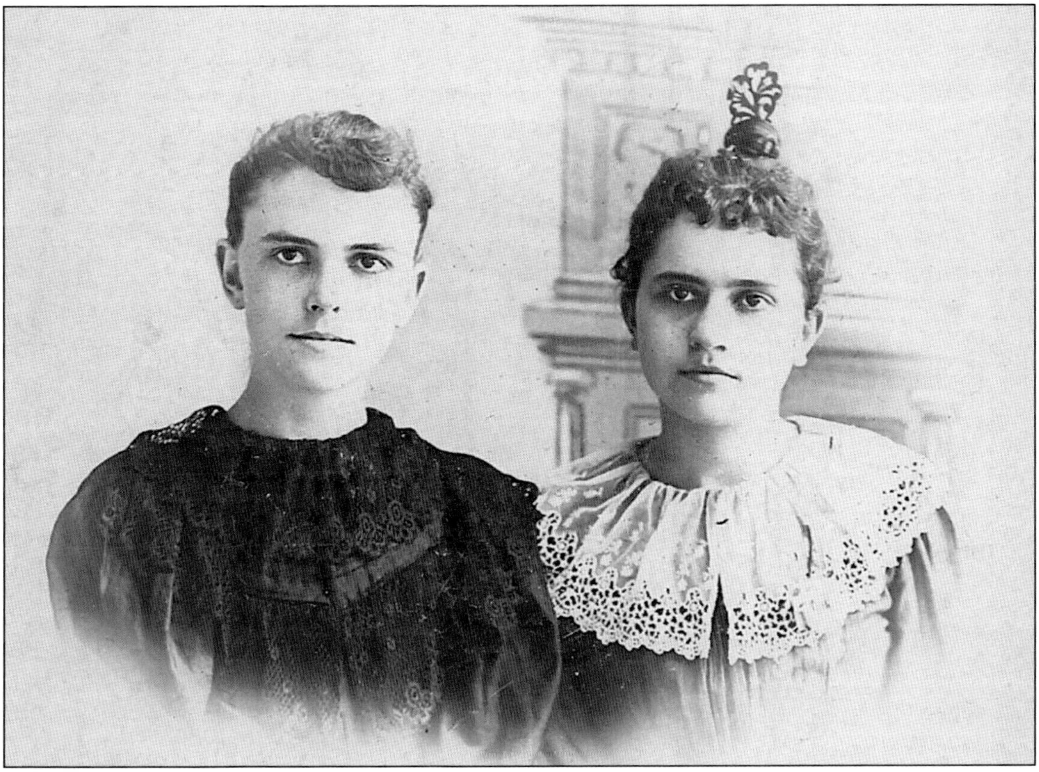

Bell, Bickley, and Knighton Dry Goods was listed among Farmersville businesses in 1887. Dr. O. D. Bell was listed as one of eight doctors who were customers of the Yeary and Rike Drug Store. Also listed was Dr. W. A. Bell, who was not practicing medicine at that time. Among firms or individuals who suffered heavy losses from the fire that began in the Tidal Wave Saloon in 1886, is listed W. A. Bell. In a small town of only 400 persons, these Bells were almost surely related in some way to the two Bell sisters, Bessie (left) and Virgie (right), pictured in 1892.

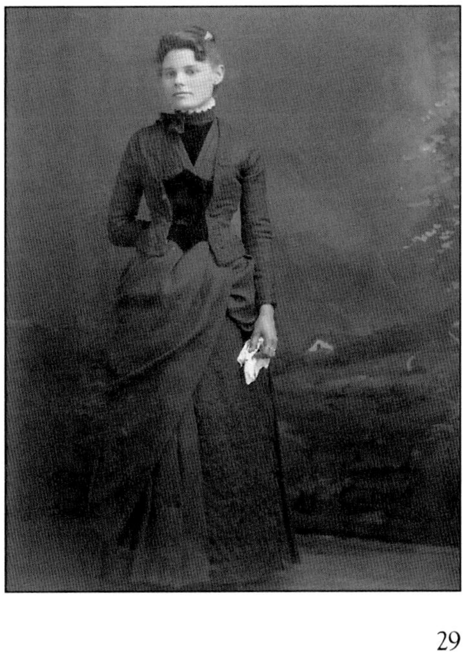

Julia Rike Pyle, another of the Rike girls, poses in her lovely dress with a beautiful background in 1891. In the 1870s, John Rike had a sawmill and wagon factory on South Main Street. That location is where city hall is located now and is a very busy place.

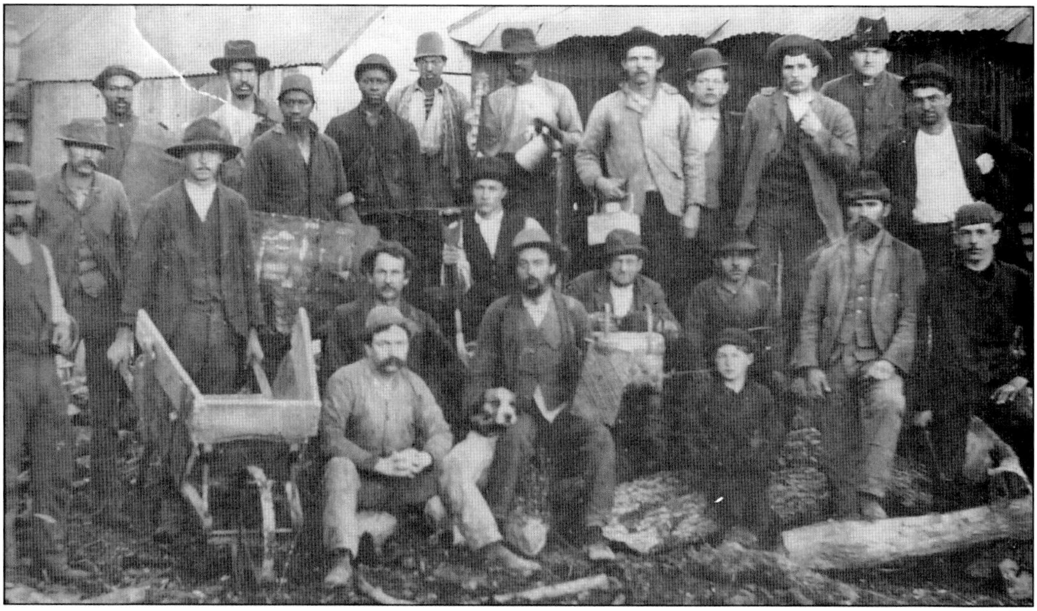

These are Farmersville men at work in the late 1800s, probably cleaning the town. Sid Nelson is pictured tenth from the left. Nelson, for whom a street is named, was the founder of one of the town's early African American families and was well loved through the years. He was born into a slave family in Mississippi in 1861. A newspaper interview with Sid was done in 1950, on his 90th birthday. He was in his twenties when he arrived in Farmersville in 1885. One of the first citizens he met was Jim Pendleton, and they became staunch friends. The only time they were separated, until Jim's death in 1933, was when Pendleton went off to college. Nelson phrased their friendship like so: "This was my man." Sid married Lissie Reed in 1887. The couple had three children, as well as several who did not survive infancy. Mary Frances Johnson, a teacher at Welford and later at the high school, was Nelson's granddaughter. He helped with the construction of the first brick school in Farmersville and many other buildings.

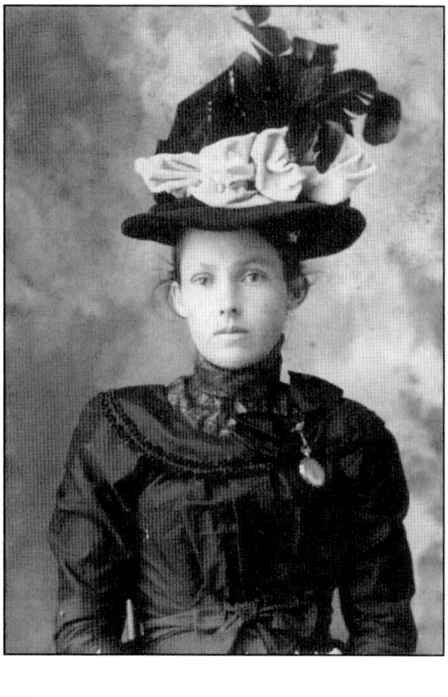

Mollie Jordan was the mother of Dora Jordan, who married Bain Honaker. Her father was William Russell Jordan, the son of Mary Wilcoxson Jordan. Dora and Bain had three children, Billy Bain, Cassie, and Margaret. Bain Honaker was killed in World War II. Dora was one of the widows who raised her children in the Bain-Honaker House on College Street. Cassie and Margaret are the Honaker sisters who gave the house to the Farmersville Historical Society. Pictured here is the grandmother of those two Honaker sisters, Cassie and Margaret, and the brother, Billy Bain Honaker.

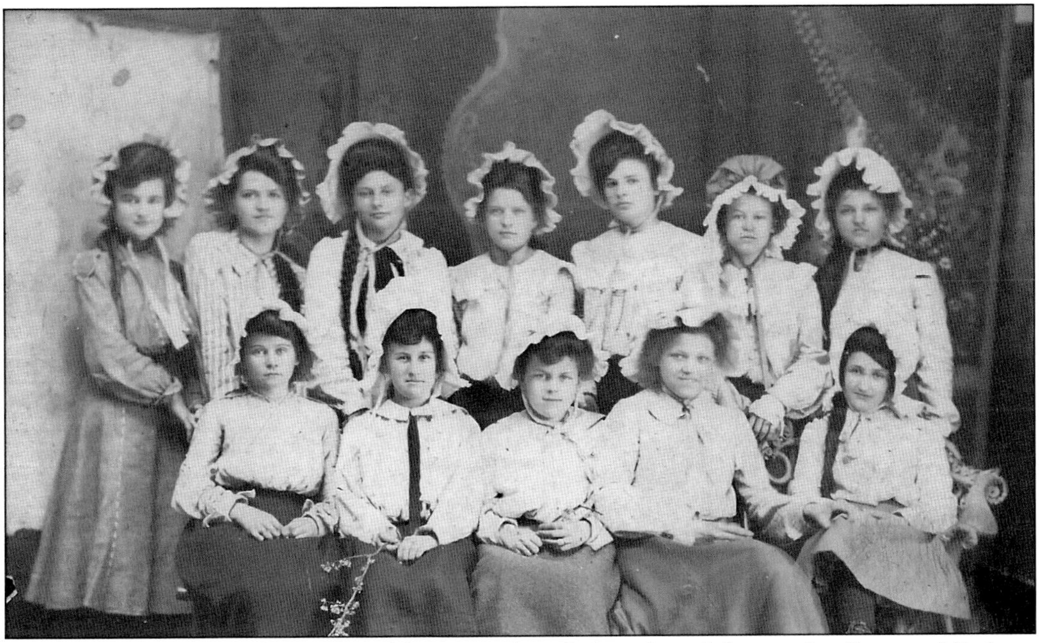

These women, in their bonnets and hats are identified as, from left to right, (first row) Esthma Wright, Ruth Fawcett, Marie Coffey, and Florence Keller; (second row) Robbie Rike, Clyde Windom, Ethel King, Annie Murchison, Bertha Haisli, Fay Neathery, and Virgie Howard.

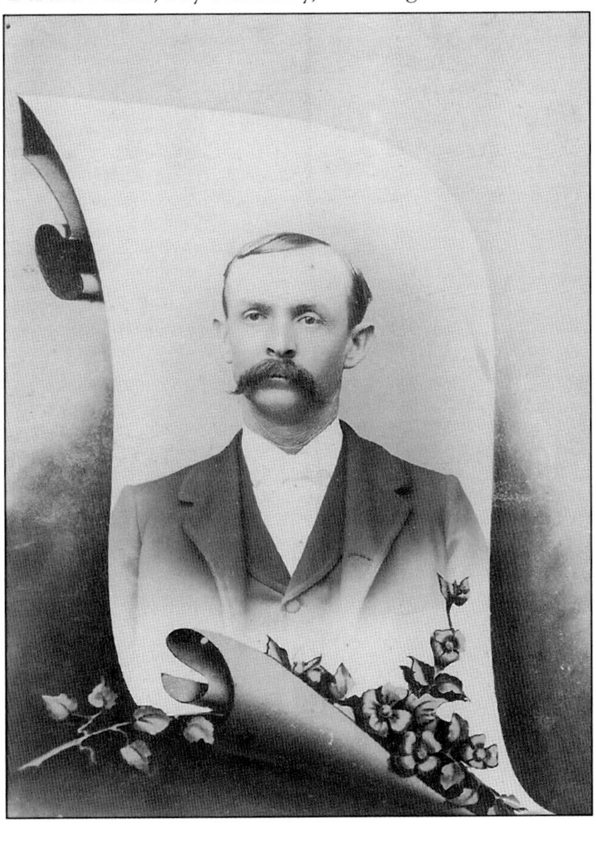

Members of the Wilcoxson family were also early settlers of Farmersville. Pictured here is Trimmer Wilcoxson. There is a street named for the family, and there are still descendants living in the area.

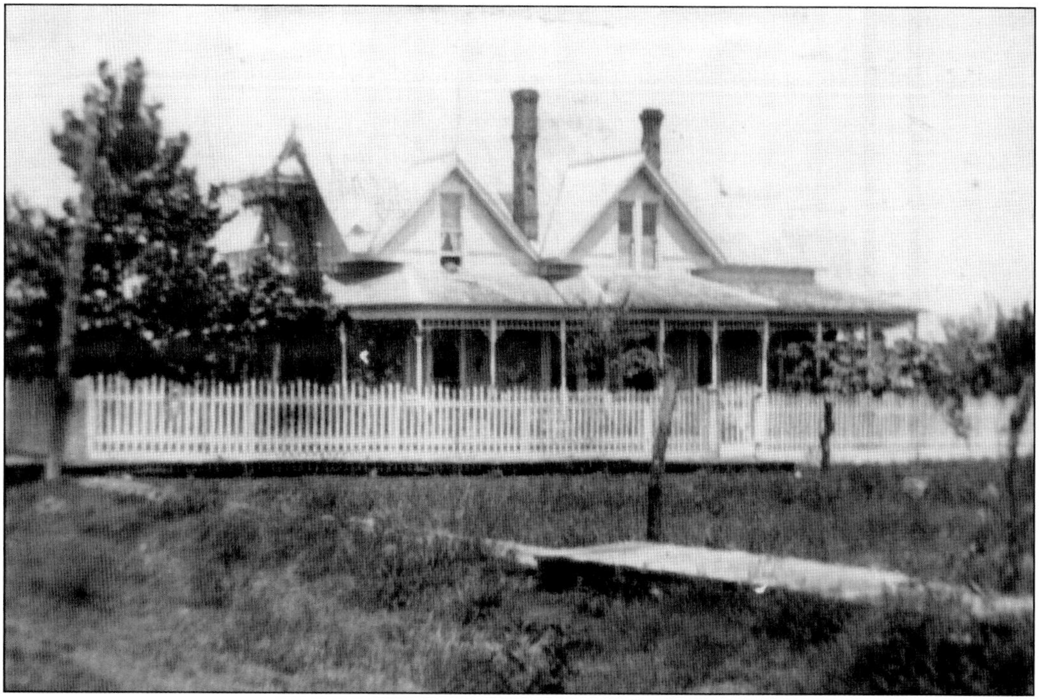

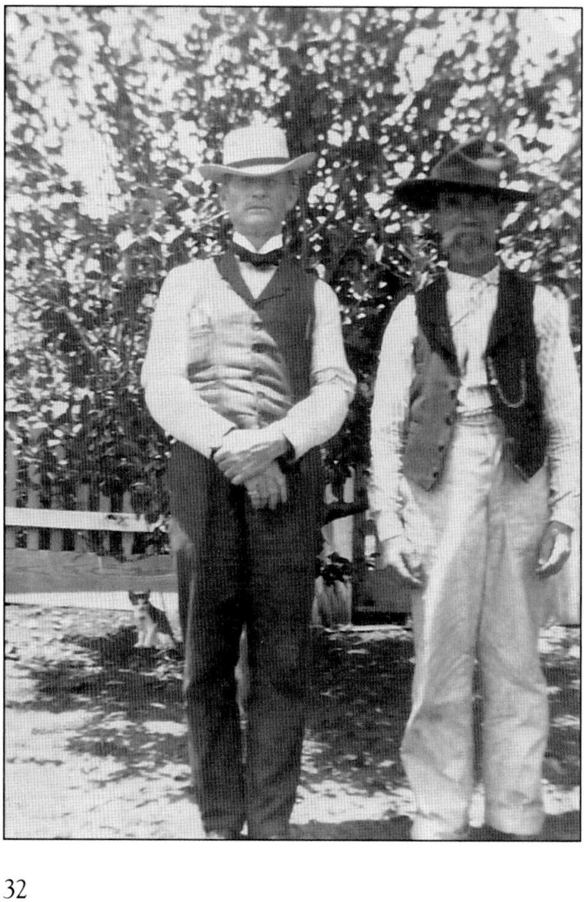

This was the home of the G. W. Rike family. It was built in 1898 and is not standing today.

These gentlemen are G. W. Rike (left) and a Mr. Gladden (right). This picture shows that many years have gone by since the younger Rike was depicted in earlier pictures.

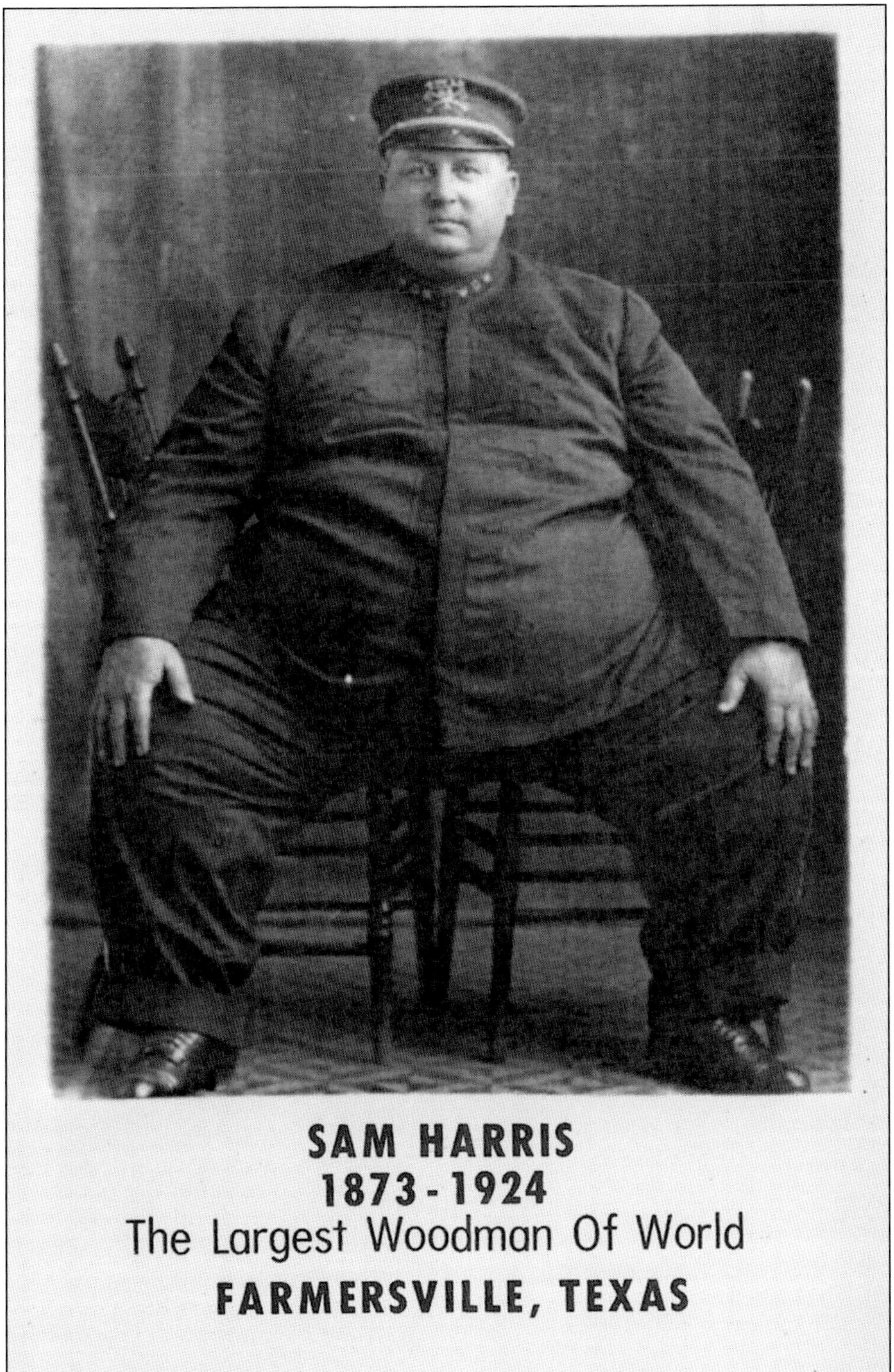

Sam Harris was born in 1871. He suffered with typhoid fever when he was a young man, after which he began to gain weight. His highest weight reached 731 pounds. When he died in October 1924, his weight was 691 pounds. After swimming across a lake in Ballinger, Texas, he contracted pneumonia, which was fatal. In 1920, Harris was included in Ripley's *Believe It or Not*! publication.

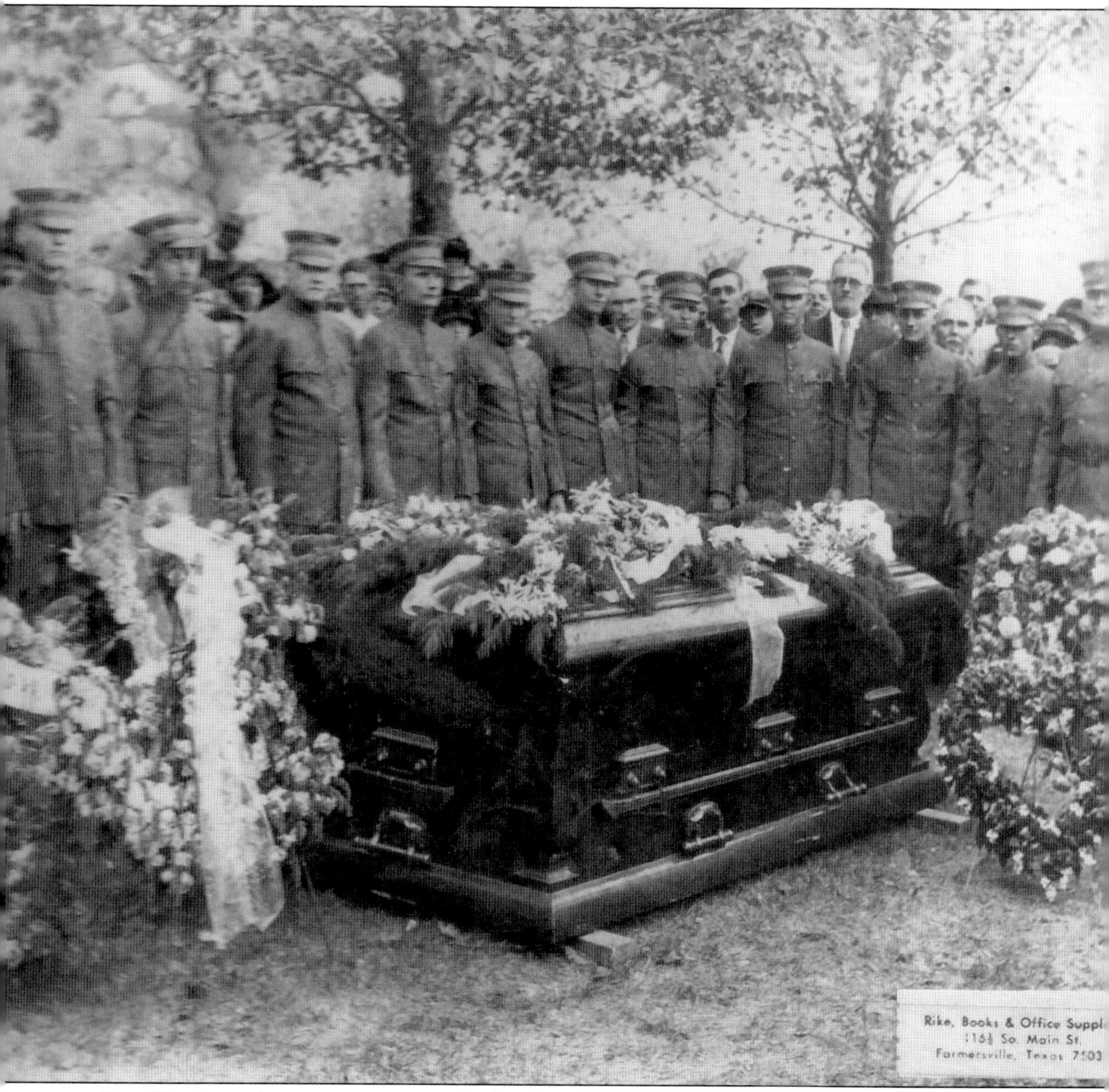

Sam Harris made arrangements with the Stringer Funeral Home in Greenville, Texas, for a burial casket made especially for him. It remained at the funeral home until needed. His funeral was conducted by the Woodmen of the World, with full honors. An estimated 10,000 people attended his funeral, probably the largest attendance at a funeral in Collin County. There were 22 honorary pallbearers and 12 active ones. They were M. T. Belew, Claude Neil, J. L. Bale, J. T. Webb, C. M. Wilhite, Elmer Worden, J. H. Nickles, C. G. McEluyes, R. C. Vicars, A. F. Yeager, J. R. Aycock, and W. W. Woodall. His casket was too large for the regular hearse, so a truck conveyed his remains to the cemetery. These remains occupy the largest grave in the Odd Fellows Cemetery in Farmersville.

Sam Harris was the father of two girls and four boys. They took these photographs in 1910 to demonstrate the enormous size of their father's pants. The three girls are, from left to right, Ola Harris, friend Eunice Ballew, and Mable Harris.

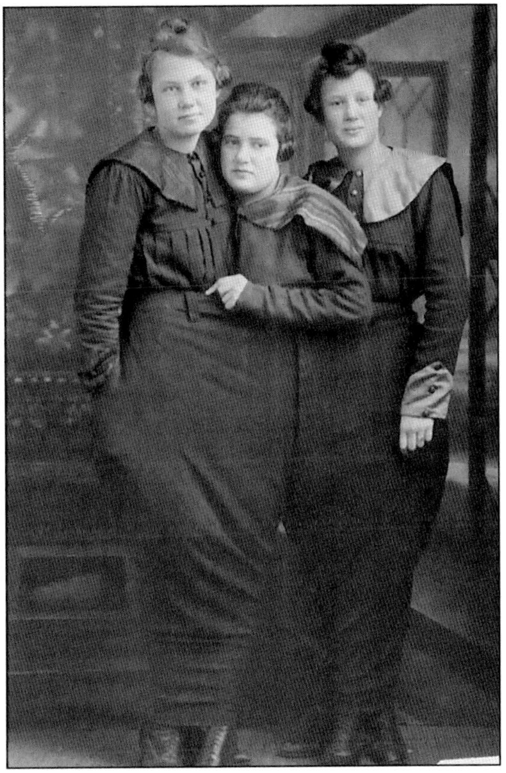

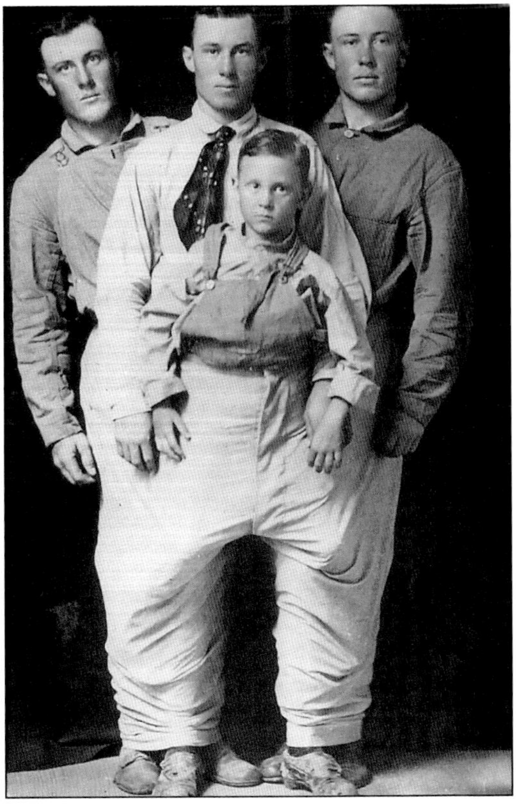

The four boys are, from left to right, Lester, "Dago," Ernest, and John Harris (the young boy in front).

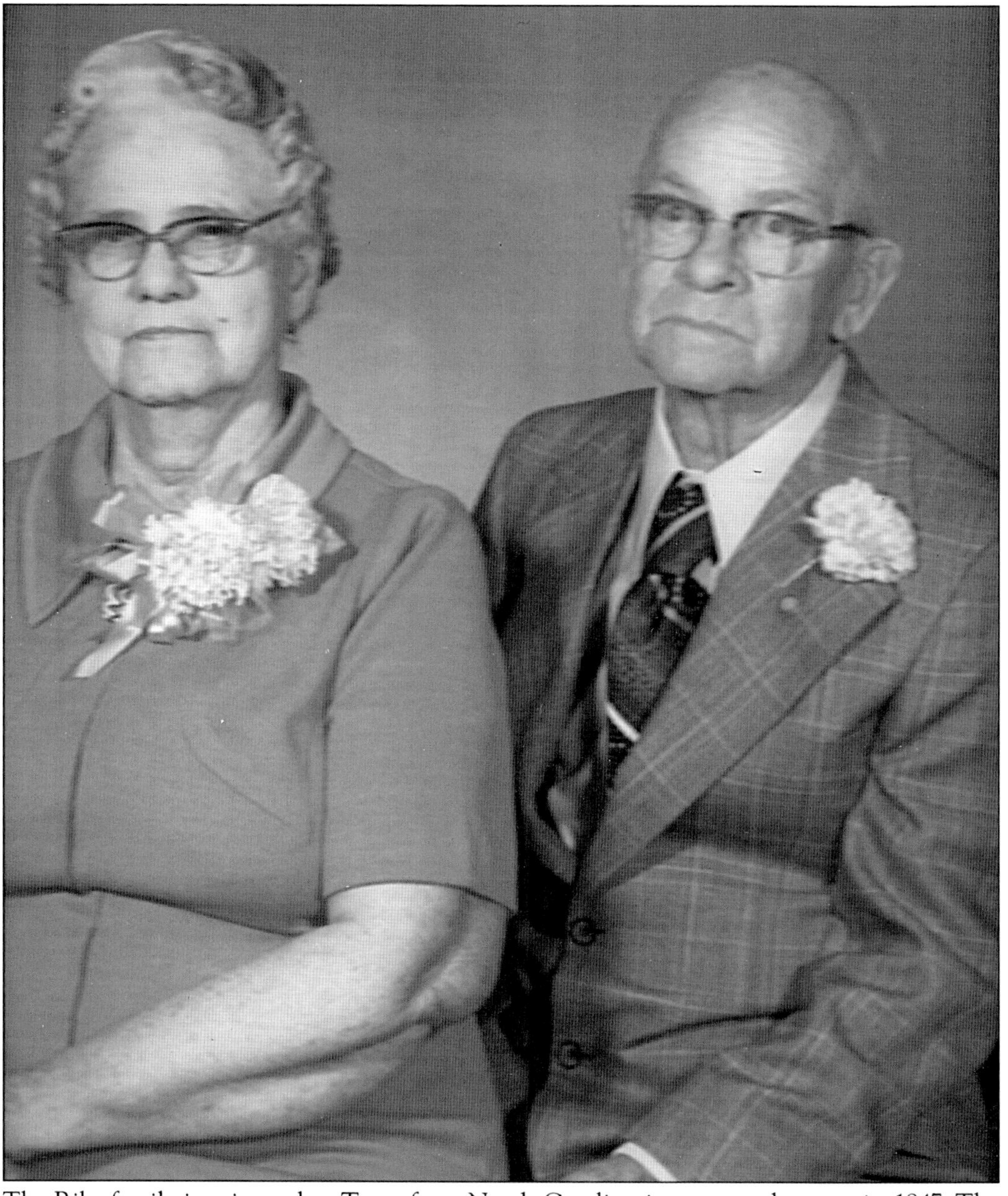

The Rike family immigrated to Texas from North Carolina in a covered wagon in 1847. The library has a copy of a diary, kept by Charles Rike's grandmother, with an almost daily account of the journey. This diary is included in a large genealogy section contained in the Charles Rike Memorial Library in Farmersville. Since 1885, members of the Rike family have operated a drugstore in Farmersville. They partnered with others in the beginning, as evidenced by the image of the Yeary and Rike Drug Store featured on page 41. In later years and generations, Charlie Rike, as he was called, operated his own drugstore in town until ill health and age forced him to retire. In 1965, he sold his stock to Bill Harrison and Rike Drug became Harrison's Pharmacy. A native of Farmersville—as was his father—Charlie spent many years collecting hundreds of bits of information about past history. Much of that history is now located in the library. His wife, Thelma, was a teacher in the Farmersville school system.

Three

Industries Came—and Some Went

Industry did, indeed, come to town. By 1881, Farmersville had seven grocery stores, three dry goods, three general merchandise firms, two saloons, two leather and harness shops, and eight private schools.

In 1885, the Exchange Bank was organized and operated for two years. It then consolidated with the newly organized First National Bank, still operating today as First Bank. Despite three disastrous fires, Farmersville survived and did well.

In the early 1900s, the fertile black land of Collin County produced cotton, cotton everywhere. It took six gins in town to keep up. Cotton ruled until onions came to town in the 1920s and 1930s. The smell of onions permeated the entire area, but townsfolk didn't mind because with it came the smell of money.

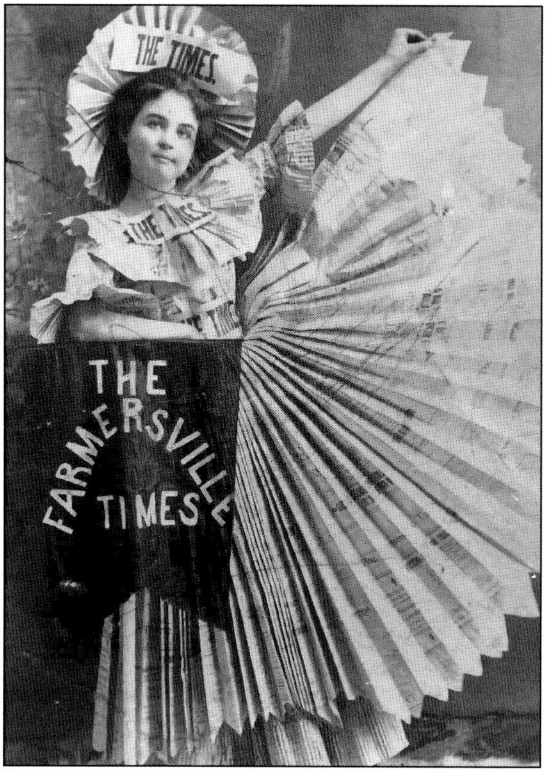

In 1897, local merchants put on an advertising show sponsored by the chamber of commerce. Most of the merchants dressed in costumes relating to their store. Ada Coffer Rike wore this dress made from the *Farmersville Times*. Established in 1885, it was and is the oldest newspaper in Collin County and still maintains its original name.

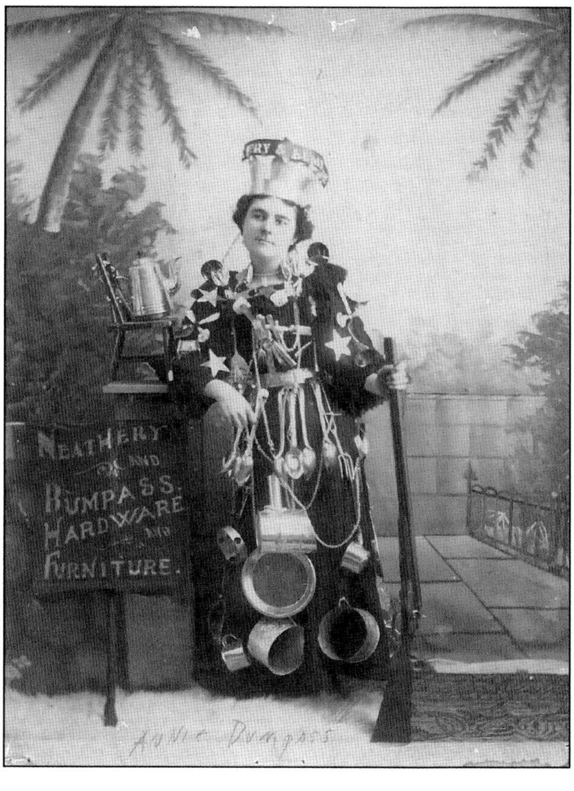

In 1897, Annie Bumpass's dress touted Neathery and Bumpass Hardware and Furniture in the chamber of commerce advertising show.

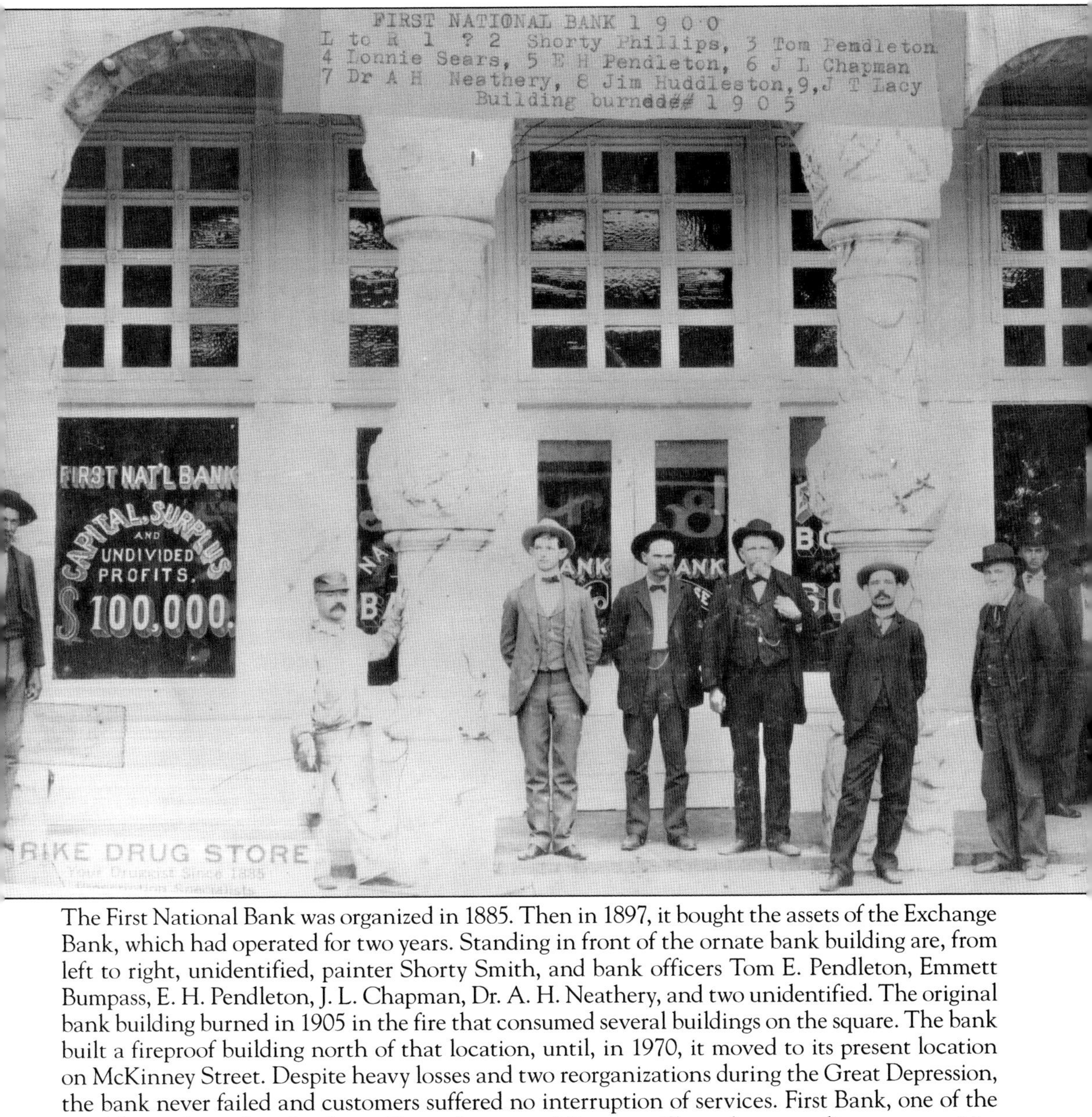

The First National Bank was organized in 1885. Then in 1897, it bought the assets of the Exchange Bank, which had operated for two years. Standing in front of the ornate bank building are, from left to right, unidentified, painter Shorty Smith, and bank officers Tom E. Pendleton, Emmett Bumpass, E. H. Pendleton, J. L. Chapman, Dr. A. H. Neathery, and two unidentified. The original bank building burned in 1905 in the fire that consumed several buildings on the square. The bank built a fireproof building north of that location, until, in 1970, it moved to its present location on McKinney Street. Despite heavy losses and two reorganizations during the Great Depression, the bank never failed and customers suffered no interruption of services. First Bank, one of the 20 oldest independent banks in Texas, has served Farmersville and surrounding communities continuously for 125 years, just recently celebrating that anniversary.

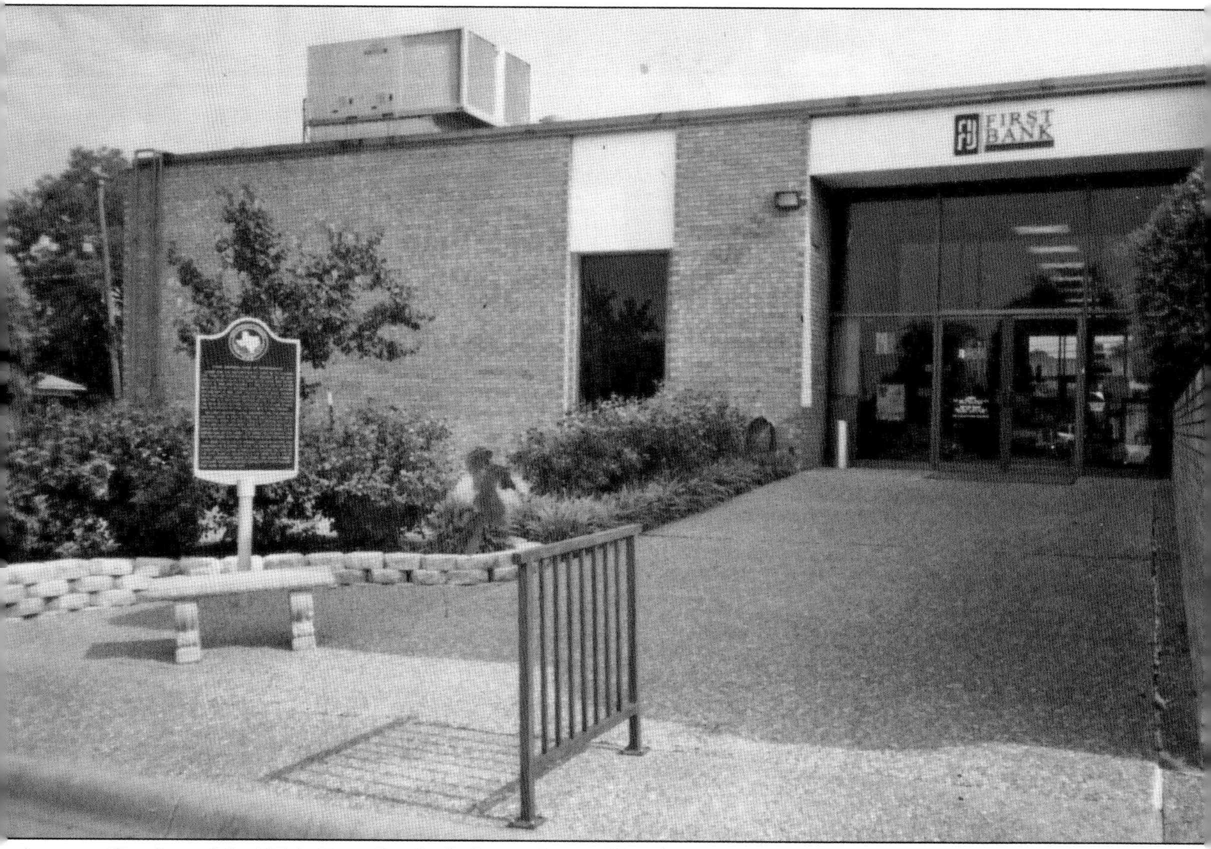

On June 28, 1996, First Bank dedicated its official Texas Historical Marker, commemorating the bank's history. Present for the ceremony were several descendants of the bank's founders, W. S. Aston, Sam Hamilton, J. E. Pendleton, Roy Phillips, Patton and Johnny Honaker, pioneer Dr. A. H. Neathery, and the bank's first president, Judge H. H. Neilson. Former bank president Ed Stuart, in remarks, gave special tribute to Oscar Carlisle, who served as director for 46 years. He stated that had it not been for Carlisle, the bank would not exist today to be honored with the marker. Stuart said, "Long before those old bricks out here on the square were put down, before most of the old buildings around it were built, before the last horse and buggy gave way to the first horseless carriage, this bank was serving its community."

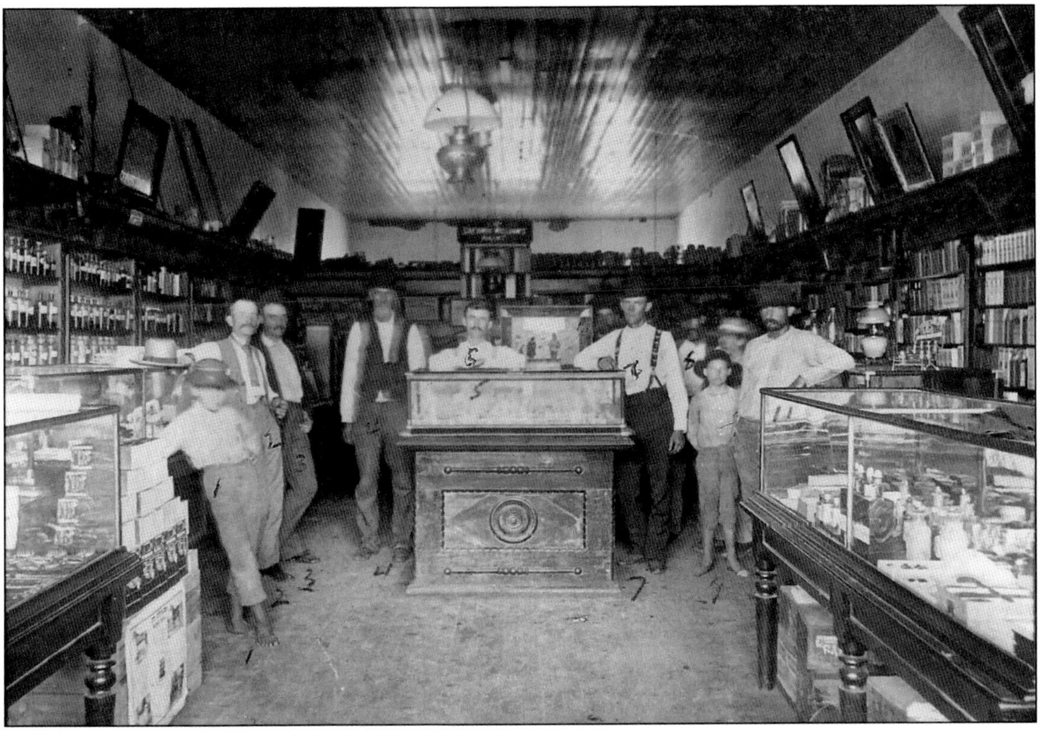

In the 1890s, before the days of electricity, this is how the inside of the Yeary and Rike Drug Store looked, located on the southeast corner of the square. Pictured above are, beginning at second from the left, George W. Rike, Mr. Wanek, D. P. Ashley, and Tom Rike. The remaining people are unidentified. The advertisement at right is for the Yeary and Rike Drug Store.

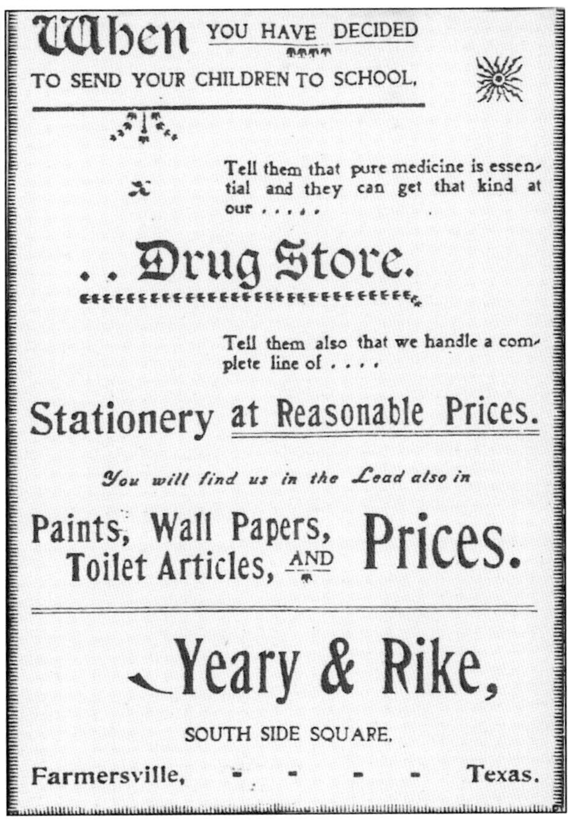

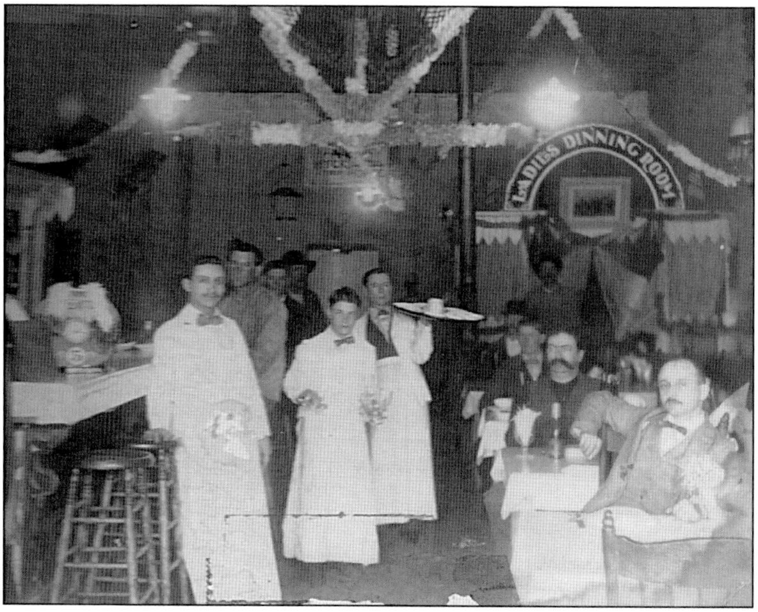

Raymond's Restaurant is shown here in 1895. The owner was Raymond Costelious and the establishment was located in the *Farmersville Times* building. Note the sign to the right that states "Ladies Dinning Room."

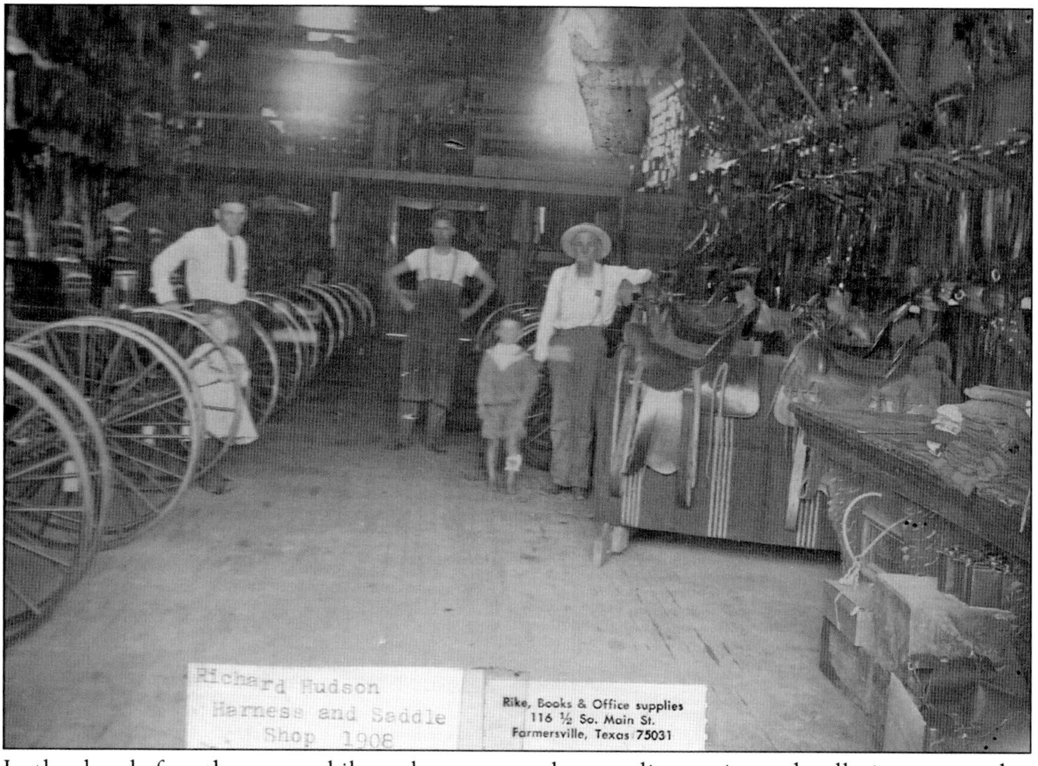

In the days before the automobile took over to make traveling easier and pollution worse, this was a familiar scene in Farmersville. Pictured is the Richard Hudson Harness and Saddle Shop in 1904. From left to right are Alice Hudson, Richard Hudson, two unidentified, and R. W. Hudson. Richard Hudson was a dealer in buggies and harnesses until 1912 at which time he sold the business to Hugo Simon. The shop was located on the north side of the square, in the third building east of Washington and McKinney Streets.

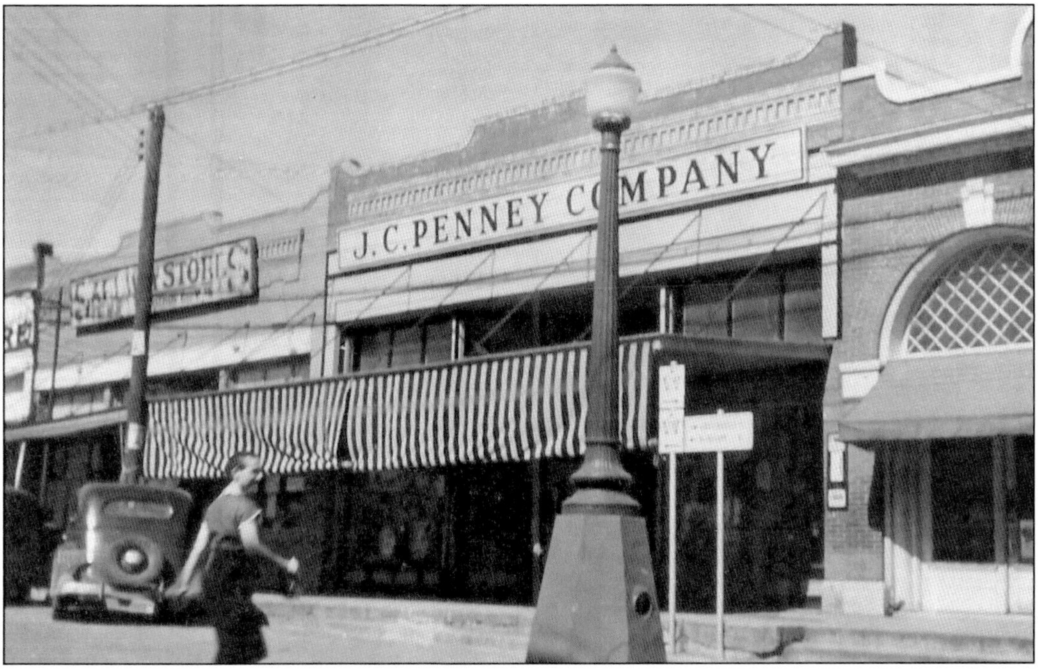

This J. C. Penney Company store was located in Farmersville in the 1900s. It was later replaced by the Neathery Hardware and Furniture Company, shown below. The location was on the east side of the square, next to the First National Bank.

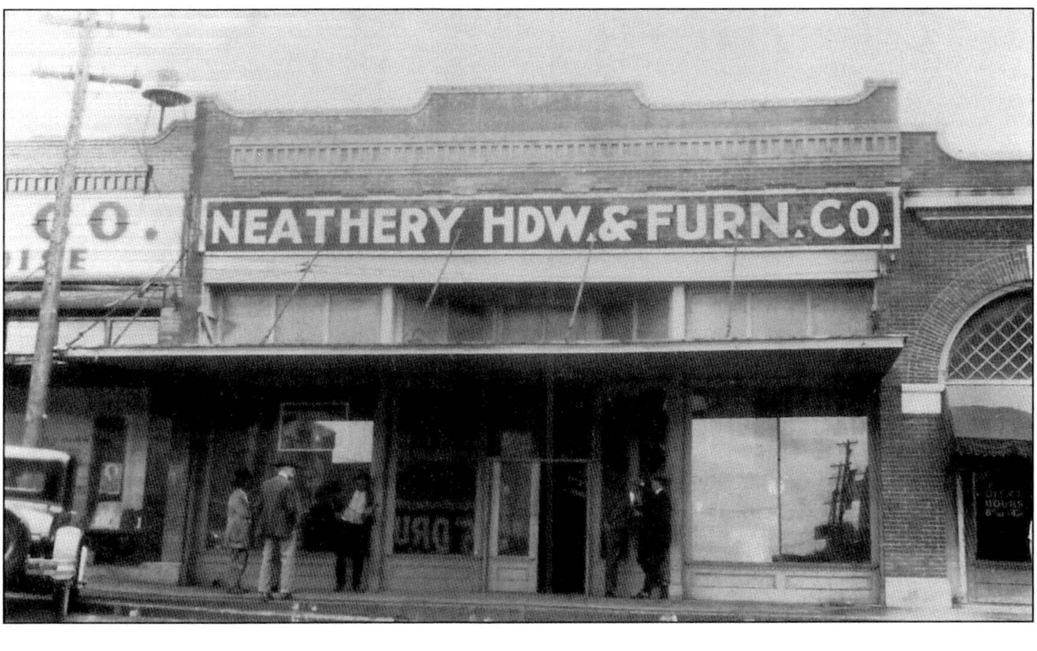

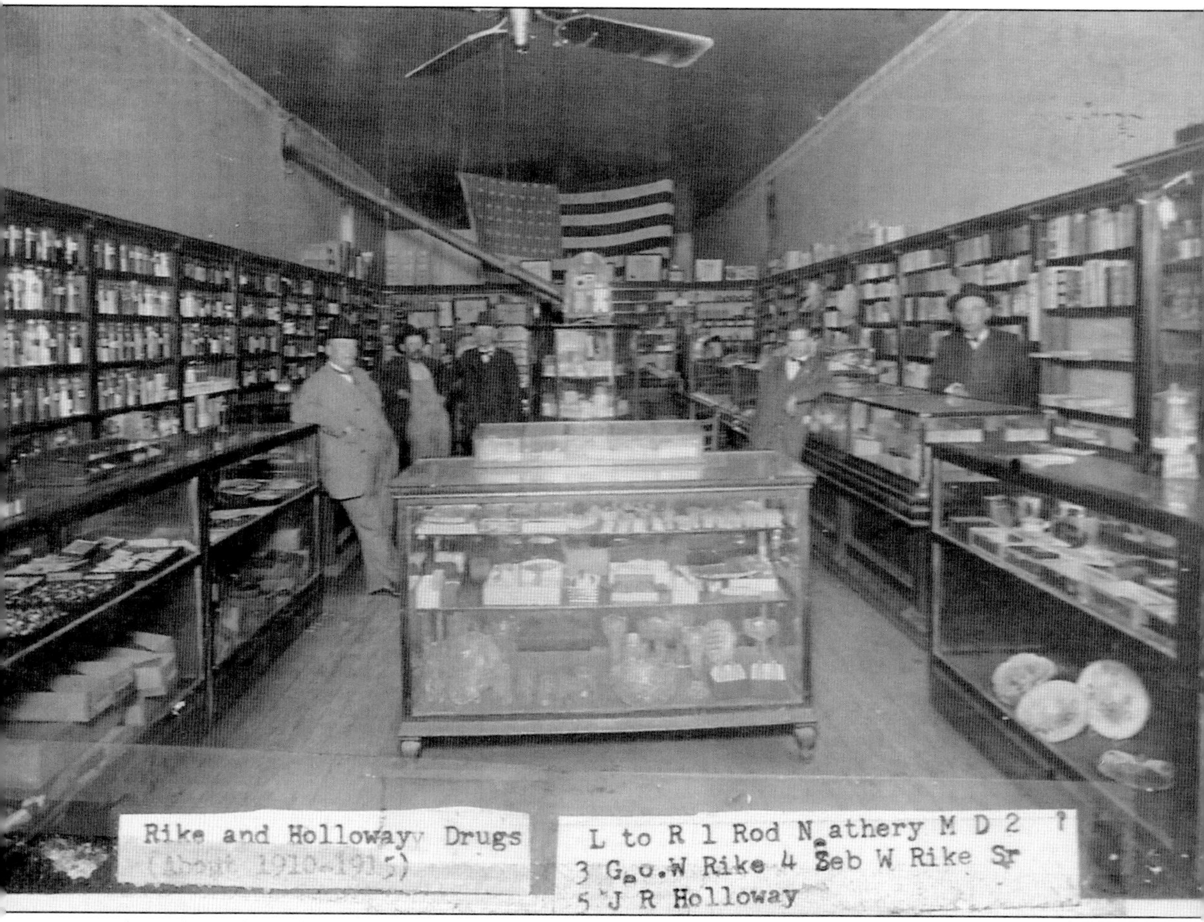

The Rike and Holloway Drug Store is pictured sometime between 1910 and 1915. From left to right are Rod Neathery, M. D. ?, George W. Rike, Zeb W. Rike Sr., and J. R. Holloway. Charles Rike had in his possession the following instrument signed by the druggists of the town and dated October 19, 1892: "We, the undersigned druggists, agree between each other, that as our license for selling whiskey expires, we will drop them and not renew them and only sell whiskey under a prescription from a physician, according to the law. The agreement to hold in effect until we all agree to go into it again. As we are, Signed: Yeary and Rike, Hope and Warden, Bell and Bickley."

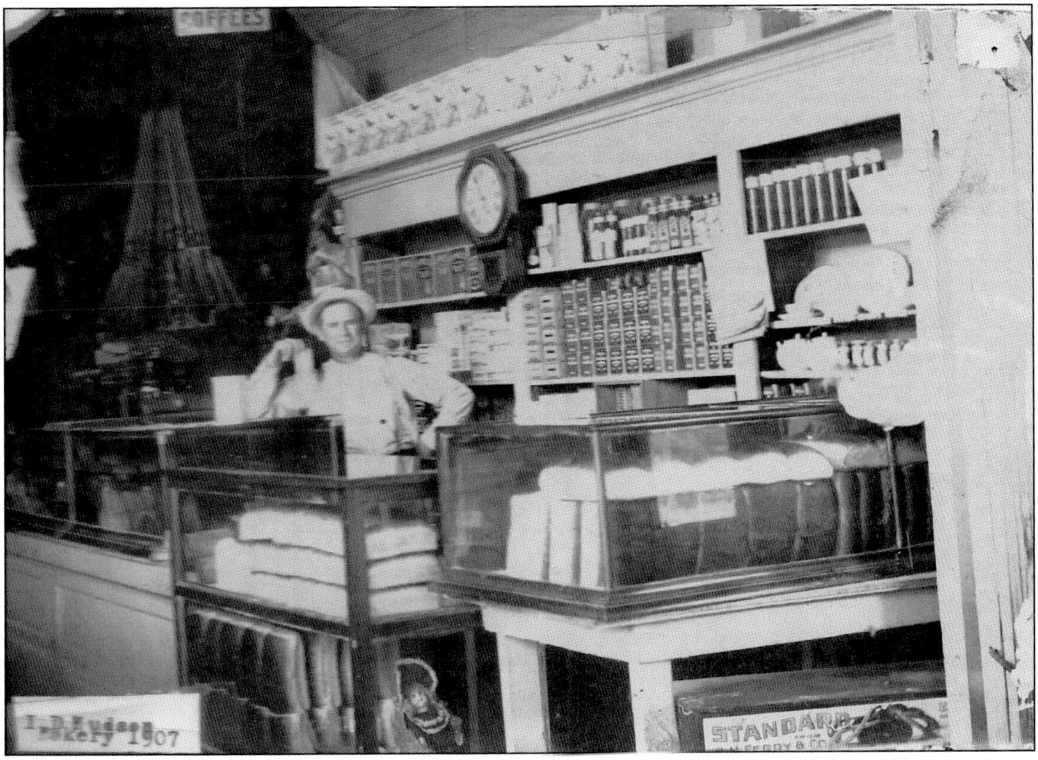

I. D. Hudson stands behind the counter of his bakery in 1907. Note the doll located in the front showcase next to the bread. The broom display above the counter is imaginative.

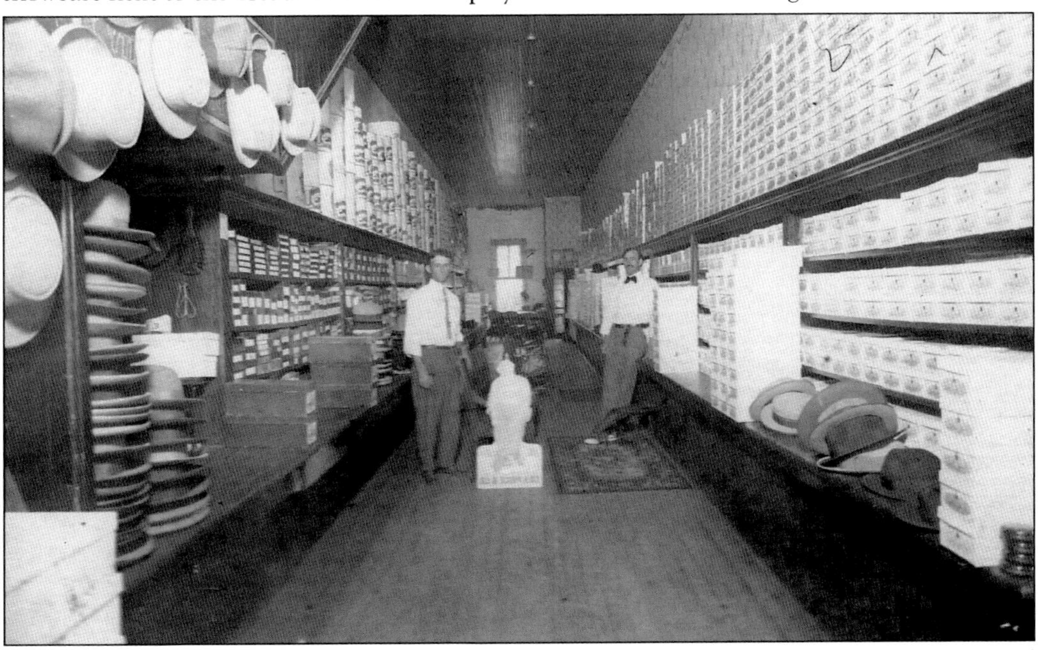

The Ed Bivens Shoe Store was located on the south side of the square in 1906. Standing is Ed Bivens (left) and Herschel Howard (right). In 1911, the store moved to another building on the north side of the square. Then in 1919, the store was sold to Thompson, Walraven, and Herron.

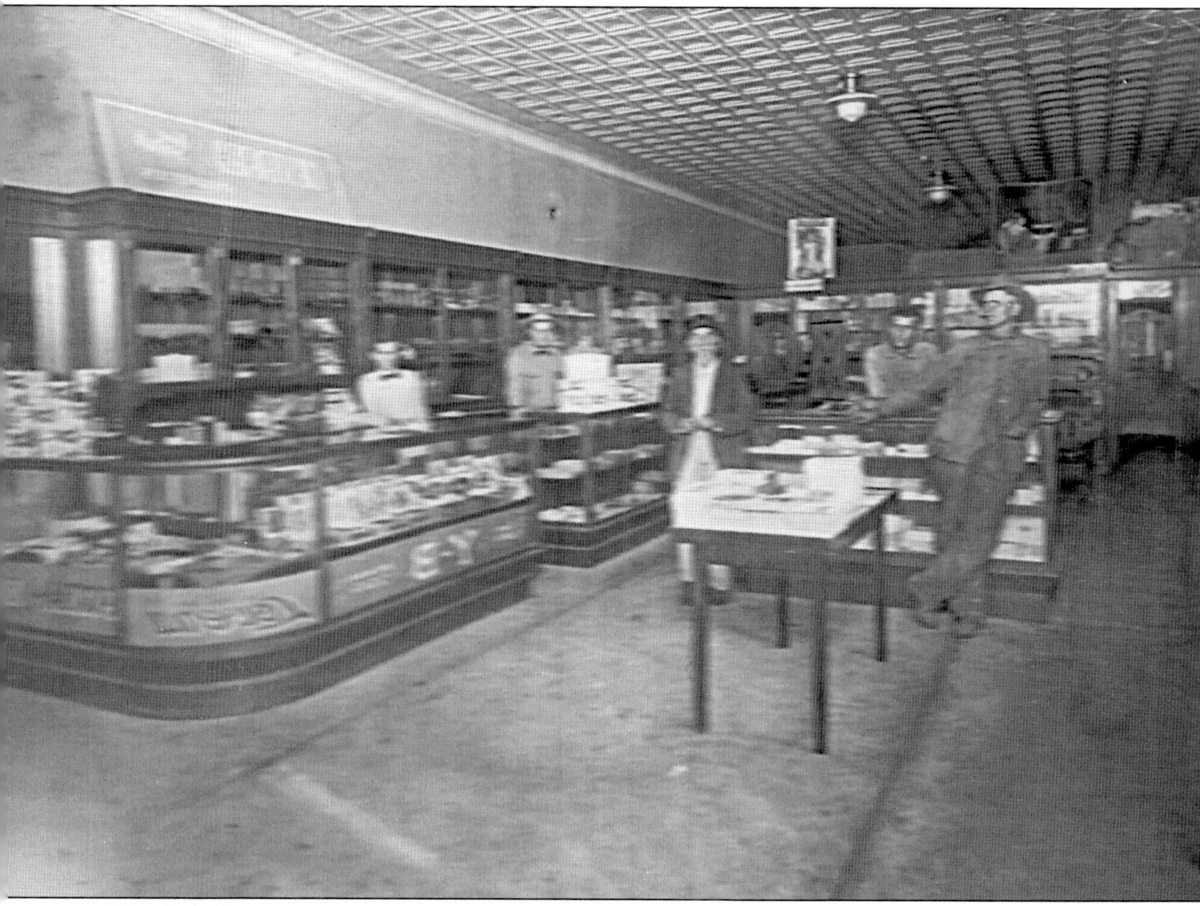

The Rike Drug Store is pictured in October 1923. Standing, from left to right, are L. C. Hart, Claude Neal, John Yeary, W. F. Hagas, and Zeb A. Rike Sr. A long line of Rikes were in the pharmacy business from the first one in 1885. At the turn of the century, many natural remedies were used. One entire side of the pharmacy was made up of shelves stocking all sorts of crude drugs, powders, barks, roots, leaves, and liquids. Even after that time, the store bought linseed oil, turpentine, crude carbolic acid, castor oil, and denatured alcohol by the 50-gallon drum. Instead of a "coffee break" in those days, "a box of snuff and a pint of whiskey" was sufficient. Records show over-the-counter morphine being purchased without a prescription.

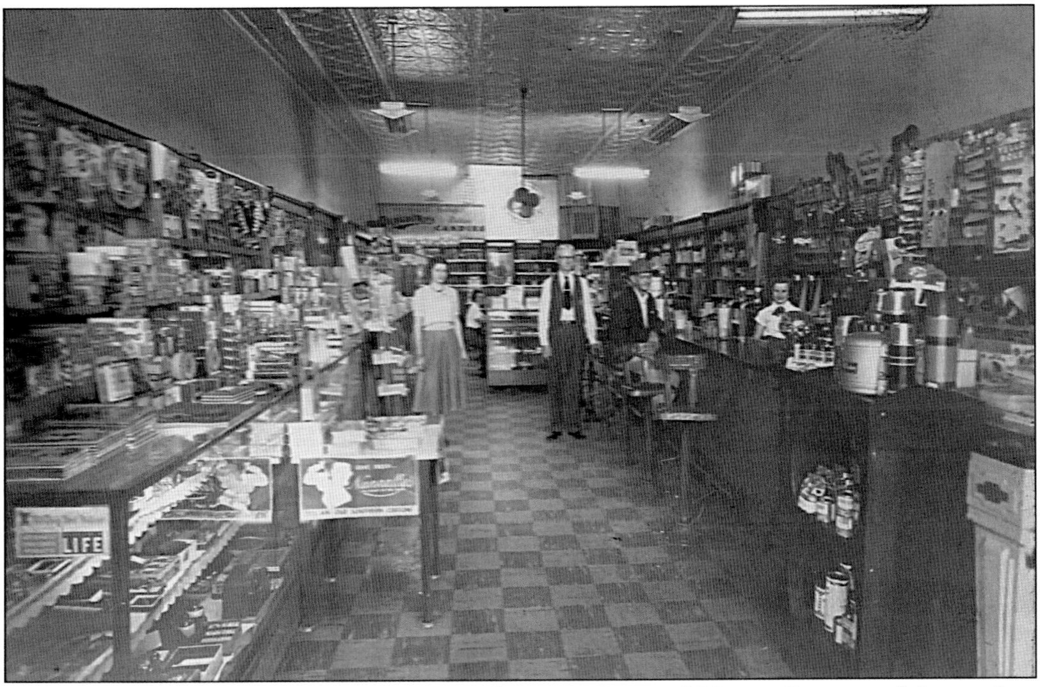

The Greenwood Pharmacy began in 1921, with owners Sam and Martin Greenwood. Located on the north side of the square, it employed eight people. In 1965, Bill and Jane Harrison purchased the store and later they also bought Rike Drug Store, when ill health forced Charlie Rike to retire.

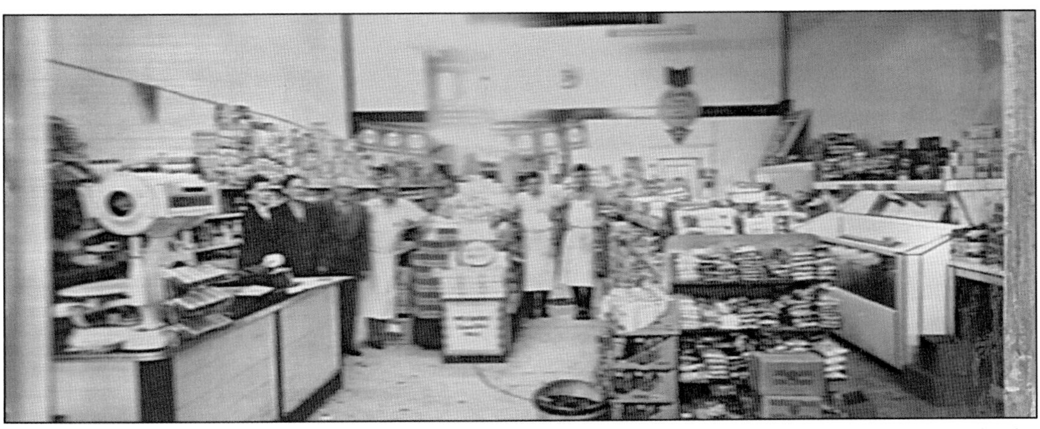

This was the B and C Grocery, which had a market and was of importance to the town. It had a cold storage in the rear of the store that opened onto Washington Street. Twelve employees kept this busy place in operation. The store was on the south side of the square.

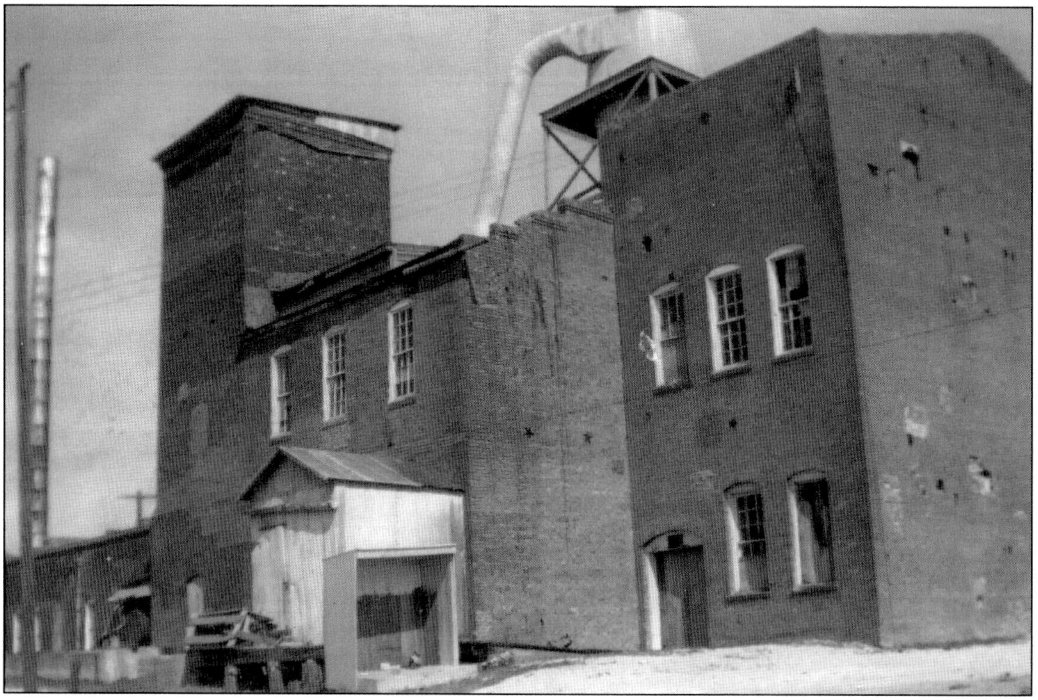

This is the oil mill site that was being used for other things. The upper stories were used as government cotton samples rooms. The lower rooms were stacked with bales of cotton. The Sweet Feed Plant is to the right. The building was located on the Kansas City Southern Railroad line, which extended from Farmersville to Shreveport, Louisiana.

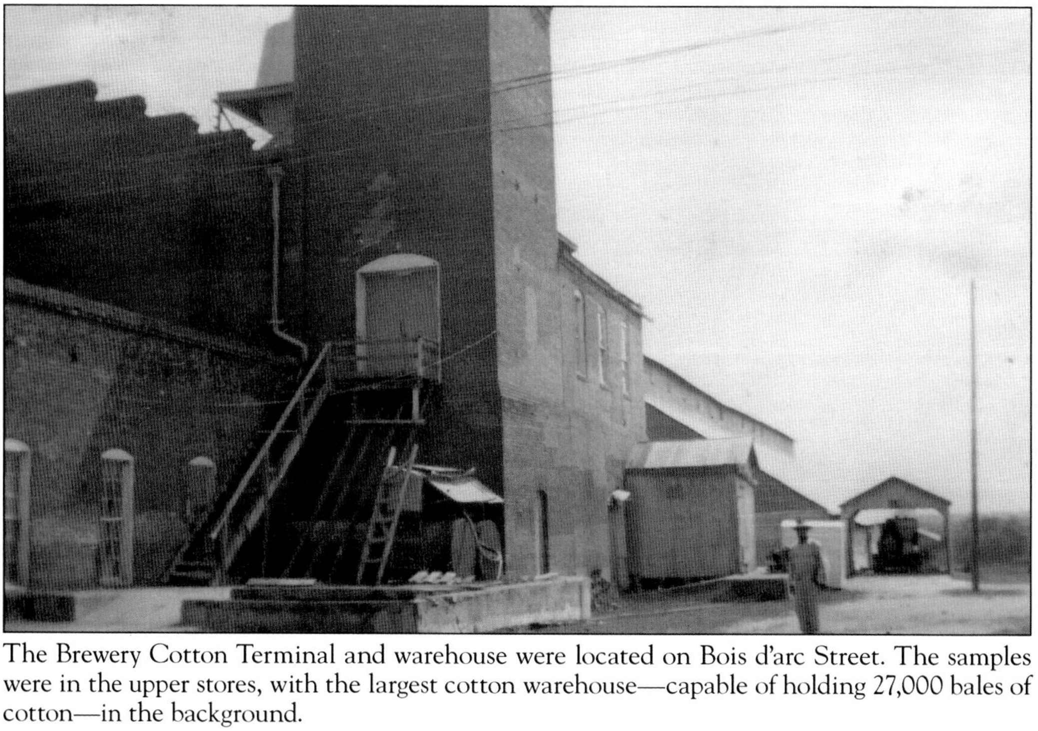

The Brewery Cotton Terminal and warehouse were located on Bois d'arc Street. The samples were in the upper stores, with the largest cotton warehouse—capable of holding 27,000 bales of cotton—in the background.

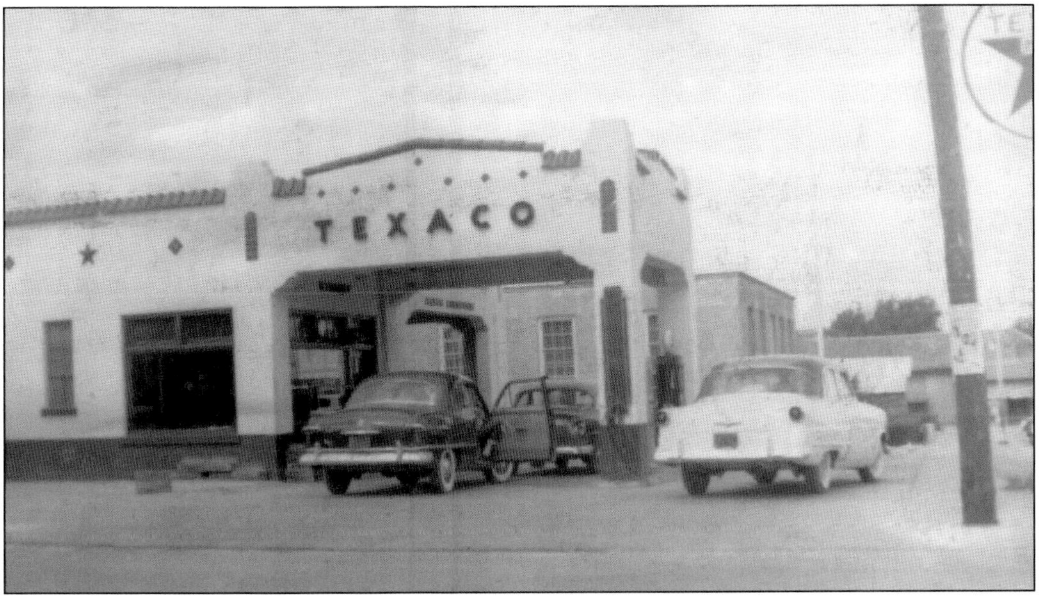

J. W. Clark once was employed at the post office. He was a very active member of the Ramblers semipro baseball team for many years. This is the Texaco Service Station that he operated in the 1950s, located next to the post office. Other service stations were at this location in later years. That station evolved into Tony's Mexican Restaurant, which may be the most popular and busiest restaurant in Farmersville in the present day. Mrs. J. W. Clark (Dorothy) was the principal at Tatum Elementary School in the 1980s.

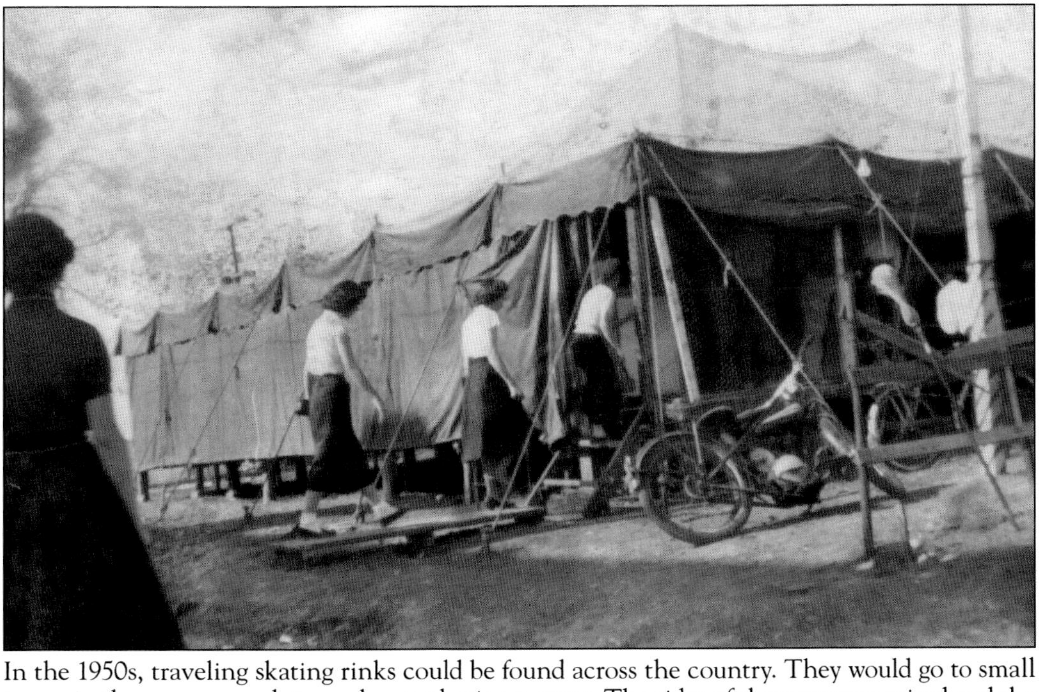

In the 1950s, traveling skating rinks could be found across the country. They would go to small towns in the summer and stay as long as business came. The sides of the tent were raised and the noise of dozens of shoe skates skating round and round could be heard. These hardwood floor rinks were very popular and entertaining for country kids who did not get much entertainment.

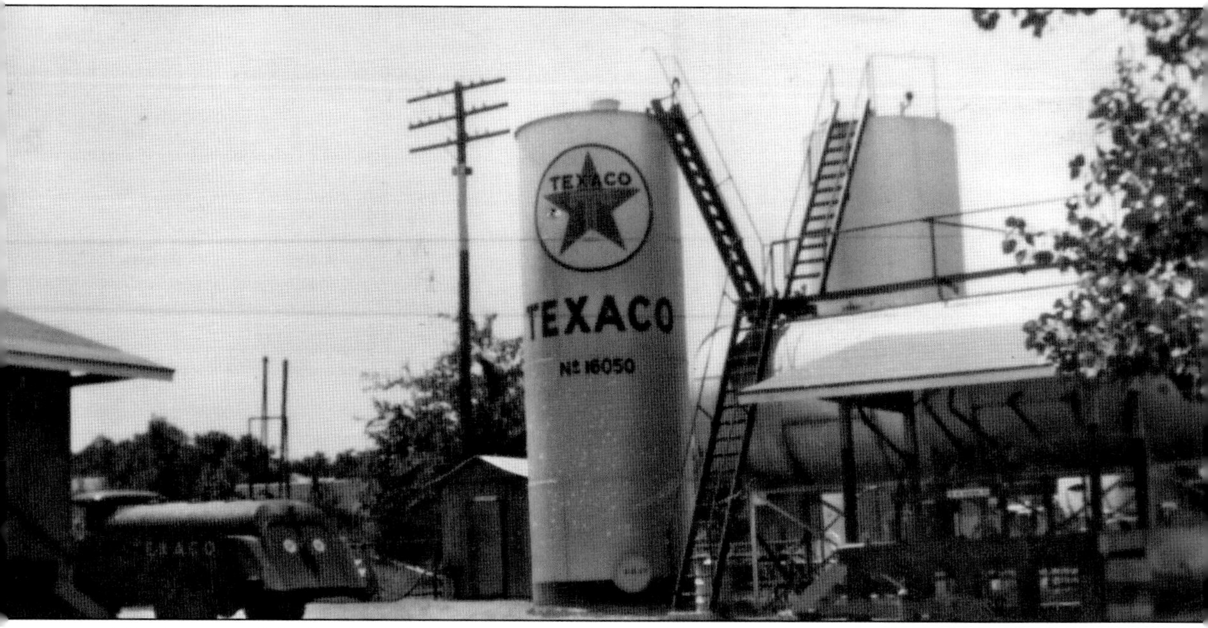

The Texaco Wholesale Oil Company was located behind what was the Public Welfare and Old Age Assistance Offices at the corner of South Main and Hill Streets, beside the Santa Fe Railroad. Four trucks worked daily from this oil company. Lee Atkins once operated it, and then later "Cotton" Wilcoxson did. After Wilcoxson passed away, there was no one available to fill his post except for his son-in-law, Mont Hendricks, who was serving in the U.S. Army. Hendricks was released early in order to come home and operate the business, which was important to the town. He operated it for many years before it closed down.

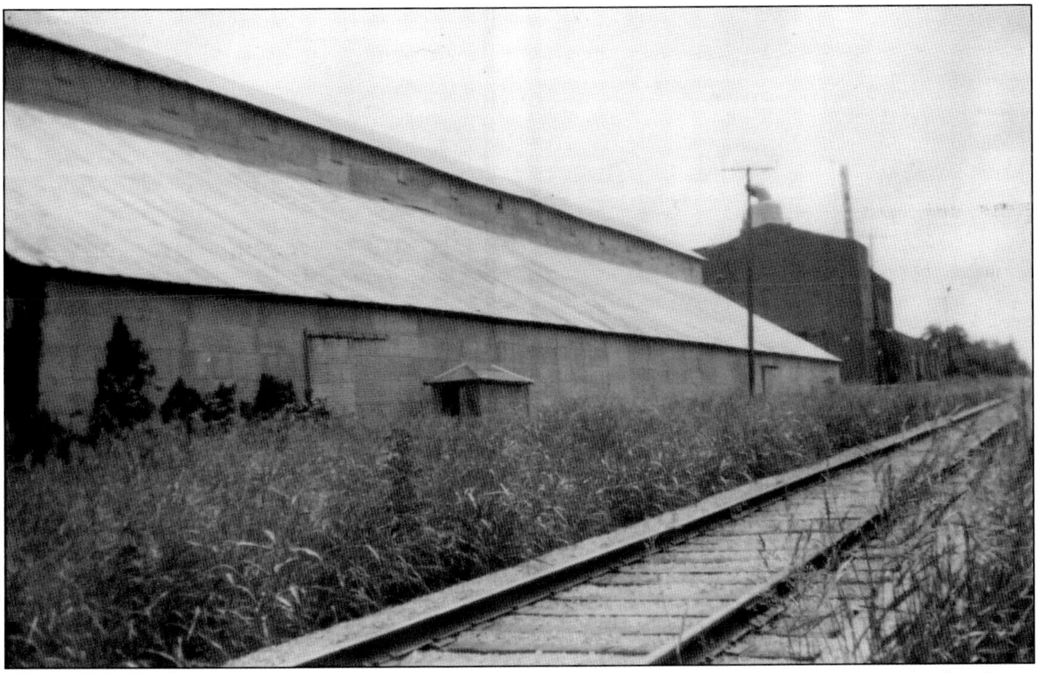

Storing 40,000 bales of cotton, alongside the Kansas City Southern Railroad stands this large cotton warehouse. The trains on this line traveled from Farmersville to Shreveport, Louisiana.

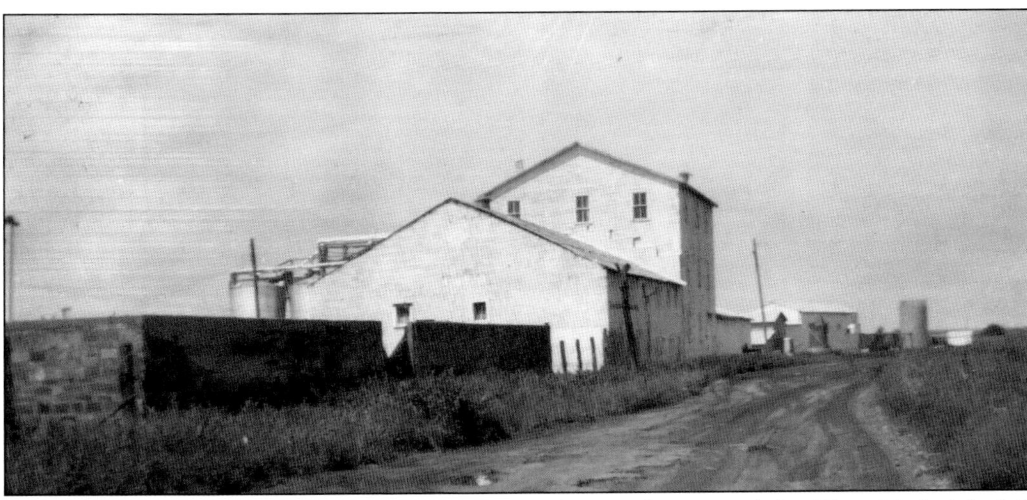

The Honaker Grain and Hatchery Company and manufacturer of the "Best Made Meal & Chicken Feed" is bragged of by this business that was located on South Washington Street, probably in the 1930s.

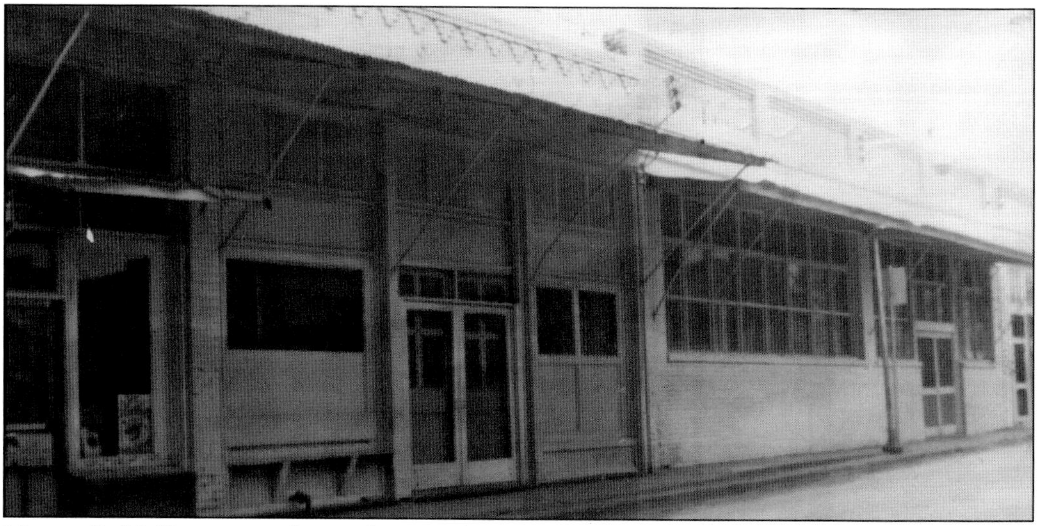

Marcus D. McCraw opened a candy manufacturing company in Farmersville in 1908. His wife, Josephine Cook McCraw, made the world's first "peanut pattie," which would later become well known in Texas and the South as a McCraw Candies product. They later produced Lance products. At one time, the company employed 100 persons. It was located on North Main Street, across from Cello-Wrap Printing Company, which was begun, in part, to produce wrappers for the candy company. The McCraws co-owned Cello-Wrap for several years. The popular taffy candy also was created at McCraw's, by Dee and Sarah McCraw. In later years, the candy company sold but the McCraw name was retained. It had two different owners, one of whom declared bankruptcy, but McCraw's was sold again. A company from Denver, Colorado, Hammond's Candies, finally bought the candy company. They still market the taffy under McCraw Candies name.

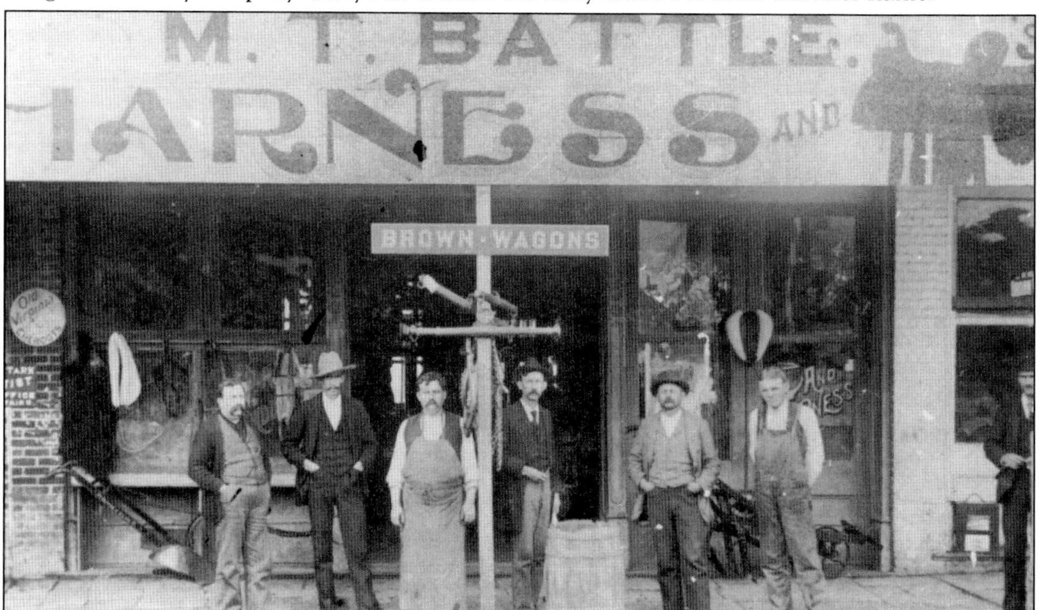

This is the M. T. Battle Harness and Saddle Shop, shown around 1890. Pictured from left to right, are A. M. Connor, unidentified, M. T. Battle, Paul R. Hamilton, Will May, Richard Hudson, and unidentified.

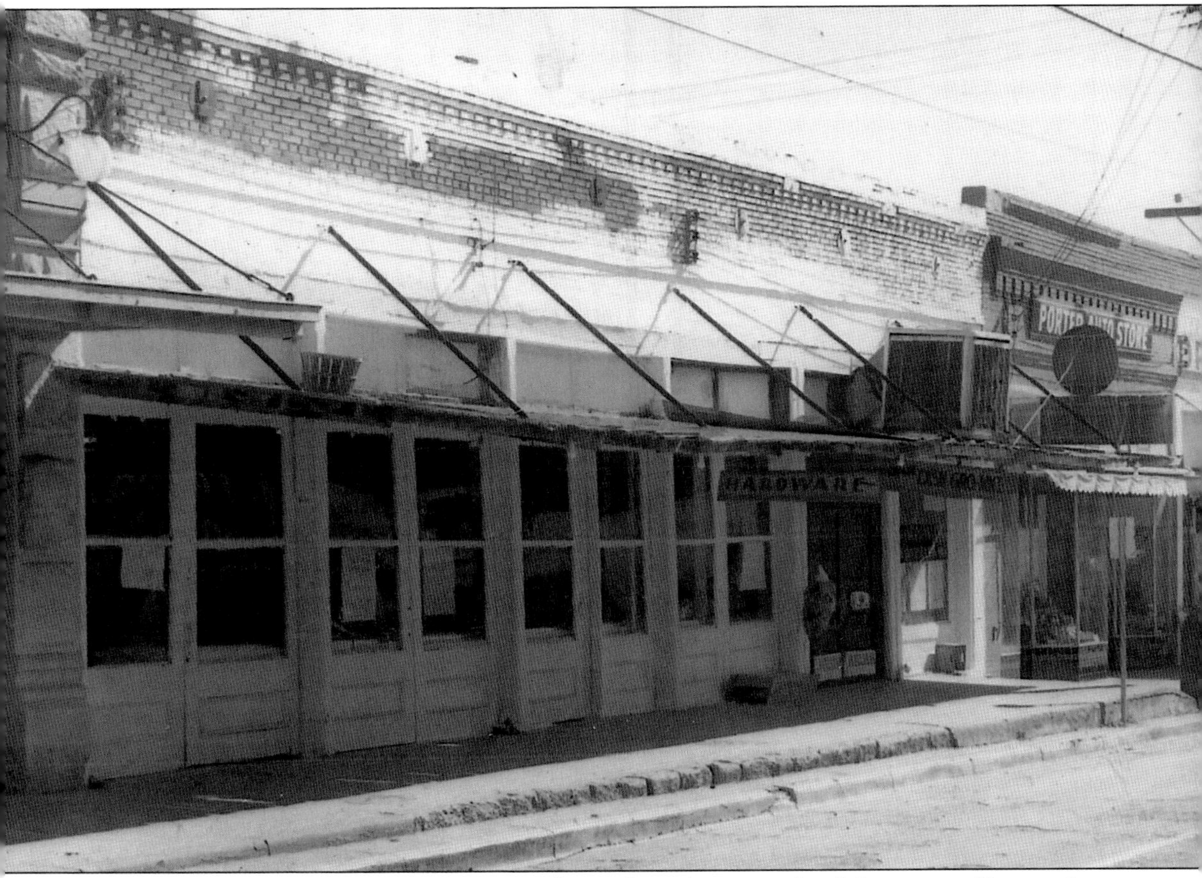

Cash Grocery and Market, shown here, was located on the east side of the square. During the 1930s and 1940s, there were seven different small grocery stores located on the square. Included, at one time, were an A&P and a Safeway store.

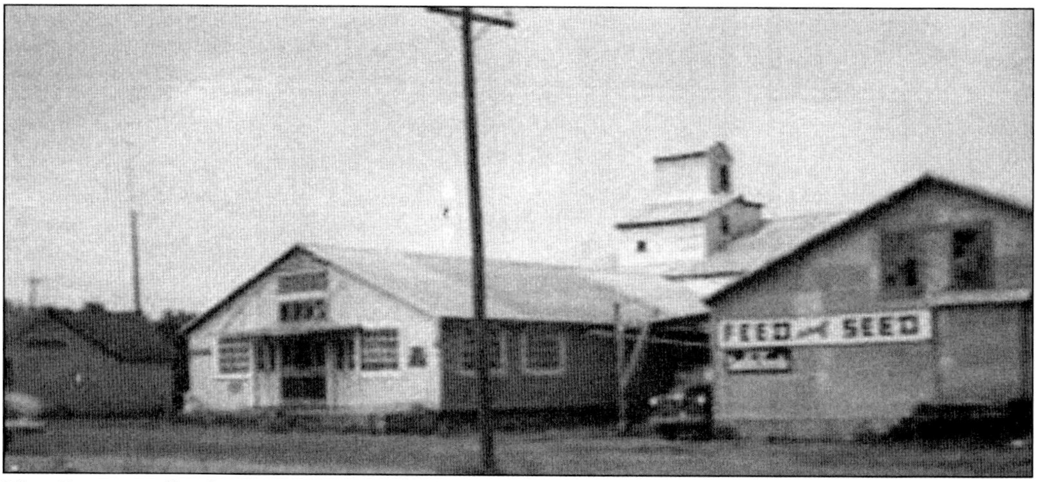

The Farmersville Grain Company was located at Santa Fe Street and North Main Street. It manufactured all kinds of dairy and chicken feeds. The company employed 20 men at that time. This photograph of the company is probably from the 1930s or 1940s. The grain company still operates today.

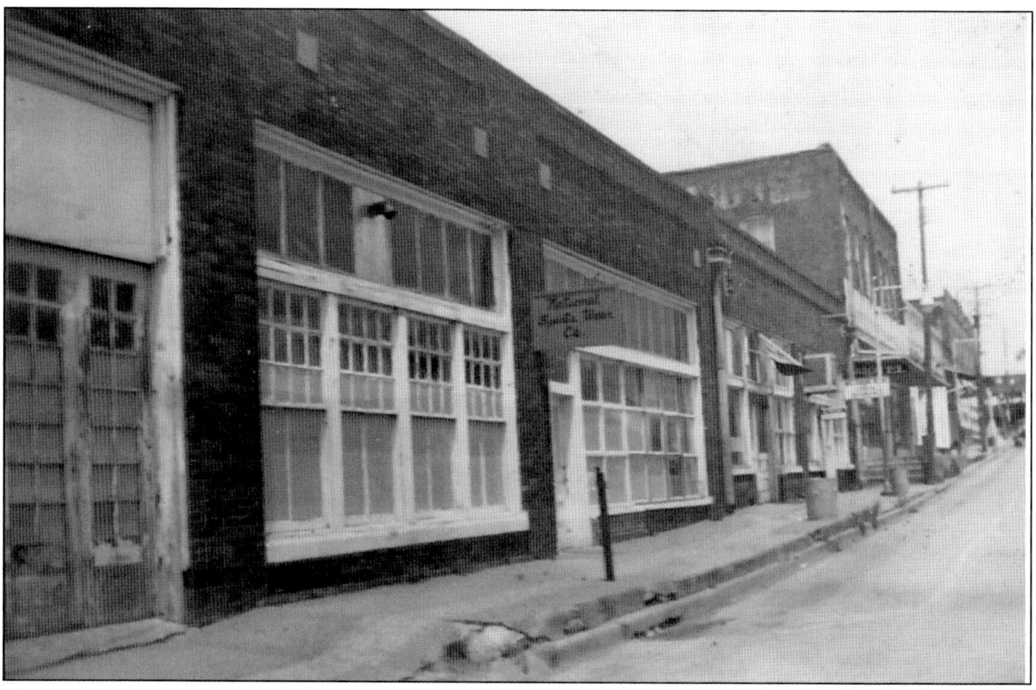

This manufacturer of men's work pants and other items of clothing was the National Sports Wear Company, located on South Main Street. It employed 62 people in the 1950s but is closed now.

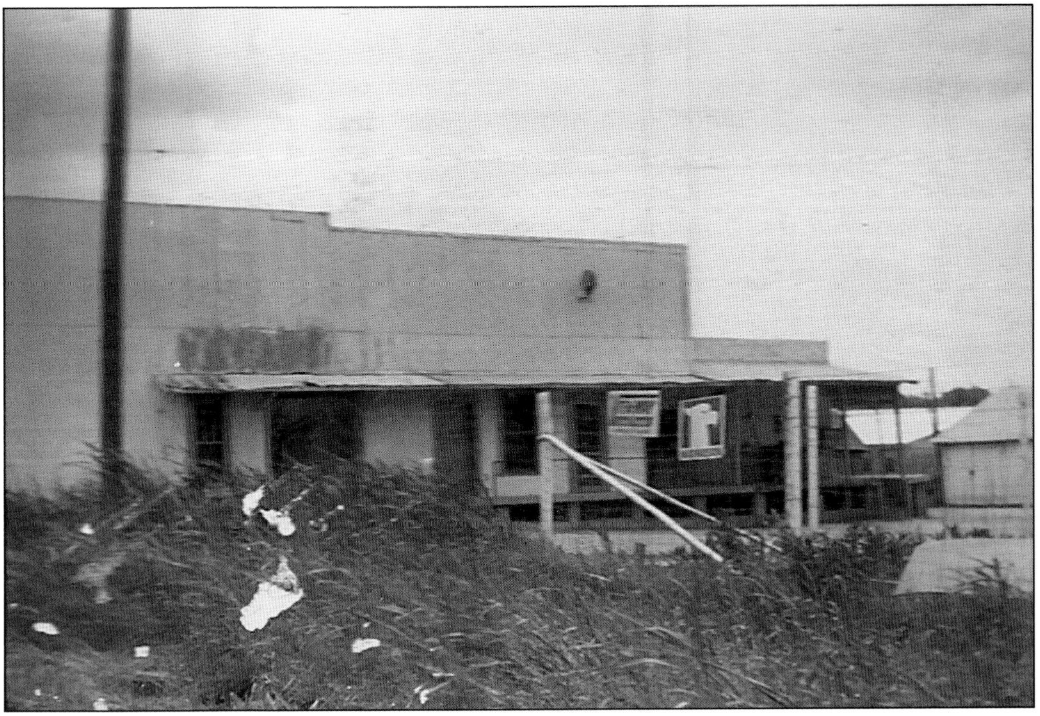

The Community Public Ice Service was located on South Washington Street. It began operations in 1908. Mr. Razor of Denton was the owner, and Charles Cobb was the manager.

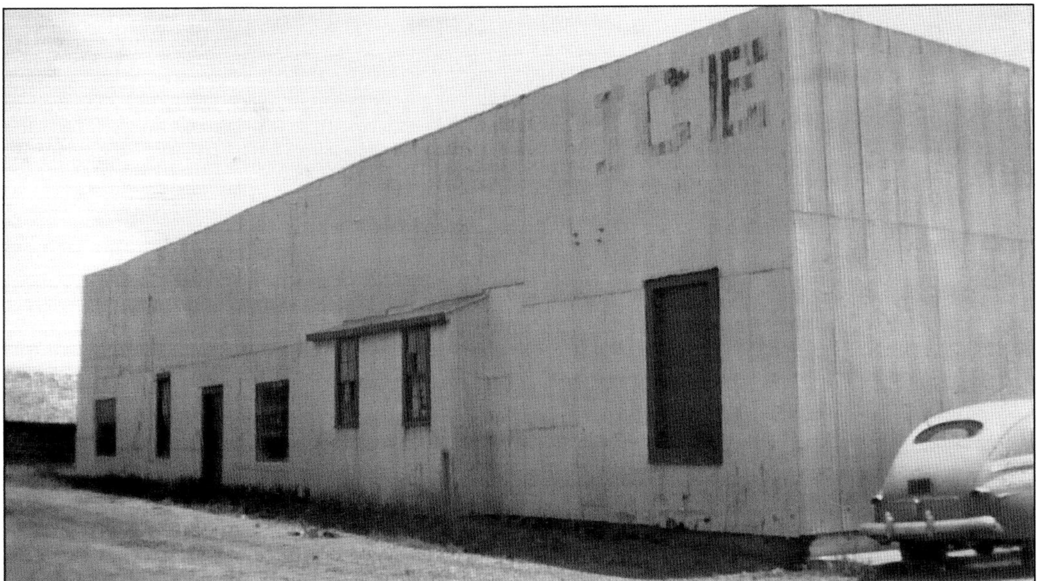

In 1916, Community Public Ice Service sold to S. J. Carver, W. A. Hall, and E. B. Hurd, who served as manager. The business supplied ice to Farmersville and the surrounding areas. Cars and trucks shipped ice daily to other towns. Merchants from Leonard, Texas, trucked ice to storage for small towns in Fannin County.

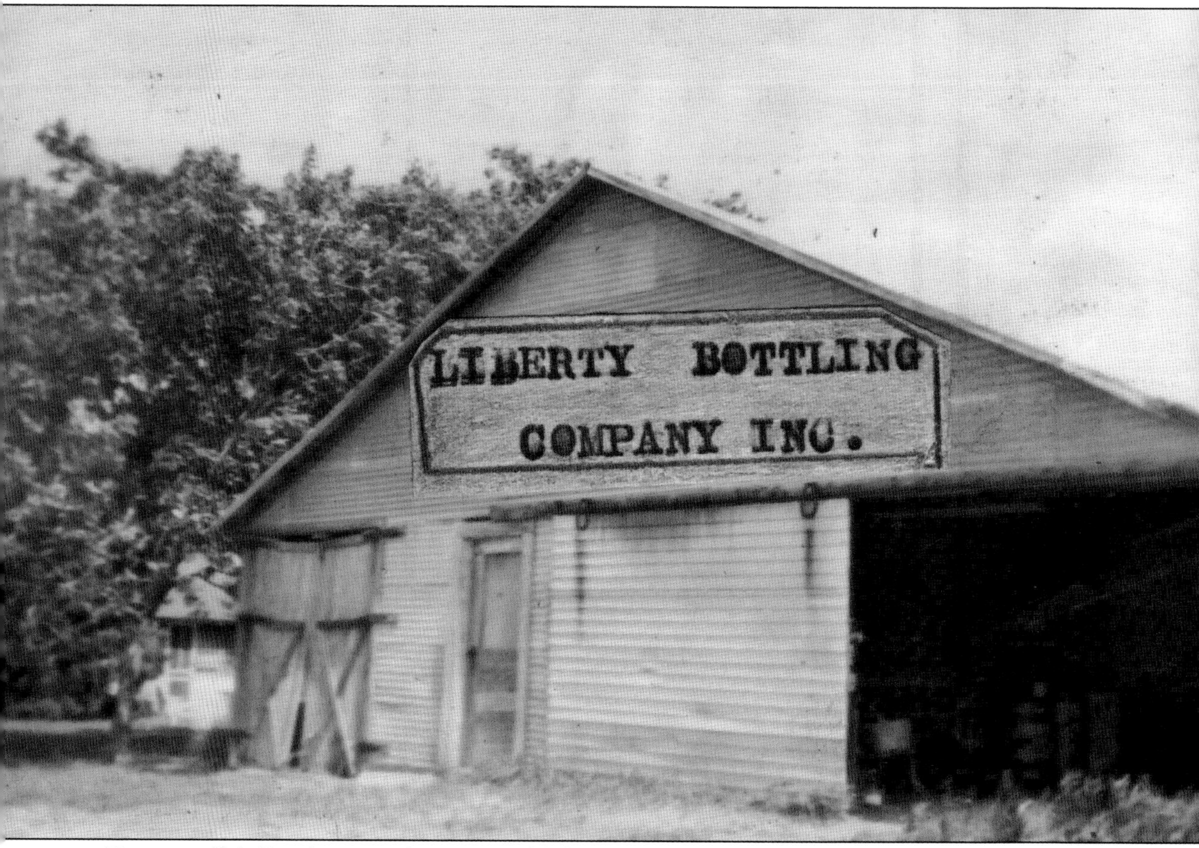

Farmersville's Bottling Works was established in the 1890s, owned by Mr. Crouse. He owned bottling works in other cities and sold to John Williams before the turn of the century. Bain Honaker owned it for about 10 years. He also owned the Coca-Cola franchise for a while, around 1908. W. P. Hogan operated the Farmersville's Bottling Works from 1912 until the1920s. E. L. Hale bought and operated it for about four years, and Frank Lenore operated it for only a year. The Liberty Bottling Works was owned by M. D. McCraw in the 1930s. Then Jason Prater owned and operated it for a number of years. It was located in northeast Farmersville on Jackson Street. Prater suspended operations during World War II, and it finally closed down for good in 1949.

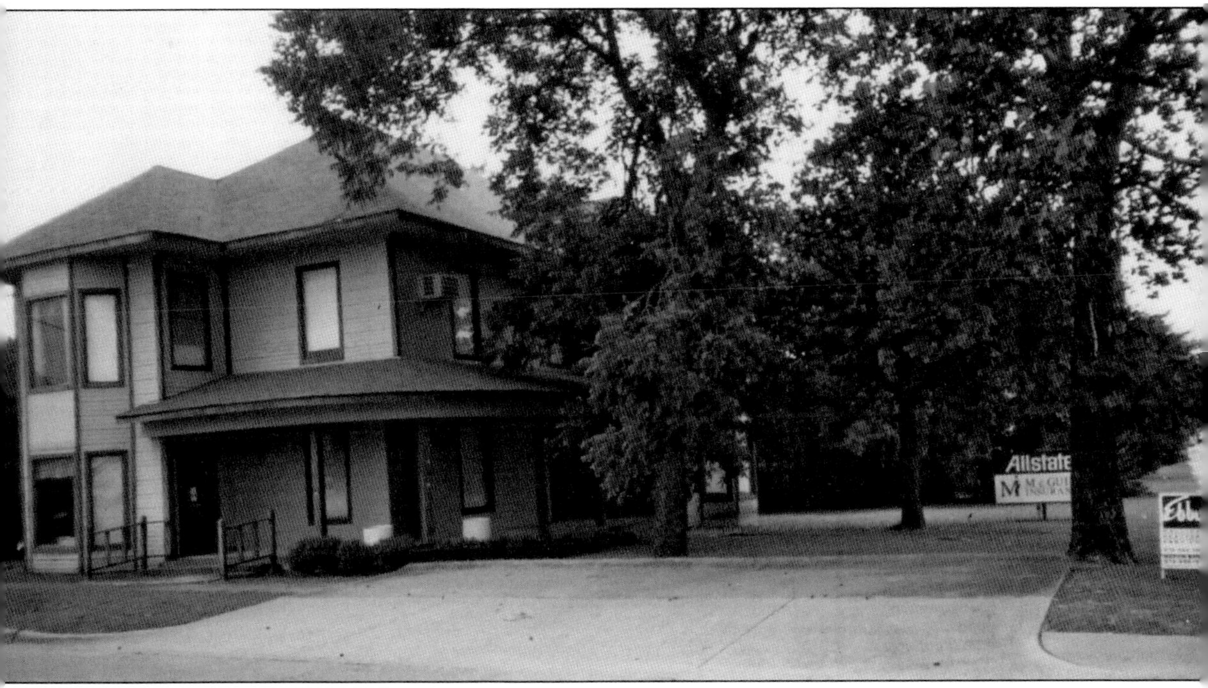

Located at the corner of McKinney and Johnson Streets was the Utt Boarding House, shown above, in 1906. In 1917, Anna Bell, wife of George Utt, sold the house to W. R. Ritch and it became the Ritch Hotel. Adah Johnson bought it in 1937, with all the furnishings, fixtures, bedding, and additional items included in the sale. The house was also owned by Byron Brumfield, W. O. Shannon, H. H. Smith, Larry Jones, and Dr. Jack Webb. Porches were added to the second and third floors on the south side. They were removed before 1945, when Nan and Zak Redwine lived there. At one time, the house was also known as the Cottage Hotel. Some remodeling was done later, and the building housed an attorney's office, an insurance company, and other businesses. Those businesses have moved, and the building was for sale in 2011. This house has had many people owning and using it for more than 100 years, though it still appears well taken care of and in very good condition.

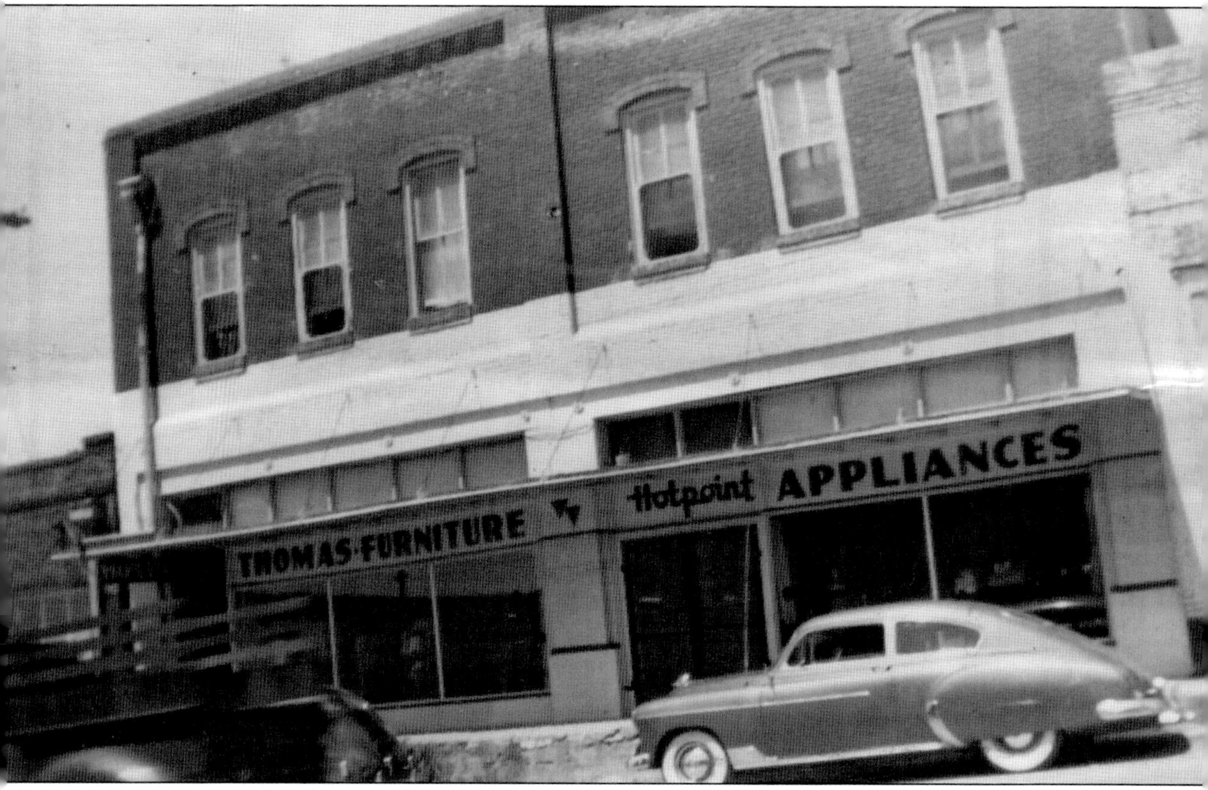

Herman May was born and raised in Blue Ridge. In 1945, he and his wife, Lynette, moved to Farmersville. Herman applied for a job as a salesman at the George H. Jones Furniture Company. He was reluctant to apply because he knew nothing about furniture. When asked during the interview, "What can you do?" May replied, "Anything, if it's honest." He learned more about furniture during the following nine years. One of his earliest memories was delivering furniture in a dump truck. Working daylight to dark, seven days a week, earned him a salary of $21 per week. In 1949, George H. Jones Furniture Company sold to Standard Furniture, and a short time later sold to Thomas Furniture. In 1954, Herman purchased the store from Thomas, and May Furniture was born. In 1966, the store began selling appliances as well. Wayne, who had delivered furniture and appliances throughout high school became co-owner with his father in 1969. After operating for 47 years, May's Furniture and Appliance Store closed in 2001.

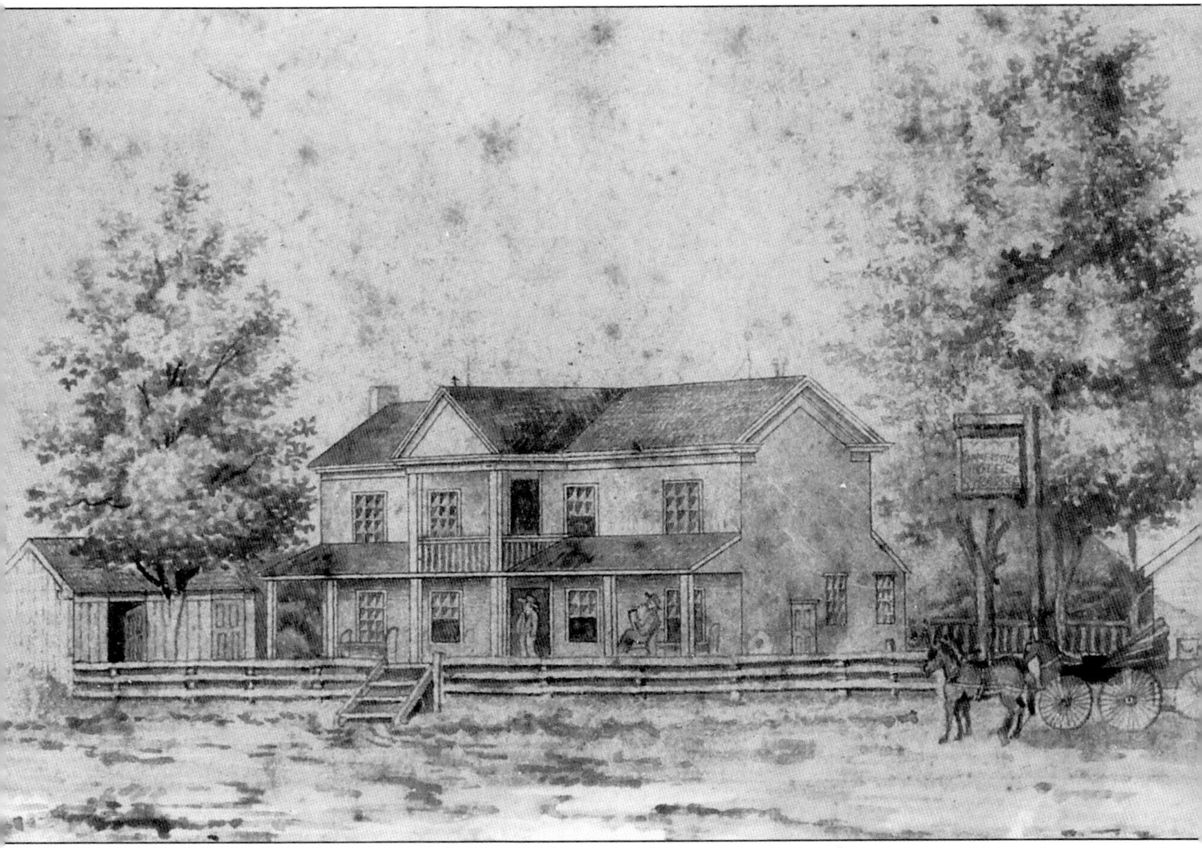

R. A. Rike owned the first hotel and tavern, with a wagon yard, in Farmersville. The Casey Hotel operated in the 1880s, the St. George Hotel from 1890 to the 1900s, and the Cunningham Hotel in 1910. Several private homes near the square served family-type meals. All did a limited boardinghouse business. The family-style meals were open to local citizens who wished to enjoy home cooking. The Rike Hotel was at the corner of College and North Main Streets in the early 1870s. Having served its purpose, the two-story building was razed in later years.

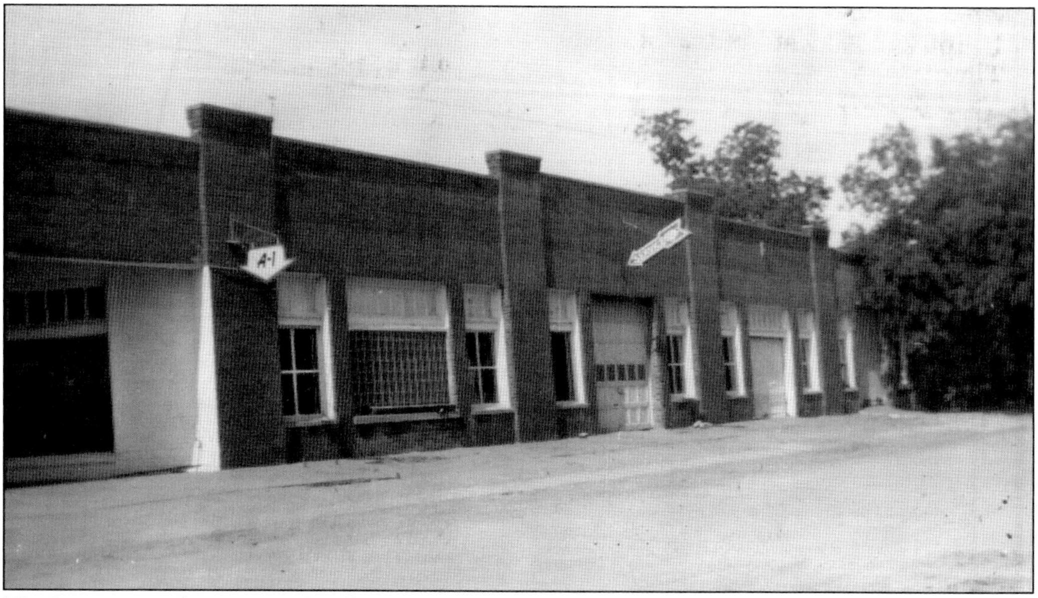

The location at the corner of College Street and North Main Street has been a very busy, versatile location for many years. Located just off the square, in the 1870s that spot was the wagon yard for the Rike Hotel and tavern. At one time, the Ford Motor Company occupied the location. Established in the 1900s, Ray Allison and Robert Holsonbake were the owners.

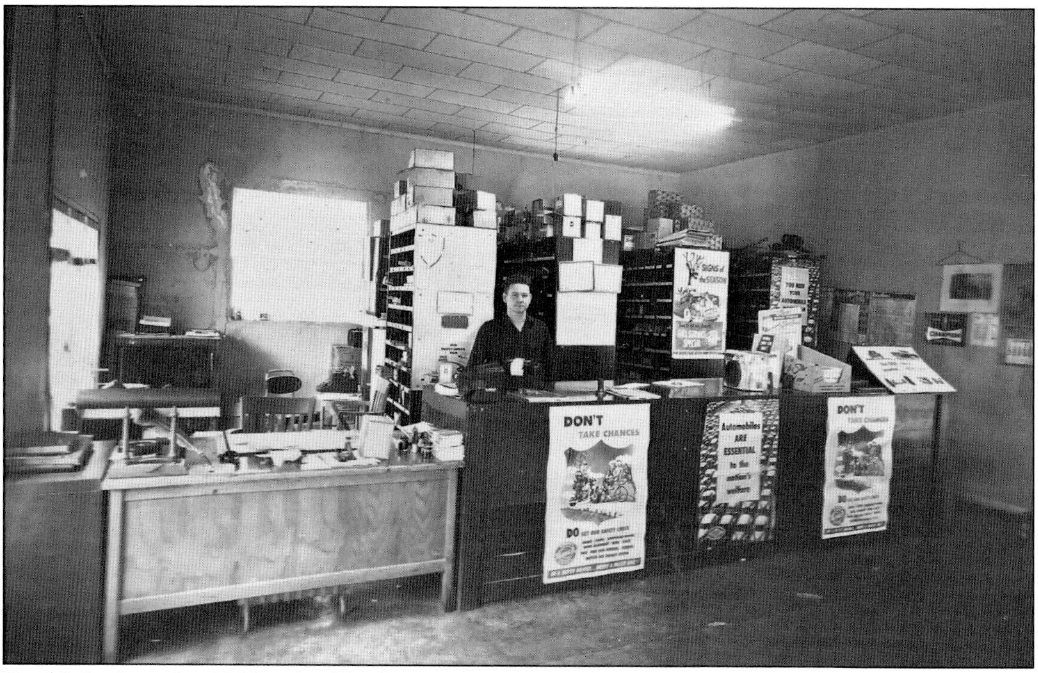

Established in the 1900s, this Ford Motor Company location was owned by Ray Allison and Robert Holsonbake. In 1915, Robert Holsonbake retired and Jack T. Webb bought out the interest in the business.

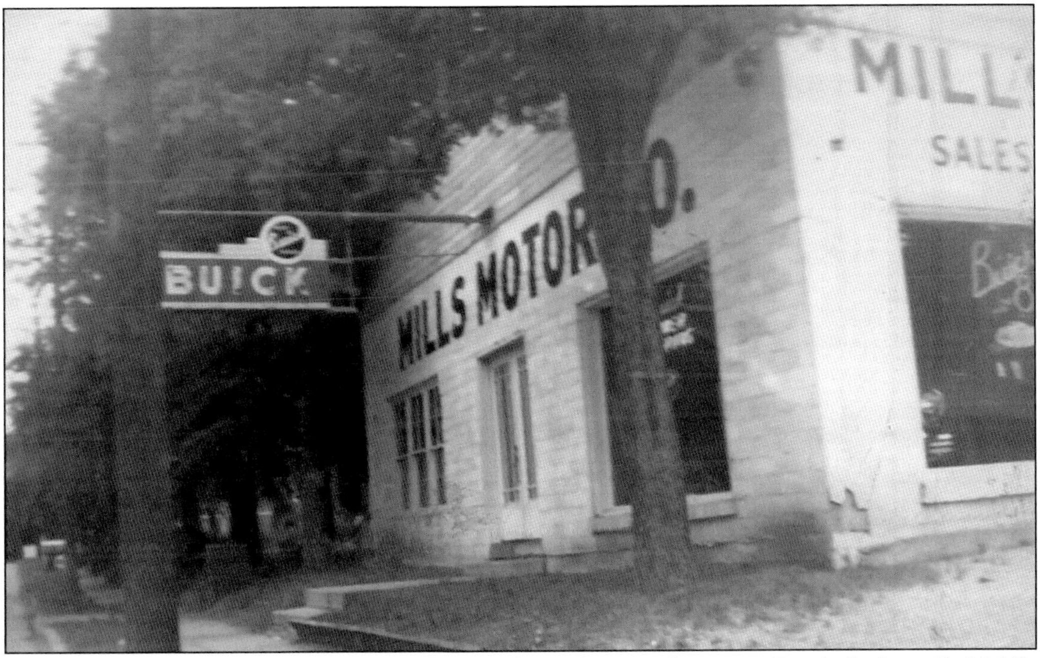

At the same location, the corner of College and North Main Streets, a Buick dealer called Mills Motor Company occupied that location for a number of years.

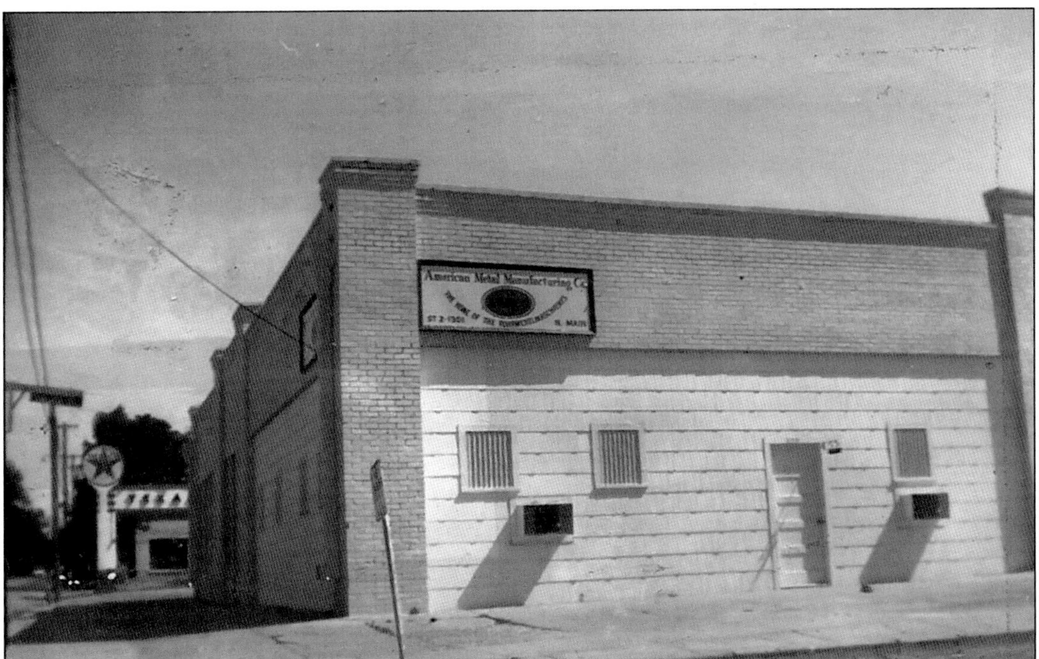

The American Metal Manufacturing Company was also located at the corner of College and North Main Streets at a later time.

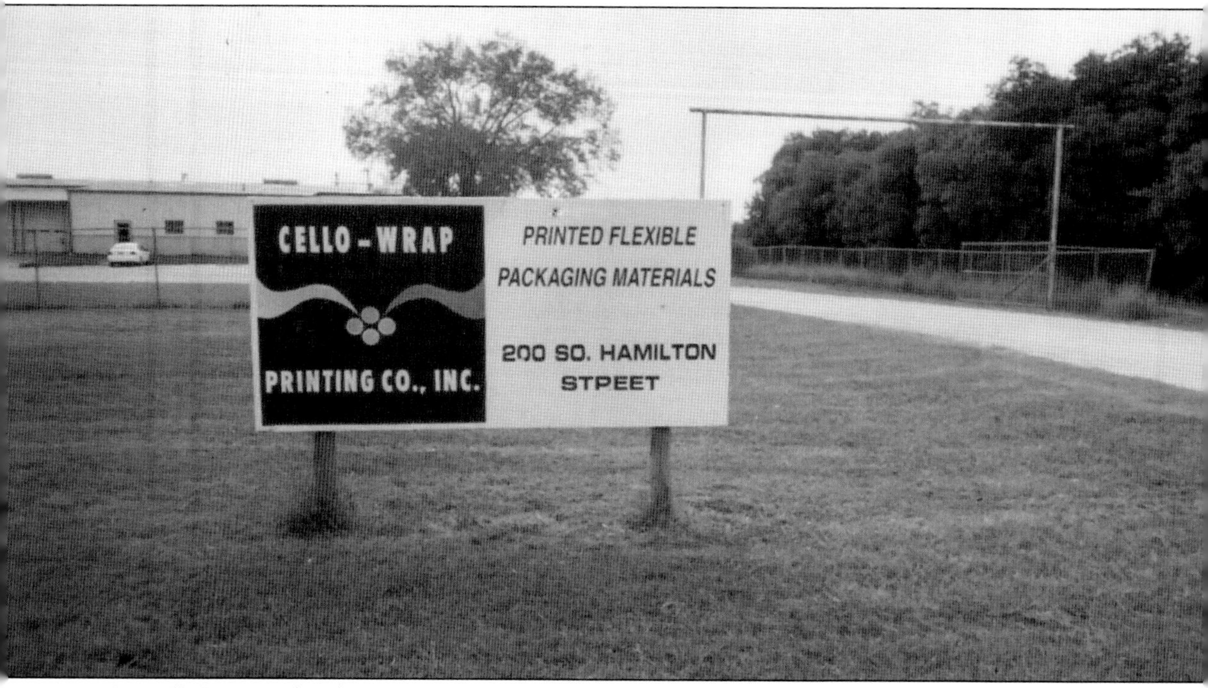

In 1953, James Whitaker moved to Farmersville from Greenville and started a one-man operation he called Cello-Wrap Printing Company, in partnership with John McCraw, the proprietor of the McCraw Candy Company, a thriving local business. The mission of Cello-Wrap was to supply McCraw's Candy with hand wraps for peanut patties. Whitaker and a machinist friend, Clyde Barnheart, conceived of and built a two-color press utilized for the work. By 1960, the company began operating its first commercially produced machine and it has only grown and progressed from there. Today Cello-Wrap stands as a Whitaker legacy. He has passed on, and the company he began has passed to his son Charlie, who is training his son Chad. The success of this business can be summed up in a statement made by Charlie Whitaker, president and chief executive officer: "Satisfying our customers by delivering whatever they are looking for remains the top priority." Cello-Wrap's major office is located at that busy corner at College and Main Streets. They have opened a second office, on Hamilton Street, pictured above.

Four

Farming the Land

The rich, fertile, black land of Collin County had no plow to break its surface until the homesteaders, the settlers, began to arrive. The Indians were driven out. The corn, the cotton, the wheat, and all manner of crops began to flourish.

As the men began to plow, plant, and harvest, they came to learn more and more. Cotton was the money crop for so many families in the area. When the cotton needed hoeing or picking, the whole family had to be out there, helping most of the time. There was no money until the crop was in and sold, so usually every one had to help.

Following closely on the heels of the cotton, onions began to get attention in the Farmersville area. A. A. Reagan planted 13 acres in 1925, harvested a good crop, and sold at a good price. Onions took over.

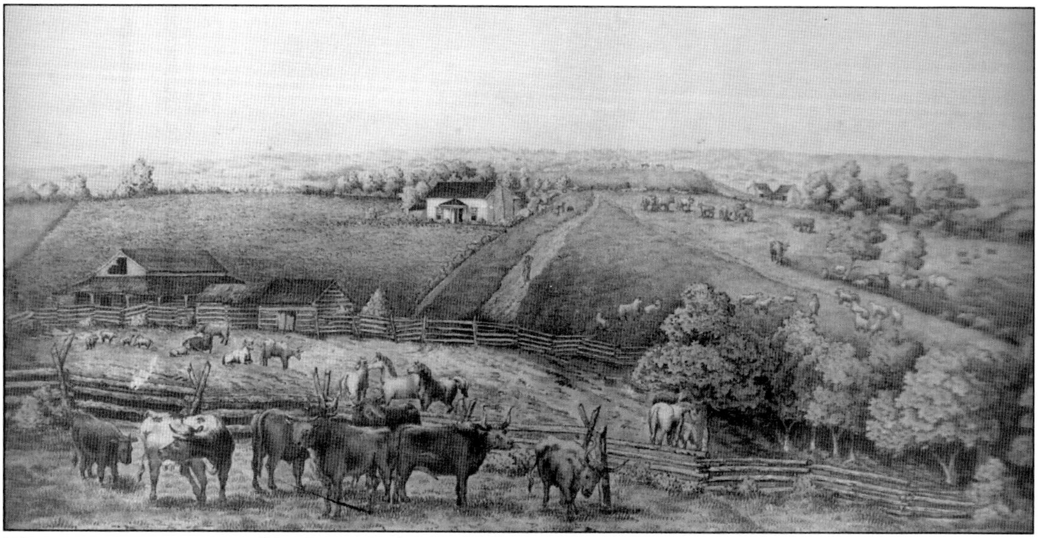

This picture was painted by R. A. Rike in 1852. It is of the Old Rike House, located three miles west of Farmersville on the old McKinney Road. The original log cabin can be seen in the foreground. It was the original home that was used for a few years. When a "modern" house was built, the old log cabin was used as a granary and a log barn was built for the cattle. The cattle pen was fenced with a split rail fence. The Rike Cemetery is located on the farm.

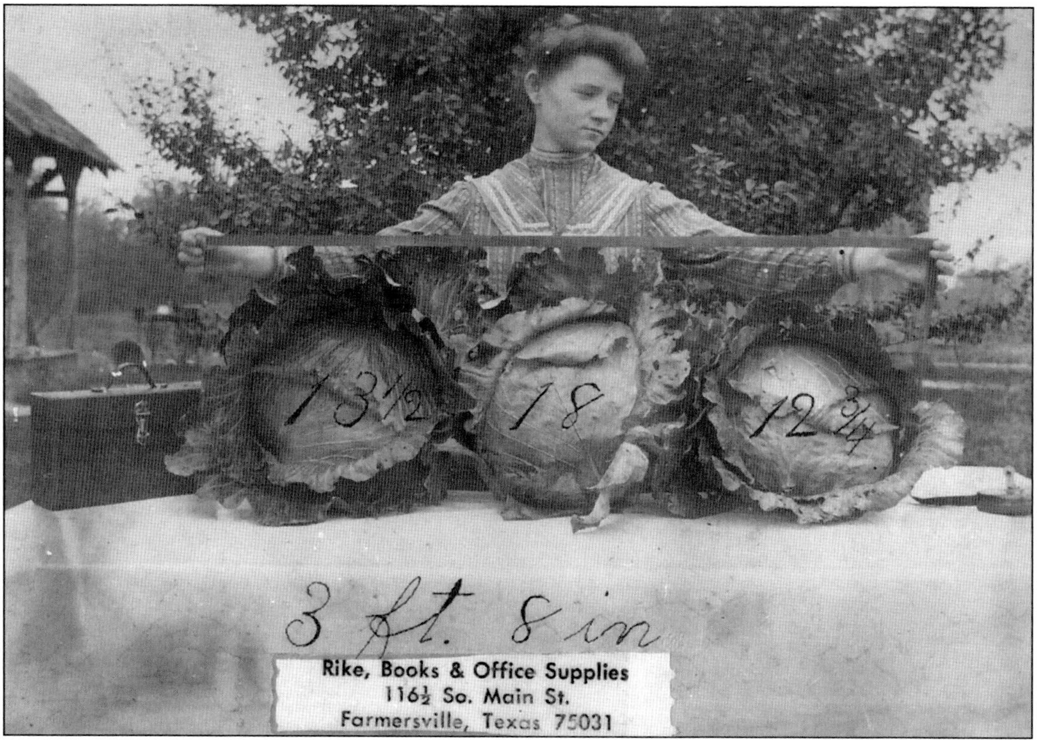

These three cabbages were raised in the fields of R. A. Rike's homestead, located west of town. The year was 1810. As seen in the photograph, one cabbage was 13.5 inches across, one 18 inches, and the last one is 18.75 inches across. The young lady is not identified but could likely be a member of the Rike family.

This gentleman is R. A. Rike, who raised these "Right Good Taters" on his farm. Records show that he took out a permit to build a bridge across Pilot Creek in the 1850s. Rike owned vast acreage on both sides of the creek. The number of acres in his homestead is not known at this time.

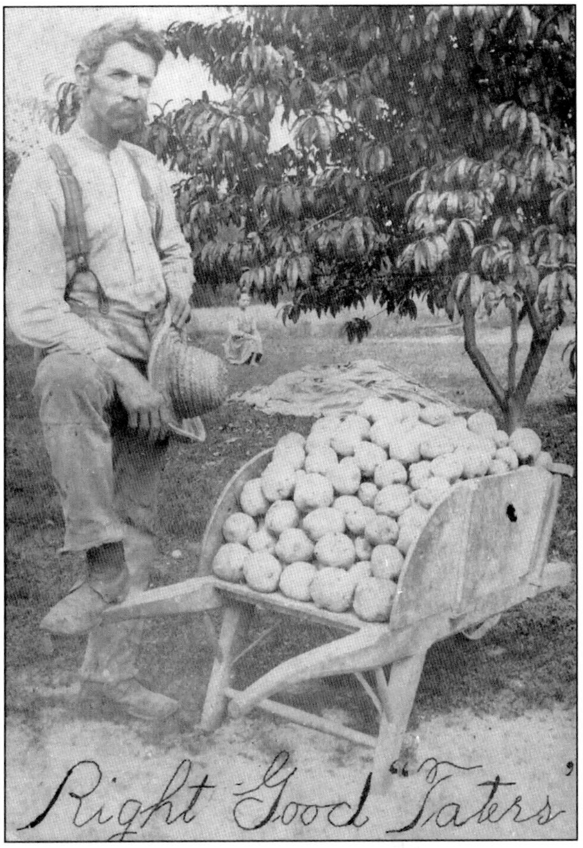

Here are two barrels of potatoes, with probably more produce in this wooden wagon of the day, ready for market. This produce was raised on the homestead of R. A. Rike, a prominent farmer near Farmersville in the late 1800s.

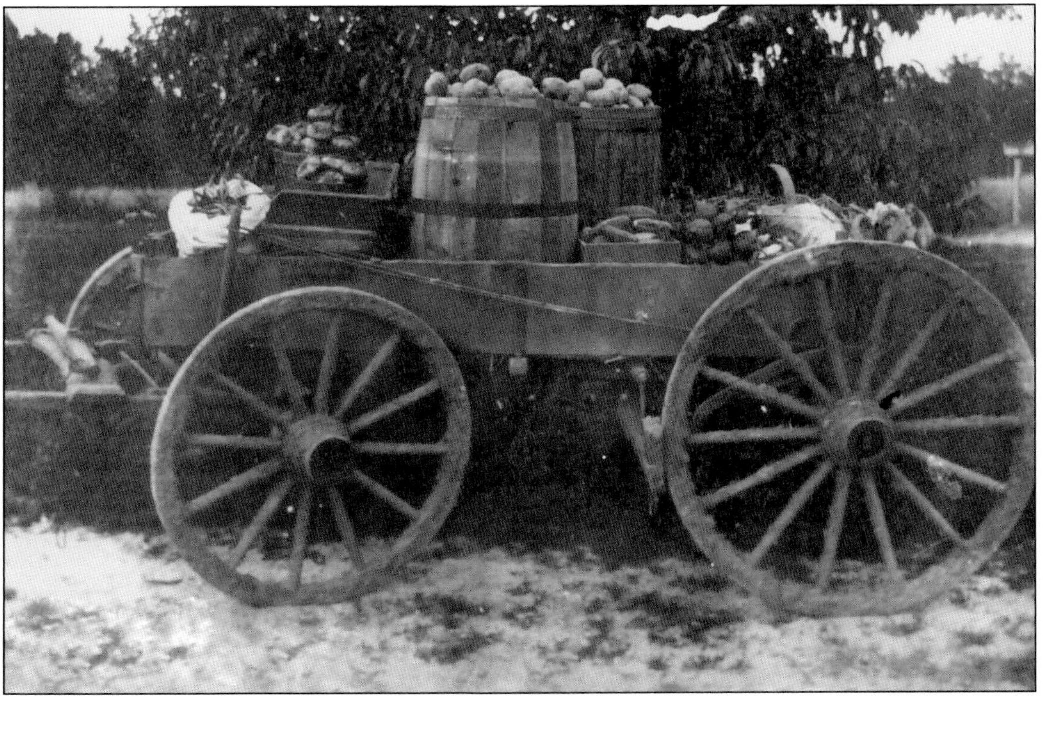

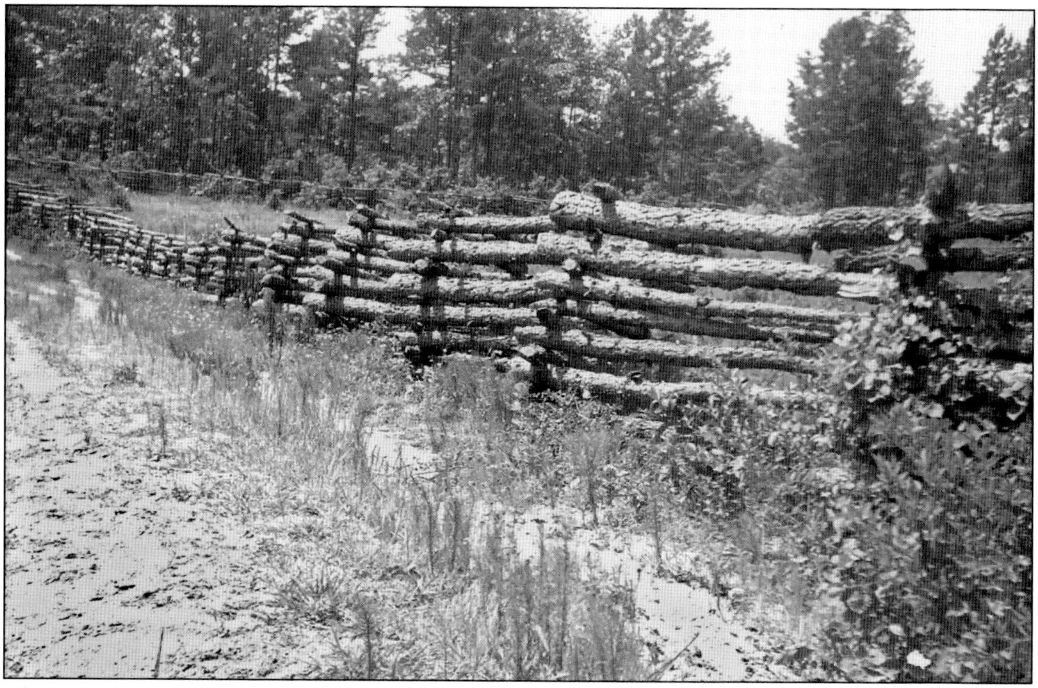

This is a section of an old wooden fence on the homestead of R. A. Rike. This fence was common in the early pioneer days, before barbed wire. There were no chain saws. The tree had to be cut down, and these logs had to be cut to the right length with either an axe or a two-man saw.

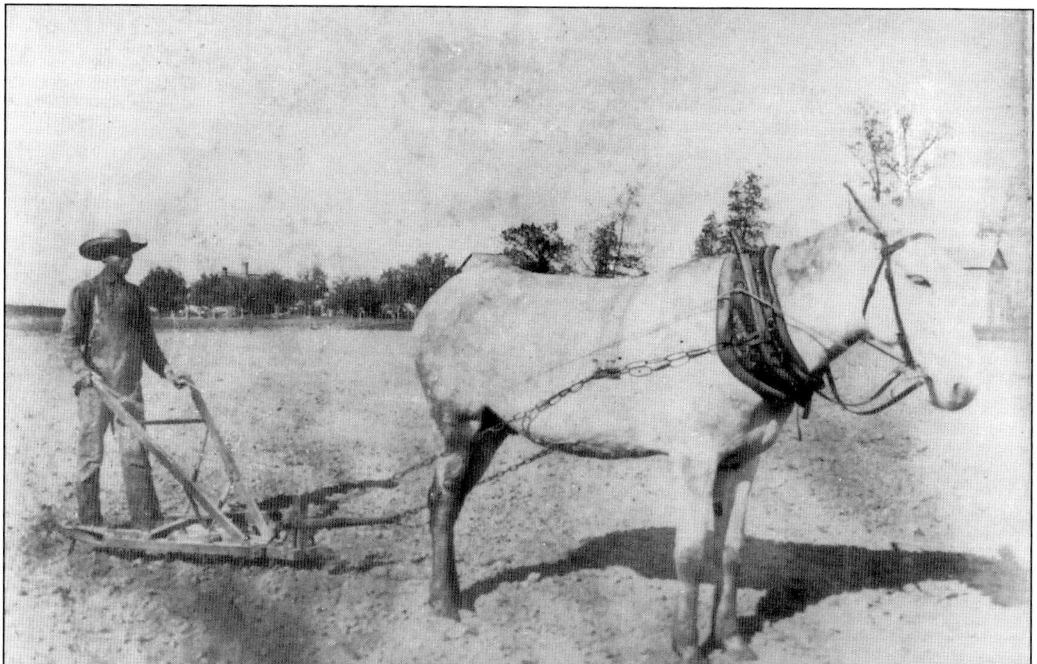

This photograph from 1850 demonstrates, yet again, the hard labor necessary to put in the crops. This land is again on the R. A. Rike homestead. Very early records show Rike being in the area in 1847. He was the grandfather of Charles Rike, of the Charles Rike Drug Store.

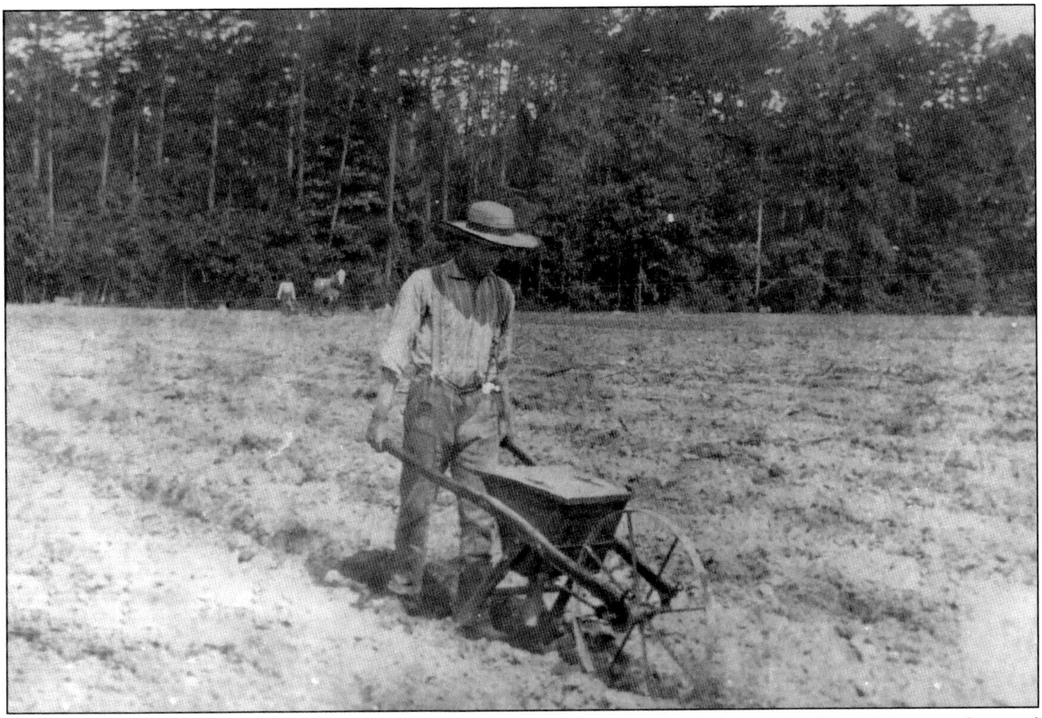

This picture taken in the 1800s shows how work was done in that time—by man, muscle, and horsepower, when possible.

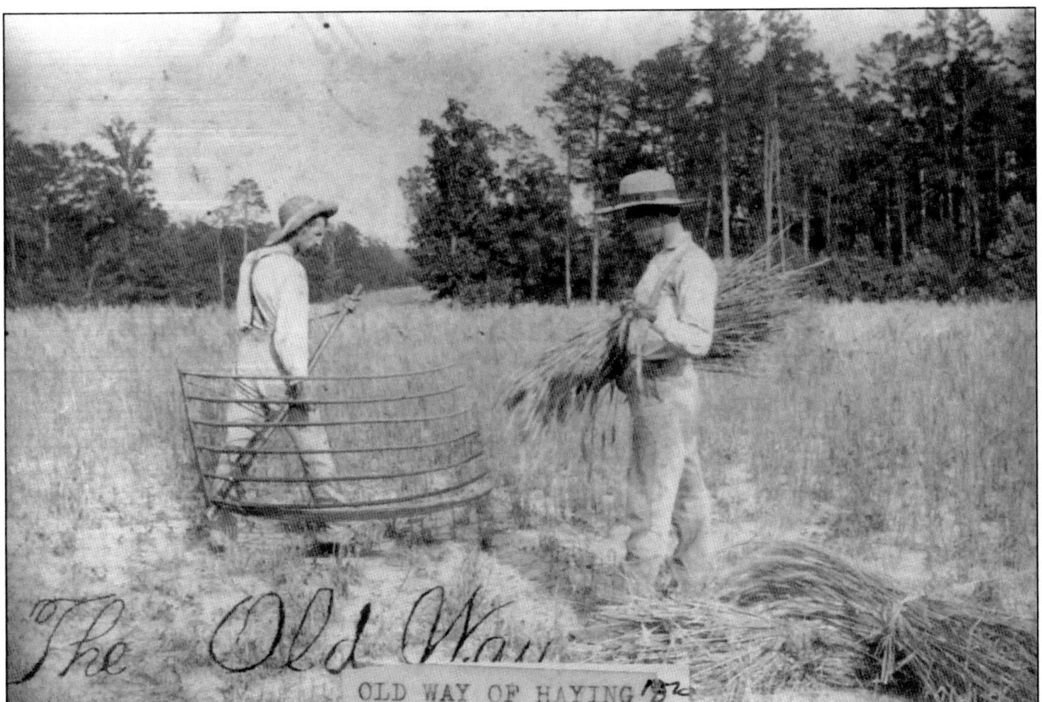

The "old way" of doing the haying was cutting it by hand and putting it in sheaves.

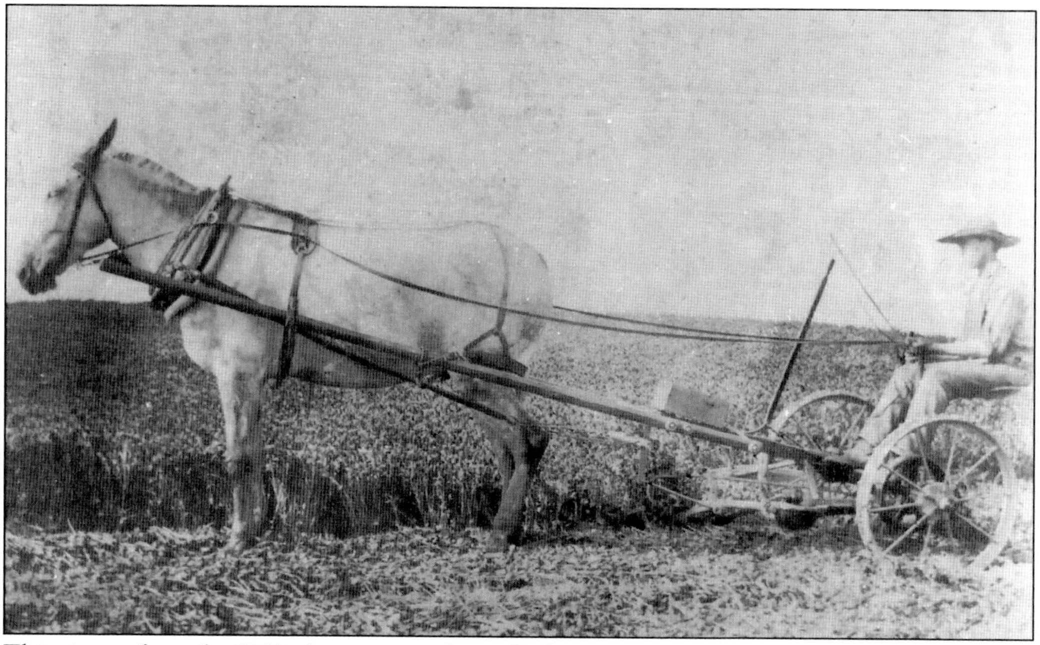

This picture from the 1880s demonstrates how all planting, much harvesting, and preparation for a new crop next year was done. A mule or a horse, hitched to the appropriate plow for each chore, slowly made its way over the ground, under the direction of the farmer. Many days of working from dawn until dusk were necessary for completion of whichever crop of field was ready.

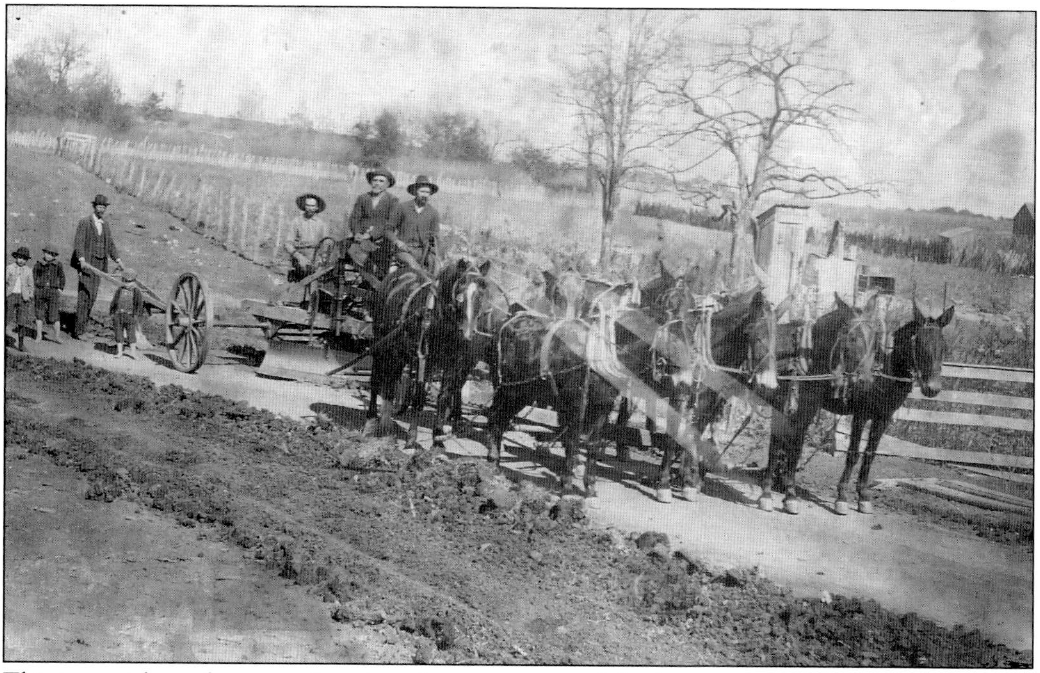

This is an eight-mule powered road grader system, one of the few types available in 1895. As with most practical living situations at that time, "necessity was the mother of invention." With no asphalt, no concrete, or very few gravel roads, it was necessary to smooth out many of the deep ruts, following a rainy time, in order to get to town for needed supplies or food.

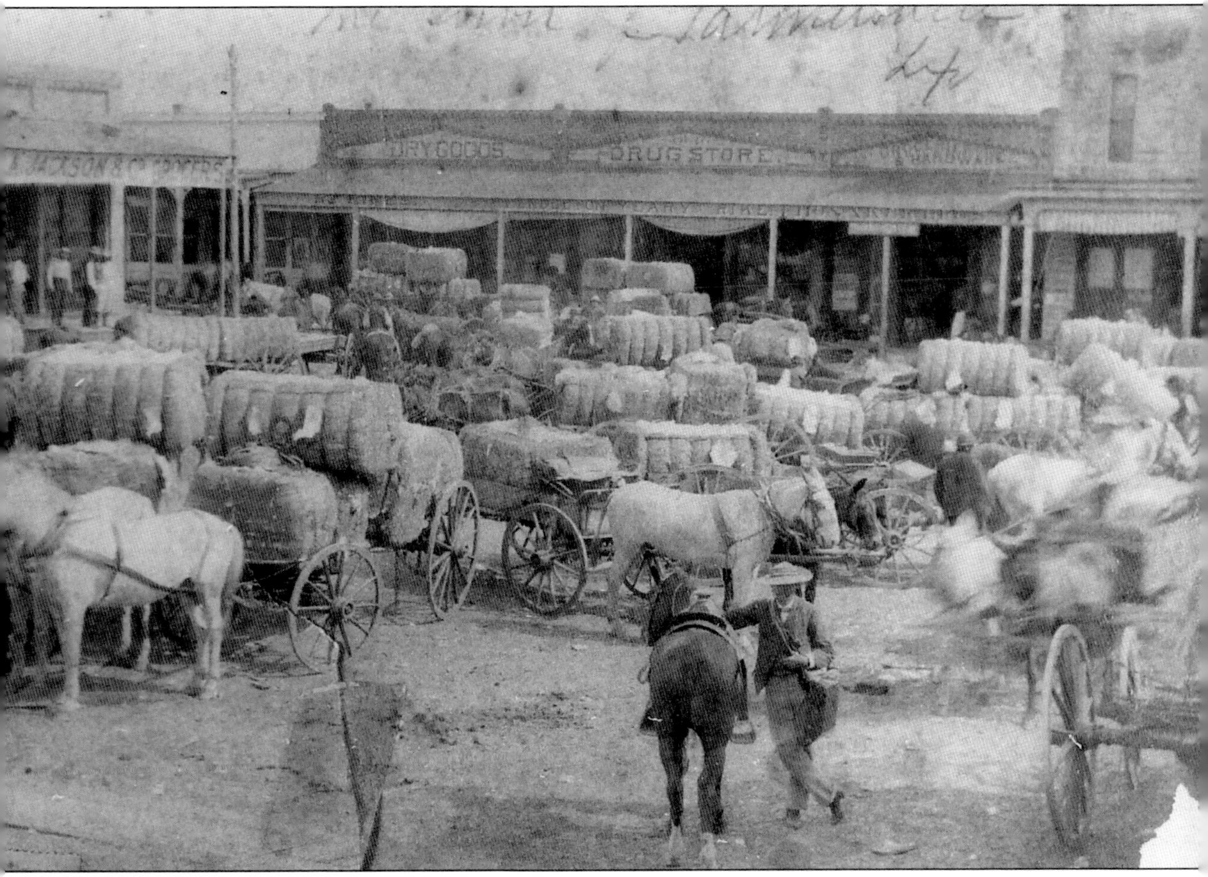

In 1886, pictured on the southeast corner of the square, are bales of cotton to be sold. Howard Crawford was the first man to plant cotton in the area. He brought the seed when he moved from Alabama to Texas. Experimenting, he planted nine acres in 1870. It produced 10 bales at a gin, which John Haven made by overhauling an old gristmill, run by oxen. Crawford hauled the cotton to Jefferson. He distributed the cottonseed among neighbors and several tried cotton planting the next year. With such good results, the cotton acreage was increased annually. In 1900, Farmersville was the center of the cotton-producing area. That year, there were 12,000 bales of cotton weighing 500 pounds each sold from the wagons. Along with those 12,000 bales of cotton, Farmersville shipped 286 cars of grain, 118 cars of livestock, 165 cars of flour, 267 cars of oil mill products, 150 cars of bois d'arc posts, and 122 cars of miscellaneous freight. Two rail lines shipped these products from Farmersville in 1900.

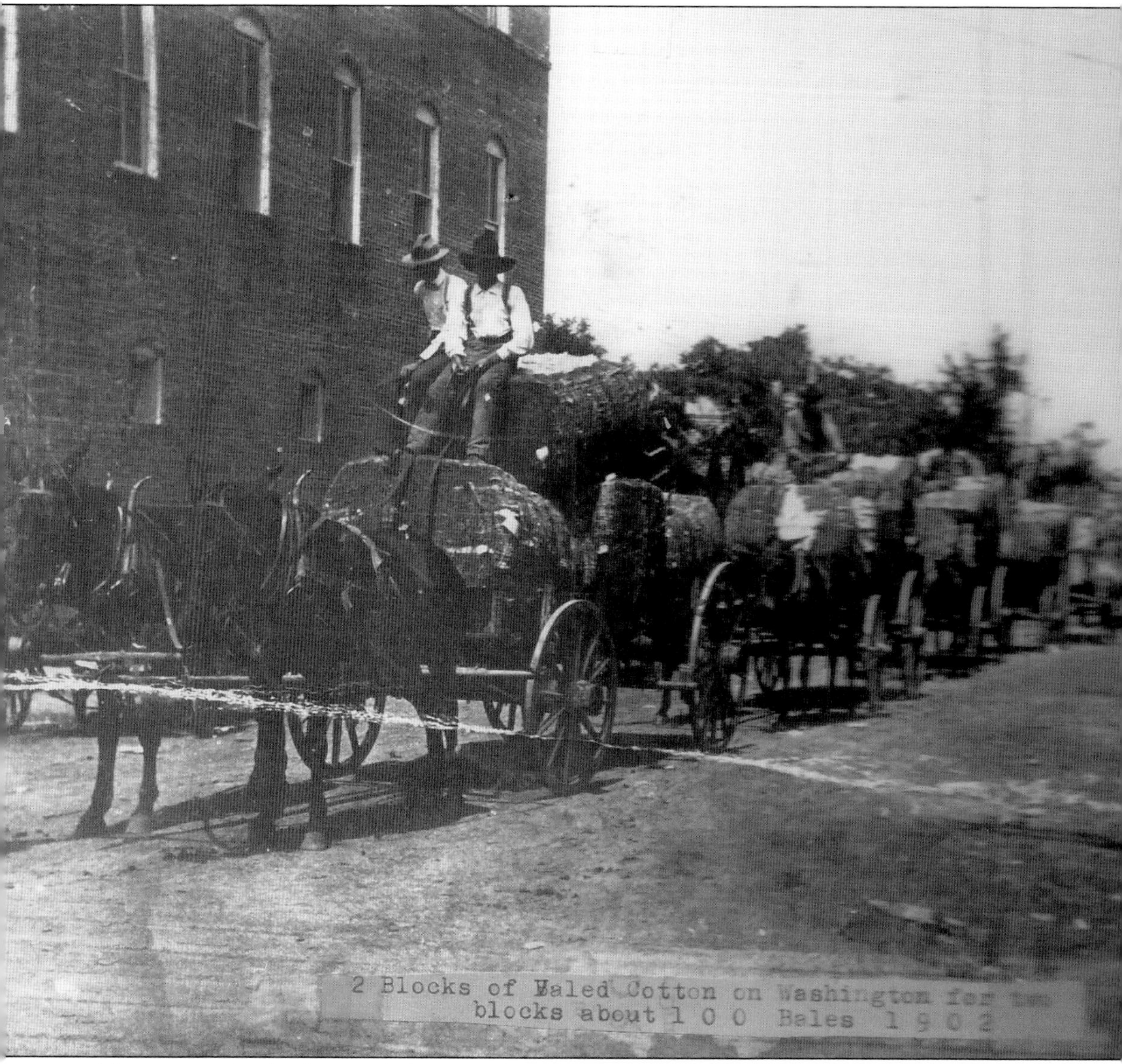

These wagonloads of cotton bales extend on Washington Street for two blocks. There are about 100 bales of cotton in this line, pictured in 1902. Cotton was grown all over Collin County, which is known for its excellent, fertile black land. These wagons, loaded with bales of cotton, have been pulled, by mules or horses, for 10 miles down country roads. They have arrived from the small town of Blue Ridge, which has no railroad, and Farmersville is the nearest shipping point to them. Cotton produced in the area during the Civil War was used in the war effort, as many other things were. A story is told of a wagonload of cotton on its way from Farmersville to Greenville that was stopped by a few armed women who were that desperate for cotton to use for spinning and weaving clothes and other things. The Confederate soldiers were so amused they let the women take the cotton.

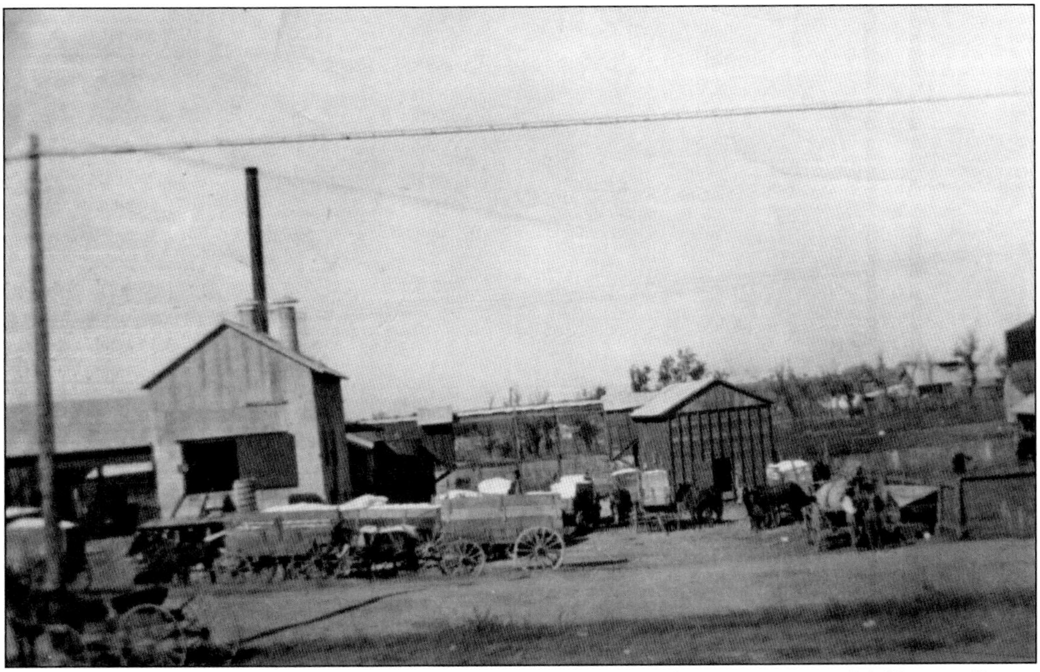

In 1910, there were six cotton gins in Farmersville. Josh Gotcher's gin was on McKinney Street where Trinity Baptist Church is now. Cotton was king and there were endless fields of cotton everywhere. In 1950, when the Korean War began, cotton sold for 50¢ per pound. The government placed a ceiling of 45¢ on it. That was probably the highest price ever paid in Collin County.

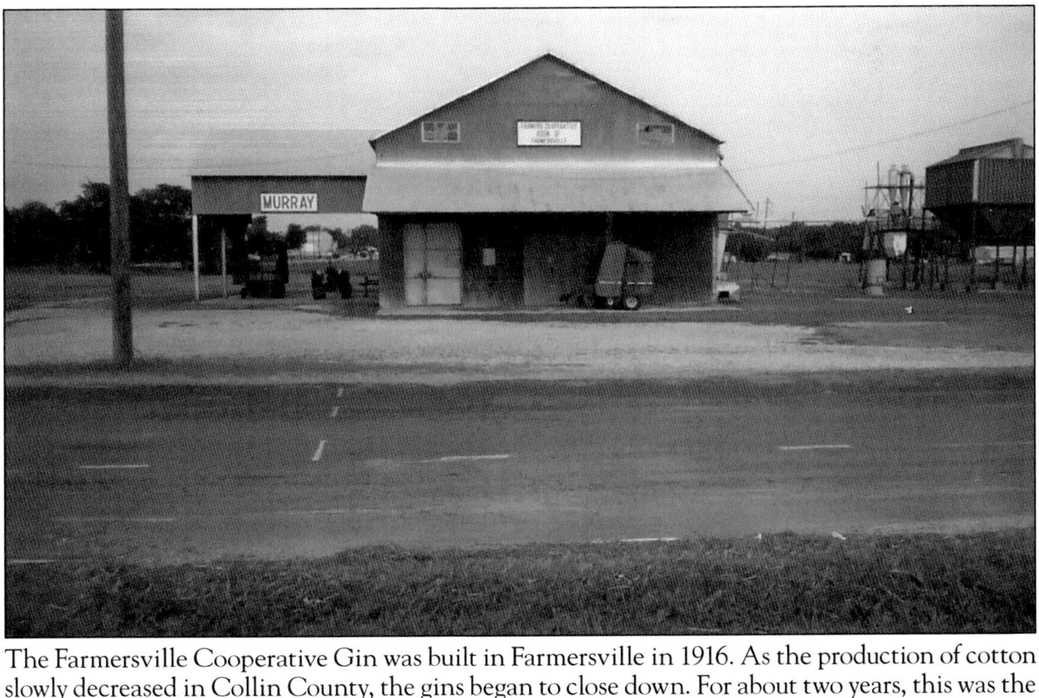

The Farmersville Cooperative Gin was built in Farmersville in 1916. As the production of cotton slowly decreased in Collin County, the gins began to close down. For about two years, this was the last gin in Collin County still operating. Then in 2005, it closed its doors as a major farming industry ended. This is that gin as it stands today, deserted and quiet, its services no longer needed.

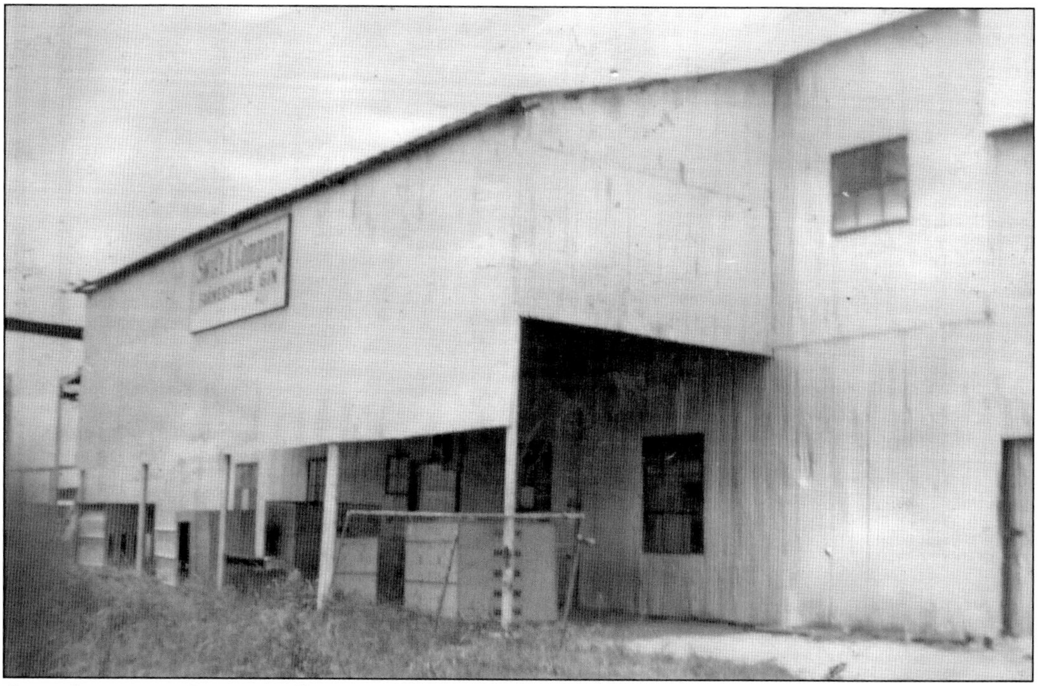

One of six gins in Farmersville at one time, this is the Swift's and Company Gin on South Johnson Street. It was beside one of the railroad tracks.

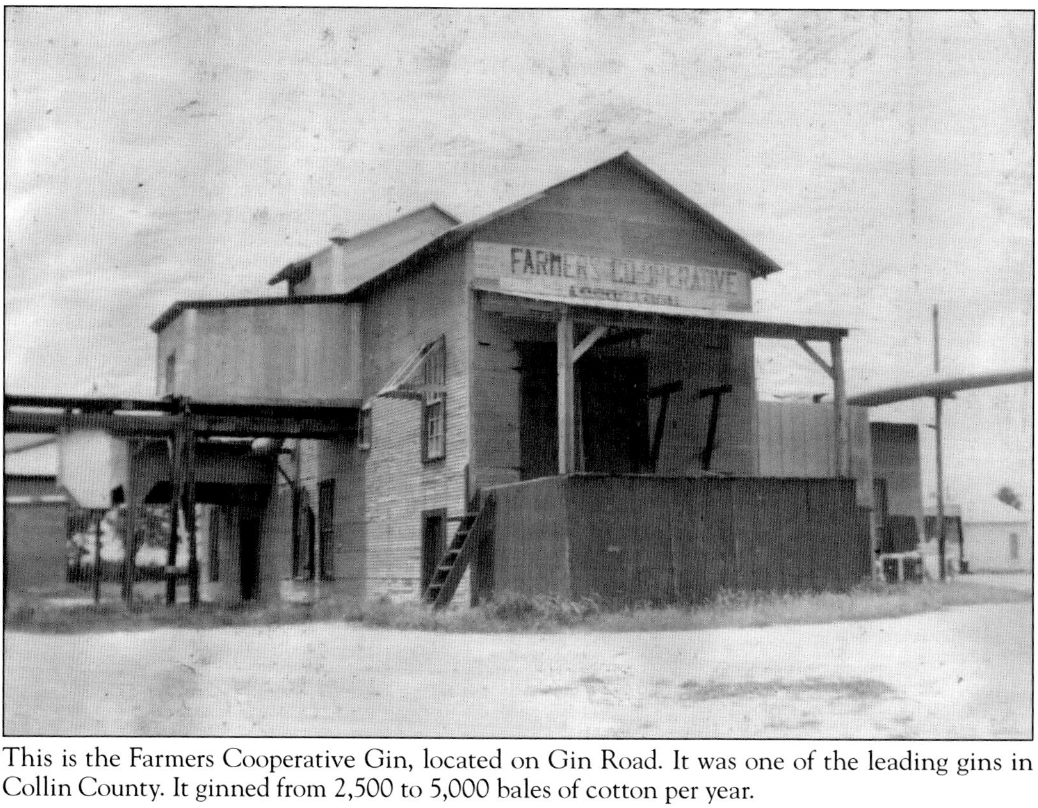

This is the Farmers Cooperative Gin, located on Gin Road. It was one of the leading gins in Collin County. It ginned from 2,500 to 5,000 bales of cotton per year.

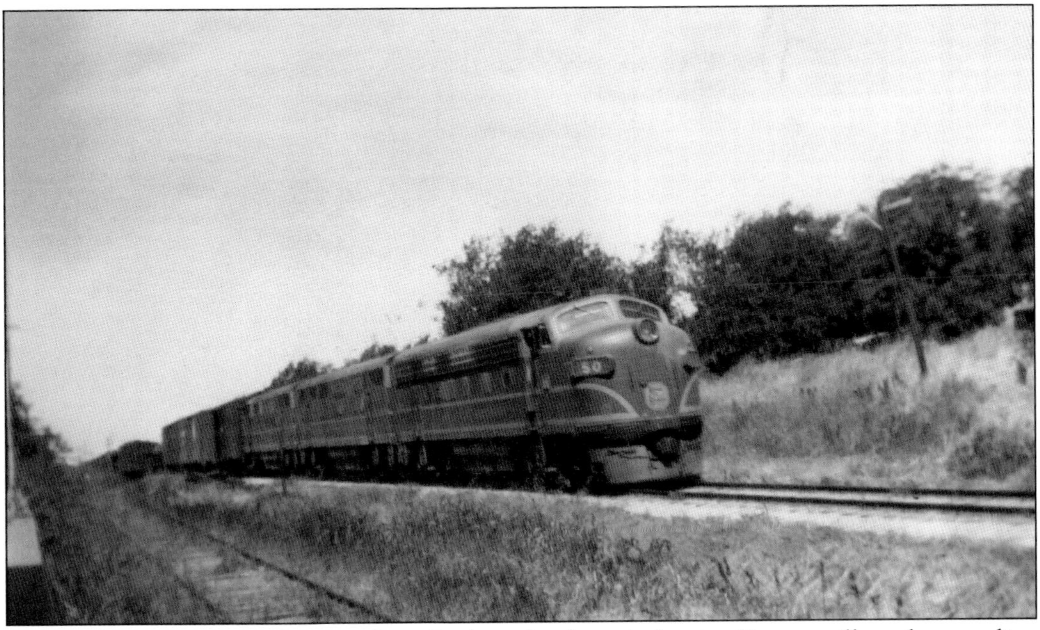

Pictured here is a Kansas City Southern Railway freight train leaving Farmersville and proceeding through Greenville, en route to Shreveport, Louisiana.

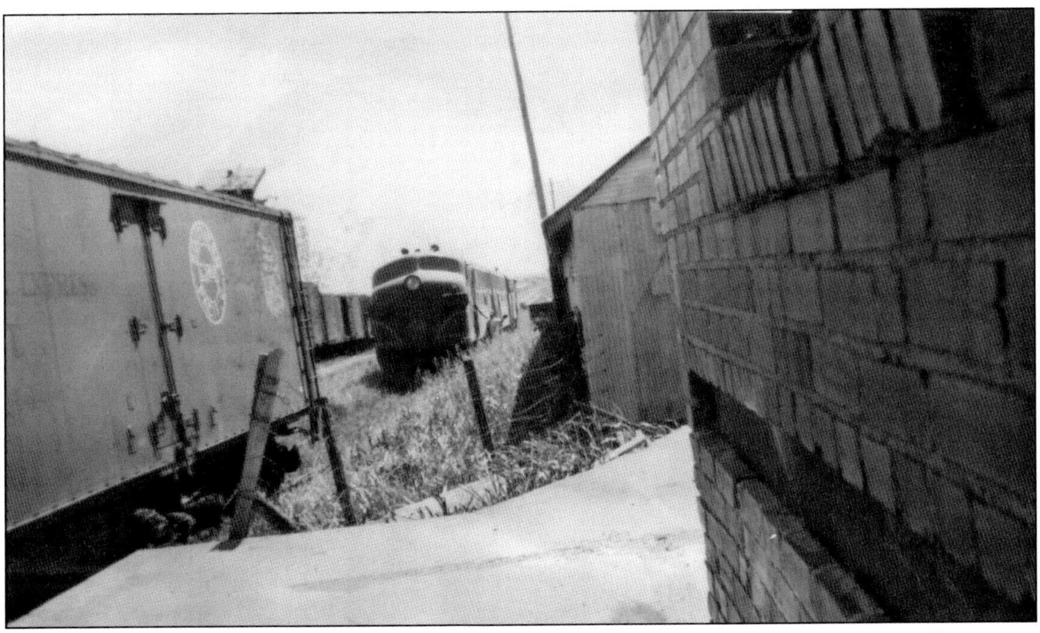

Located at the Texas Cotton Terminal in Farmersville, these trains are switching tracks.

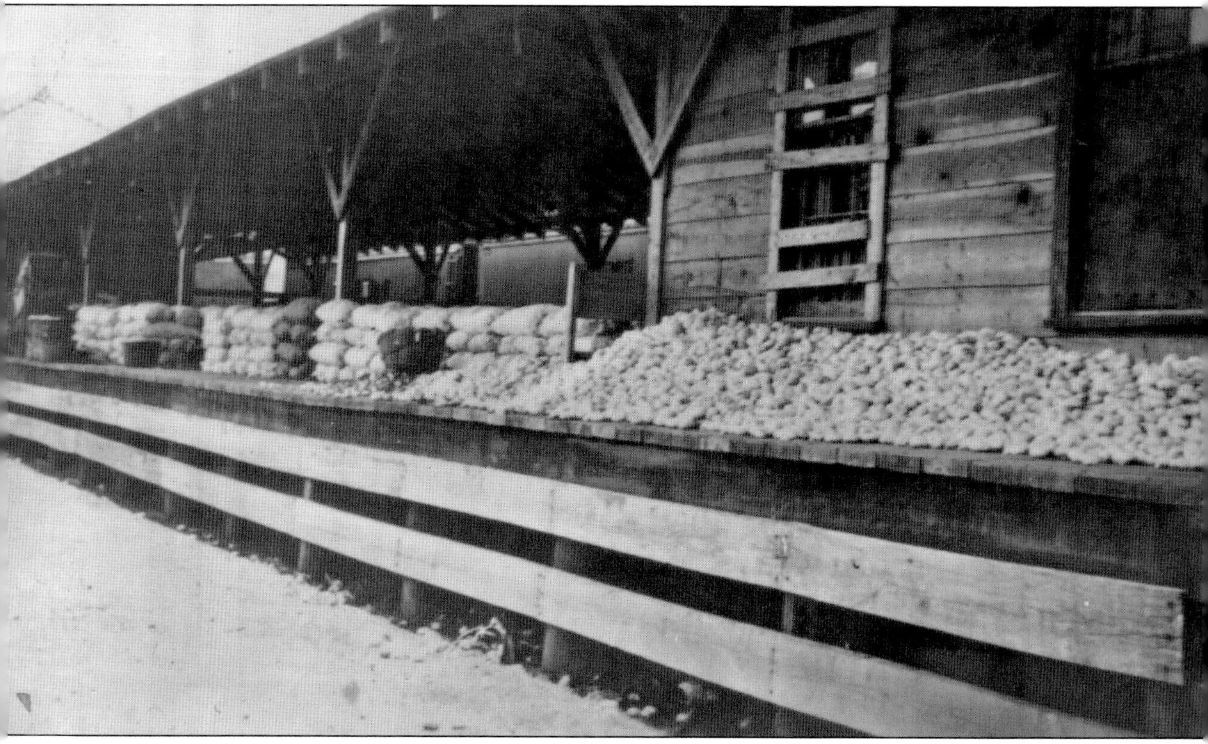

In 1935, and several years previously, Farmersville had slowly come to be the geographical center of the great black land belt of North Texas. Since the Bermuda onion was first grown there, it proved to be of the highest quality and had gained the reputation for being the sweetest and best onion grown. Farmersville was well known as the "Onion Capital of the North Texas." More than 1,000 carloads of "East Collin Sweets" were shipped annually. In 1935, the first North Texas Onion Festival for Friendly Farmersville was held, sponsored by the junior chamber of commerce. The annual festivals continued for several years. Onion buyers from all over the United States came to attend that event. People came from miles around and the festivities went on for days. There was a parade with floats from surrounding towns, an elected onion queen, area bands, and—at the first festival—the Whirlwind Fliers. They were famous stuntmen and passenger fliers that came to thrill the crowd with daring stunts. However, due to the outbreak of World War II, the festival was eventually suspended.

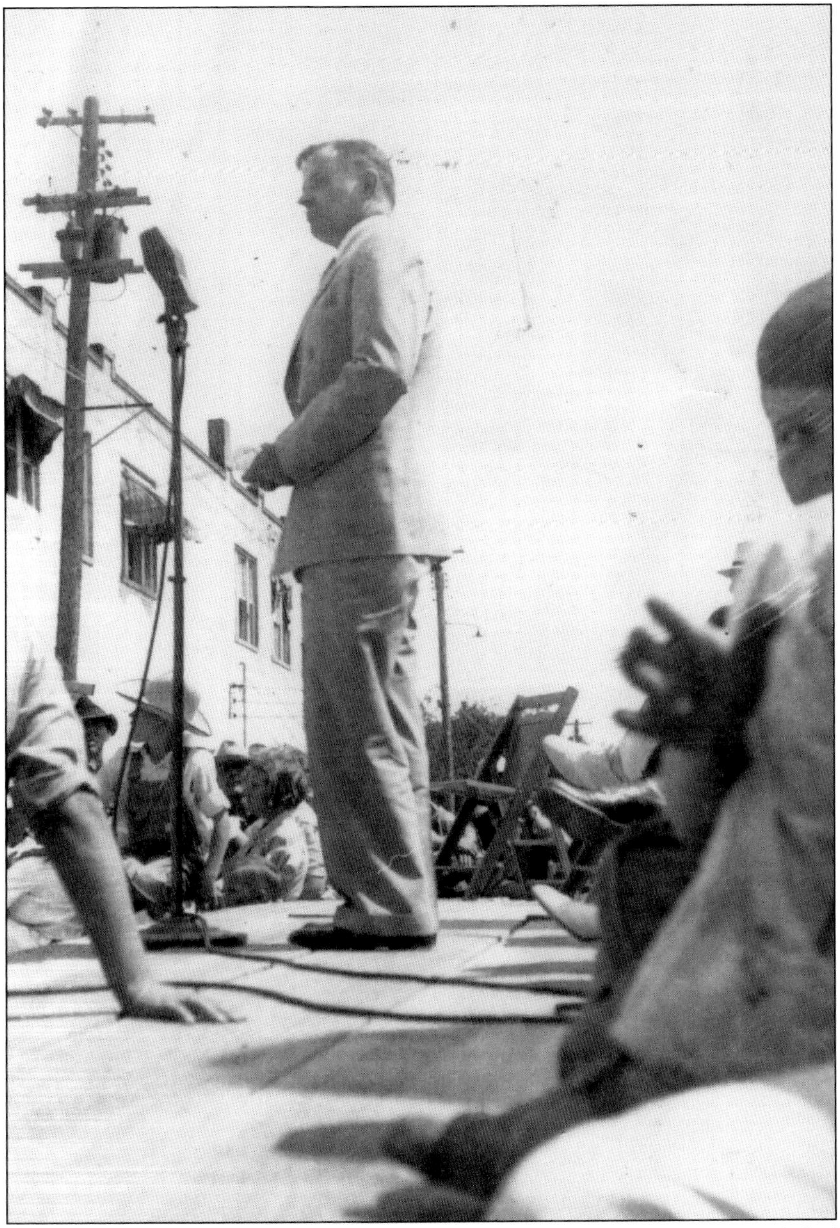

The governor of Texas, James W. Allred, was invited to the first Onion Festival, held in June 1935. He accepted the invitation and the local program committee placed him on the program to speak at 4:00 p.m. from the platform on the square. On that Tuesday morning, a committee of six Jaycees met Governor Allred in Dallas. They joined the governor and his party, including Justice Richard Critz of the Supreme Court, Rev. Pat Moreland, secretary to the governor, and Capt. A. S. Johnson, for a luncheon on the roof garden of the Adolphus Hotel. Leaving for Farmersville, the governor's party was given a patrol escort out of Dallas. At Copeville, the governor was met by a caravan of 20 cars from town, and Mayor Rike. They welcomed him and his party, and the caravan was led to Farmersville. Through this two-day event, a total of 30,000 people attended from all sections of Texas and adjoining states. That first North Texas Onion Festival was an amazing event for the area and all concerned.

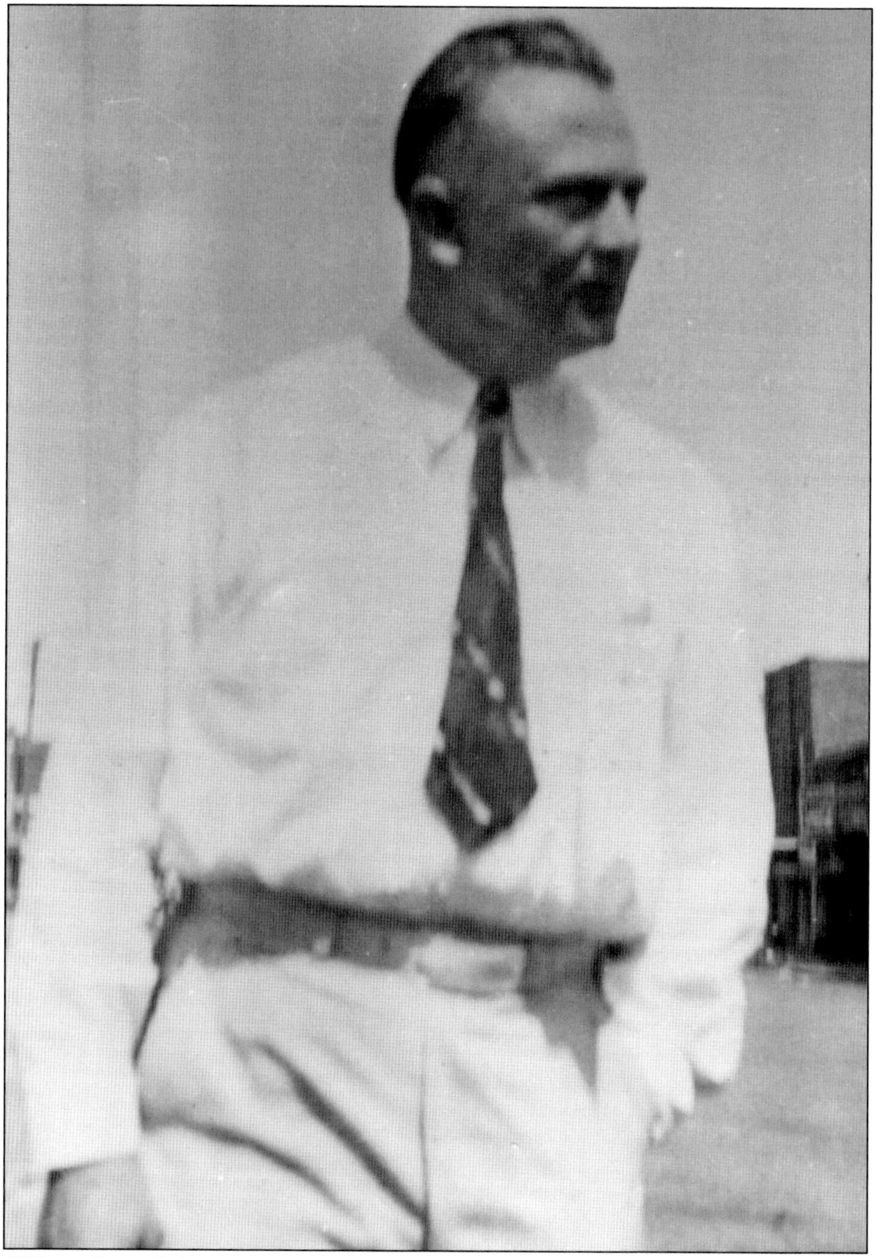

W. Lee O'Daniels, with his musicians, were at the first Onion Festival in 1935. He was born in Ohio and moved to Fort Worth, Texas, in 1925 to take a job with Burrus Mills, who produced Light Crust Flour. O'Daniels, who ran the company's radio advertising, in 1931, put together a country band. The band was christened the Light Crust Doughboys and featured Bob Wills. Both the band and singer very popular in Texas. Later O'Daniels formed his own band called Pappy O'Daniels and His Hillbilly Boys, named after O'Daniels Hillbilly Flour Company. In 1938, O'Daniels ran for governor of Texas, winning by a 51-percent majority. He won reelection in 1940, ran for the Senate, and defeated a very young Lyndon Johnson. O'Daniels was ineffective as a senator and stepped aside in 1948. He attempted a comeback as governor twice in the 1950s, to no avail. He died in Dallas in 1969.

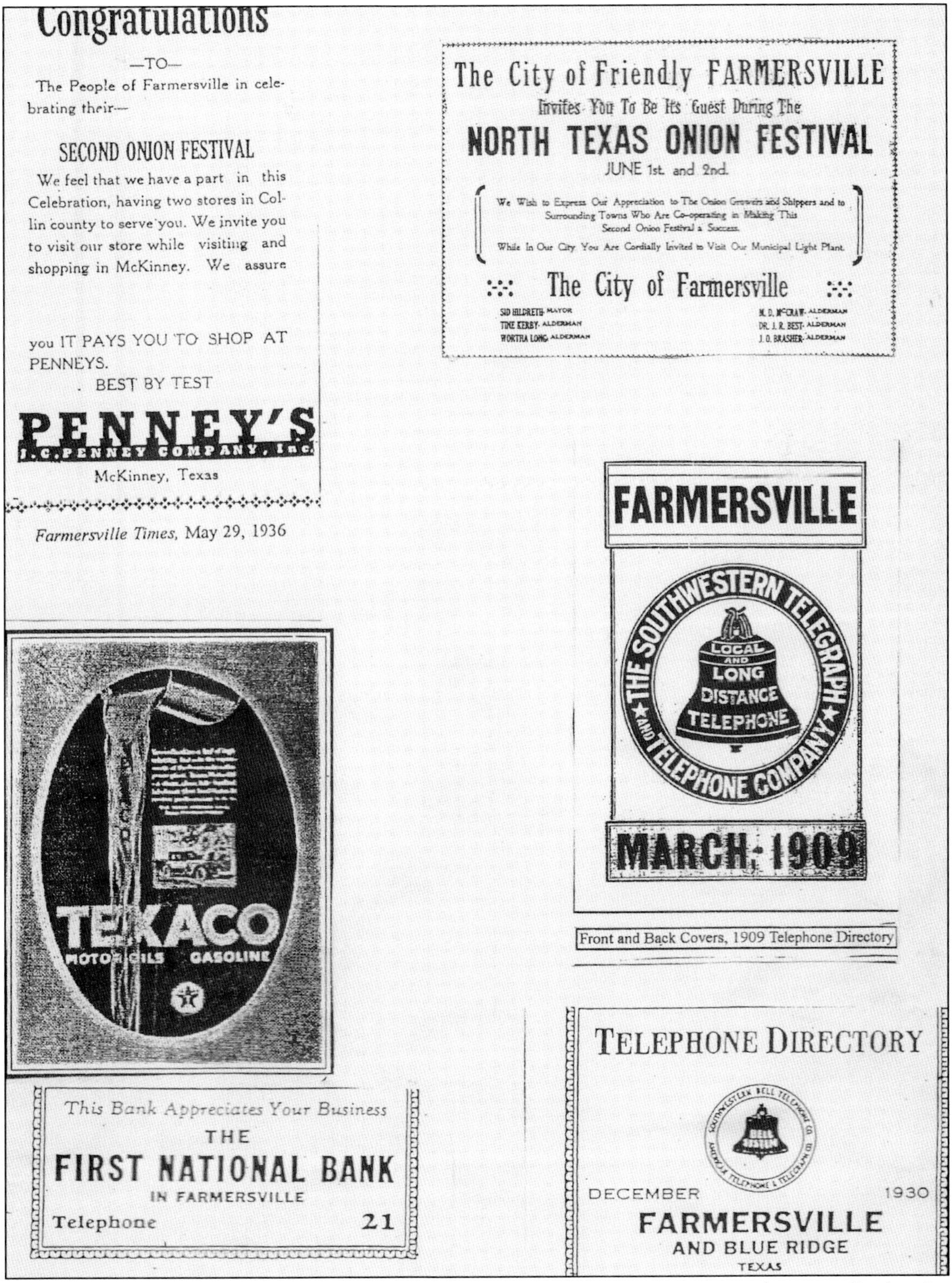

These are advertisements for many of the businesses in town in 1936, and especially for the second Onion Festival.

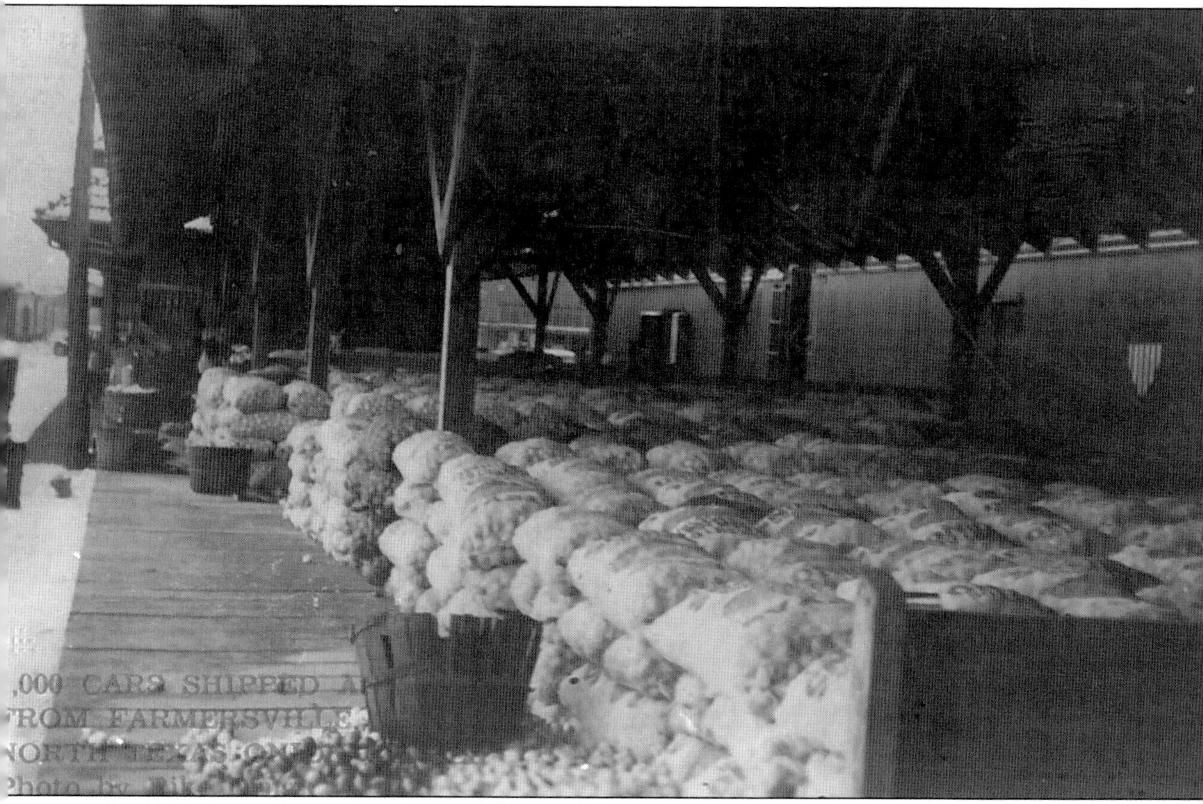

In 1926, Hugo Simon, secretary of the local Lion's Club, came up with a program to advertise the "Large Collin County Sweets." The club hailed the plan with great enthusiasm. An onion deluxe was wrapped in tissue paper, telling of the unequalled quality of the onion, especially the "Large Collin County Sweets," and the expected production for the year. Approximately 1,000 Lion's Clubs received a sample of the popular onion. The onions for the stunt were furnished free by the members of the Farmersville Onion Growers Association. The printing was done by the *Farmersville Times*, as its contribution.

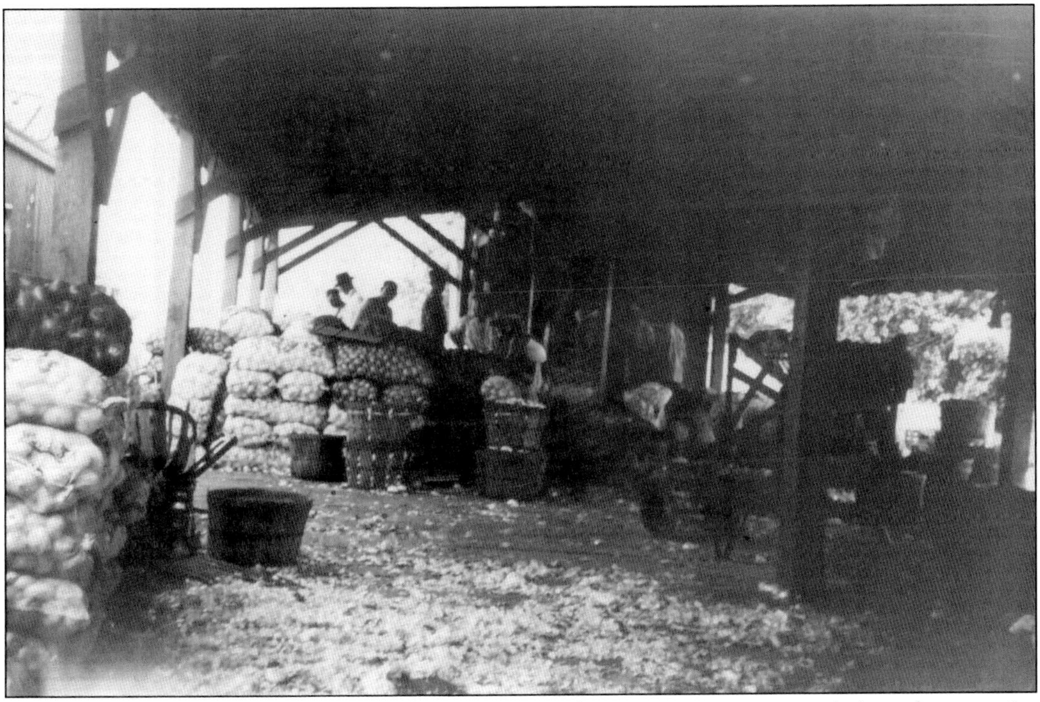

The onions grown in Farmersville and many surrounding communities provided employment for old and young alike. In addition to helping plant, care for, and harvest, many men—who were boys at the time—reminisced about working in the onion sheds, stacking, loading, and handling onions all day, every day. For many, those were all the jobs available in a small town, especially for high school-age boys.

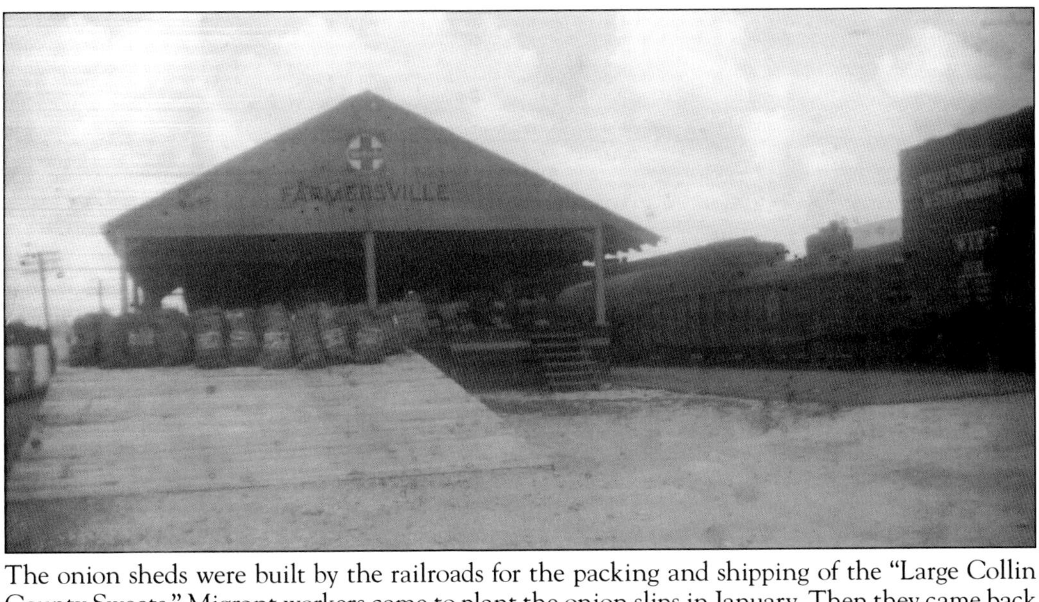

The onion sheds were built by the railroads for the packing and shipping of the "Large Collin County Sweets." Migrant workers came to plant the onion slips in January. Then they came back to harvest them in late May and June.

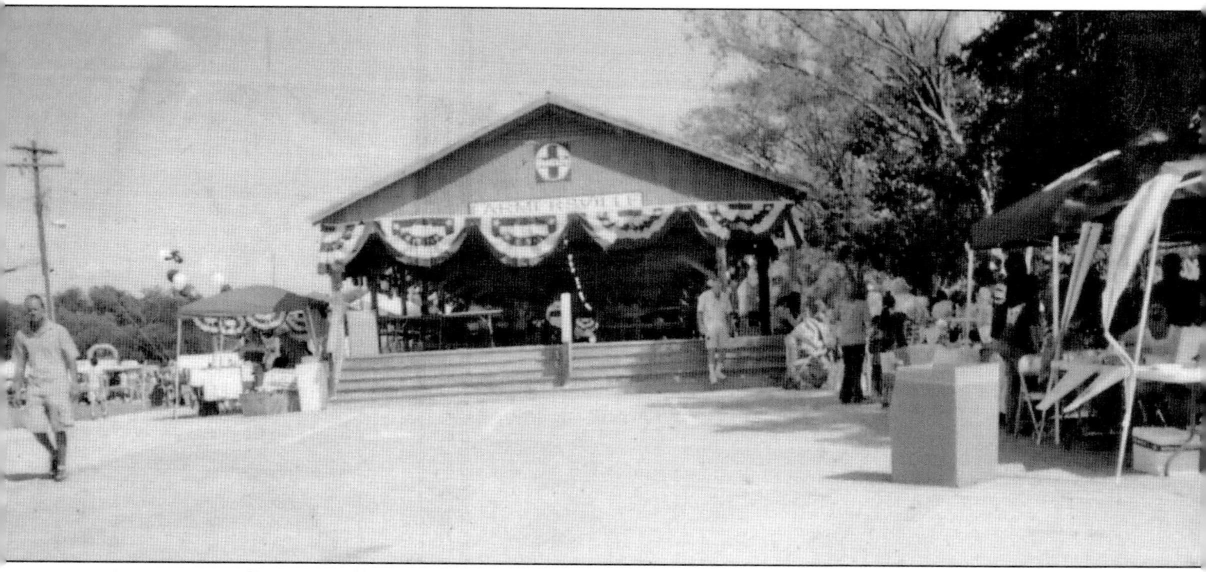

At one time, Farmersville was home to eight onion sheds built for the storing and distribution of huge onion crops that were grown in the area. Those sheds stood next to railroad tracks where onions were shipped to different locations; 1,000 such carloads were shipped annually. Built around 1935, those sheds have stood empty over the years or were used for various things. One such shed, located on Main Street next to the city park, was purchased by the Centennial Committee, a local committee created for the centennial celebration of Farmersville in 1973. In the interest of preserving the historical significance of that shed, it was purchased and later donated to the city. With restoration and some remodeling done, the shed was made into a location to be rented for community events. It is used annually for the Old Time Saturday celebration that is staged in October. In June each year, Audie Murphy and veterans of all wars are honored for their services with the celebration headquarters located there. Also the Farmers and Fleas Market is held there on the first Saturday of each month.

Five

Organizations and Clubs

As population increased and people had a little more leisure time, different clubs and organizations began to form. Such groups as the Rotary Club, the Lion's Club, and Woodmen of the World began to organize.

The Culture Club was the oldest social club for women in Farmersville. It began in 1912 in the dining room of the historical Bain-Honaker House.

One particular group of men formed a semipro baseball team called the Ramblers. They were very active for many years and had their own ballpark near one of the cotton gins, where there was a large area that gave them plenty of room for a field and stands.

Also in this chapter, the Farmersville's Centennial is celebrated as well as Old Time Saturday, which came to be an annual fund-raiser.

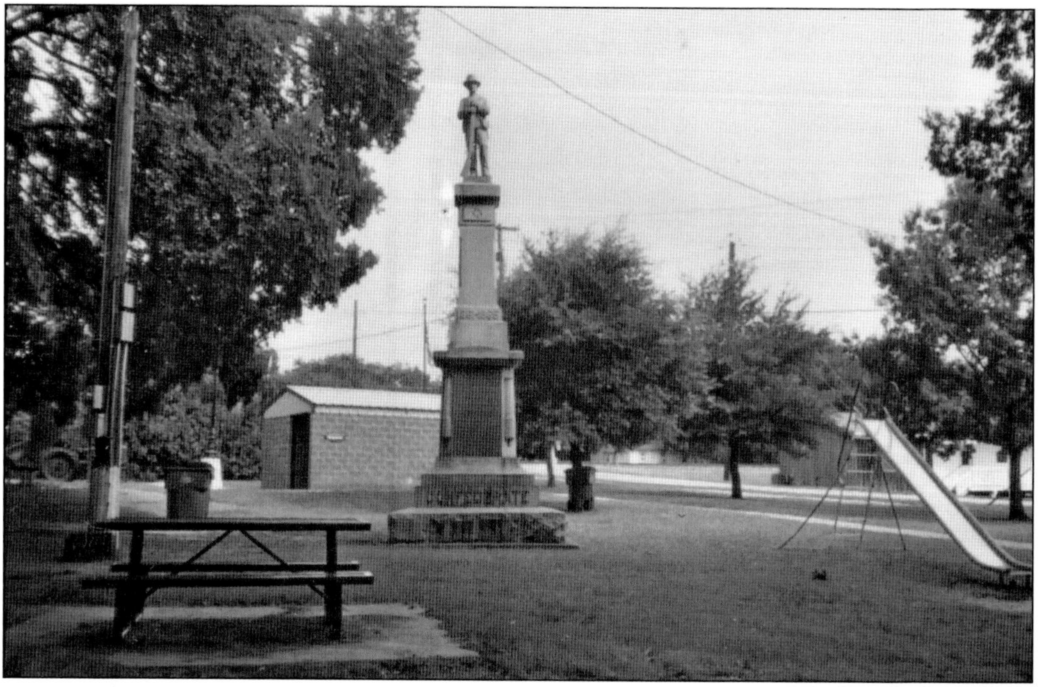

In November 1912, a collection was begun in the community to assist the United Daughters of the Confederacy in erecting a large monument in memory of the soldiers of the Confederacy. The monument was an endeavor to make a permanent remembrance for generations to come. A copy of the two pages of contributors listed is in the Charles Rike Library, provided by the granddaughter of the woman who made and kept the list. There are 112 names on it, with the majority of the donations listed as $1, $2, or 50¢. That list of individuals includes names that have been in Farmersville since the early establishment of the town, such as Rike, Murchison, Honaker, Pendleton, Yeary, Bumpass, Bickley, Neathery, and Wilcoxson, to name a few familiar signatures. In 1917, with $2,500 raised, the 25-foot-tall statue was placed in the city park, constructed entirely of Texas materials. The wording on the statue reads, "In Memory of All Confederate Soldiers. Erected by Stonewall Jackson Chapter 1208, Farmersville, Texas 1917 A.D. Lord God of Hosts be with us yet, Lest we forget, Lest we forget."

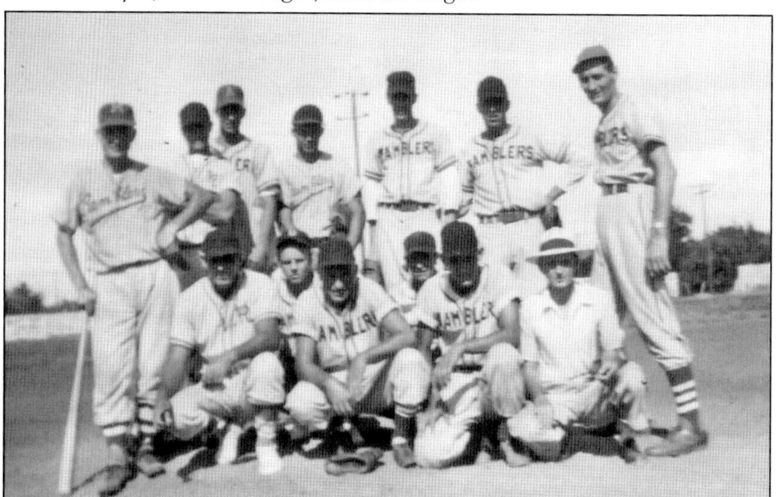

The Ramblers, the Farmersville semipro baseball team, was organized around 1948. In six playing seasons in the league, the Ramblers won 287 games and lost 91. They took two pennants after Shaughnessy playoff victories and finished in fourth place. In 1953, the Ramblers finished first but fell to Anna in the playoffs.

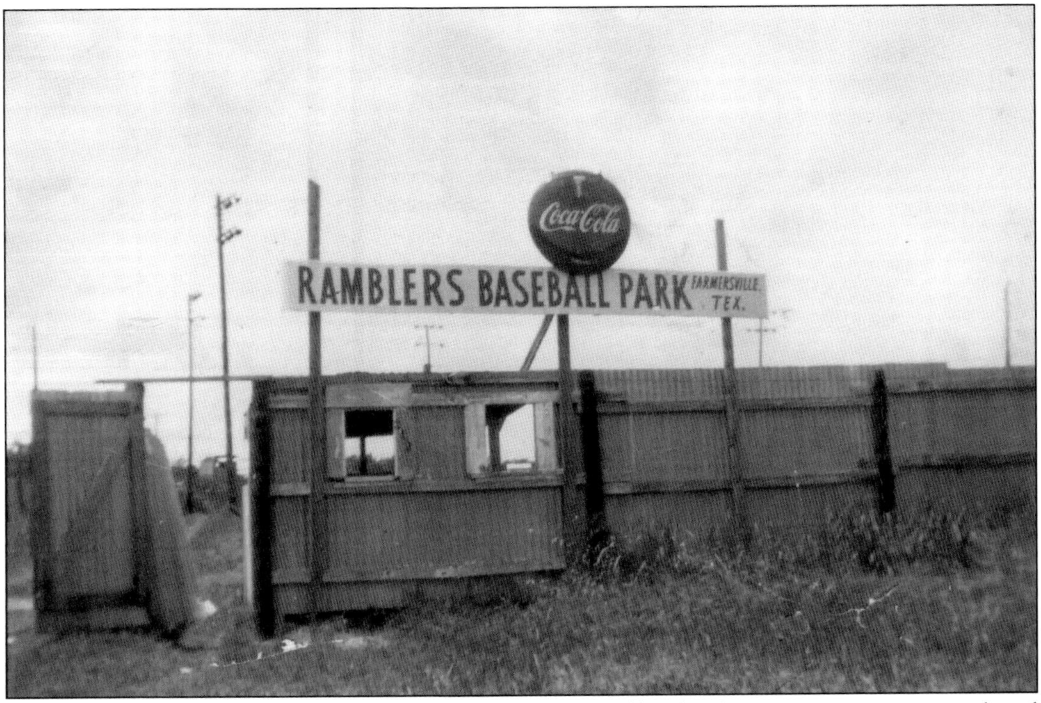

This image shows the home of the Ramblers, Rambler Ballpark, where many games were played over the years. It is not a fancy ballpark and they were not a fancy ball team, but they did make a name for themselves.

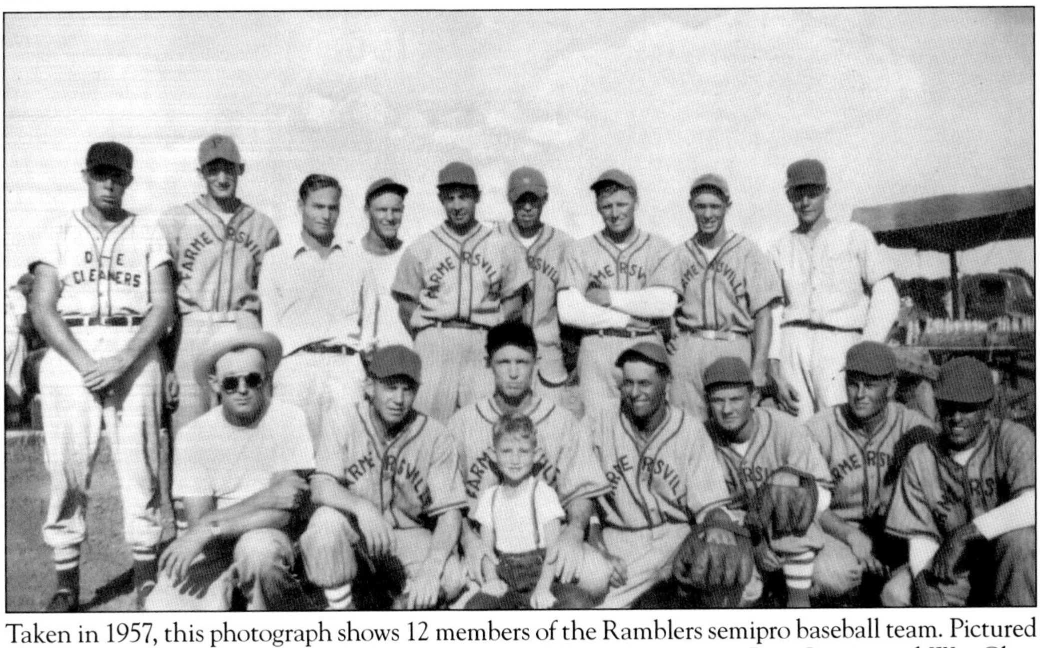

Taken in 1957, this photograph shows 12 members of the Ramblers semipro baseball team. Pictured are, from left to right (first row) A. V. Currin, J. White, C. Brown, Rex Curtis, and Wig Clay; (second row) Don Anderson, Blaine Hall, Charles Smith, Jim Hess, Wayne Tilley, Theodore Moss, and Sim Lewis. Other players were not available for this picture. The team disbanded in 1962 after several team players moved away.

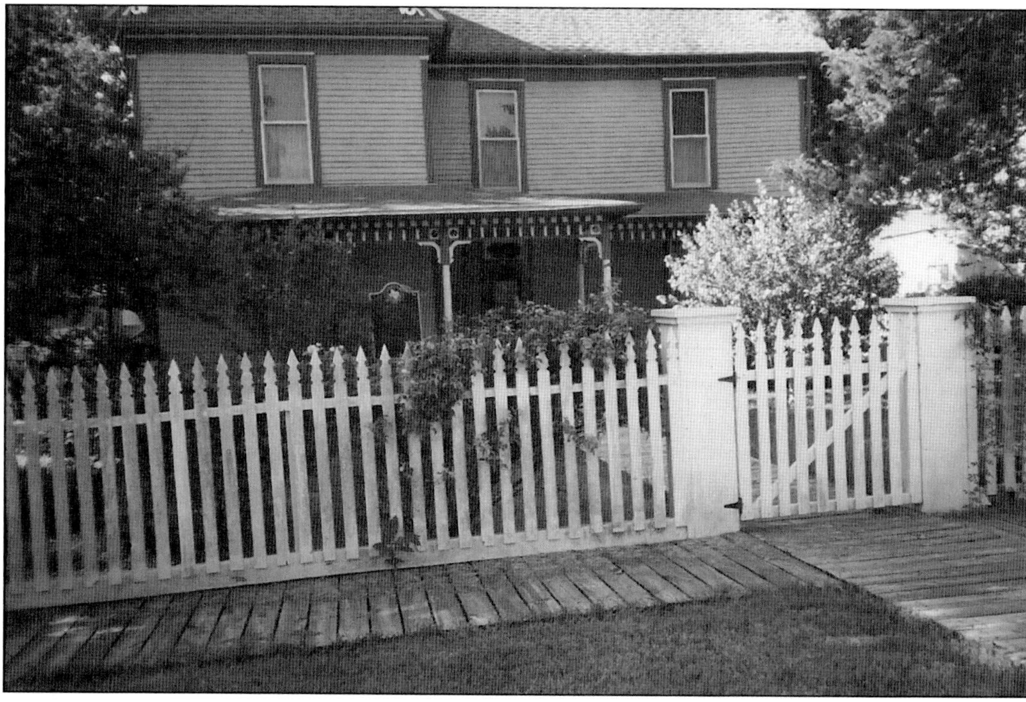

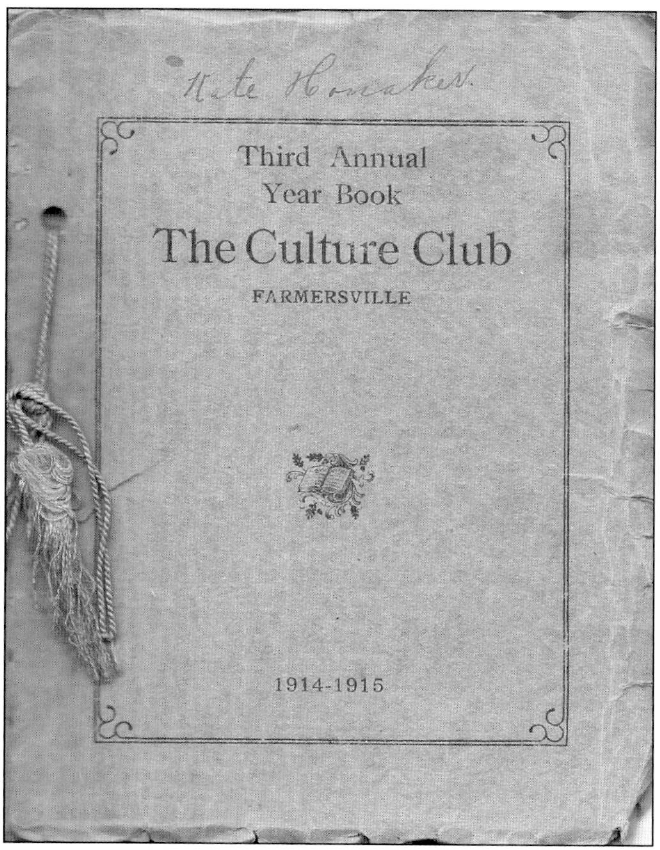

The Culture Club was the oldest social club for women in Farmersville. Formed in the dining room of this Bain-Honaker House in 1912, it was organized as a study club and it gave assistance and support to worthy causes. The State Hospital of Terrell was a recipient of gifts from this organization, as well as the Helping Hand Nursing Home in Farmersville. Its motto was "If I rest, I rust." Pictured at left is the club's 1914–1915 yearbook. The club disbanded in the 1990s. Their organizational records are in the Charles Rike Library in Farmersville.

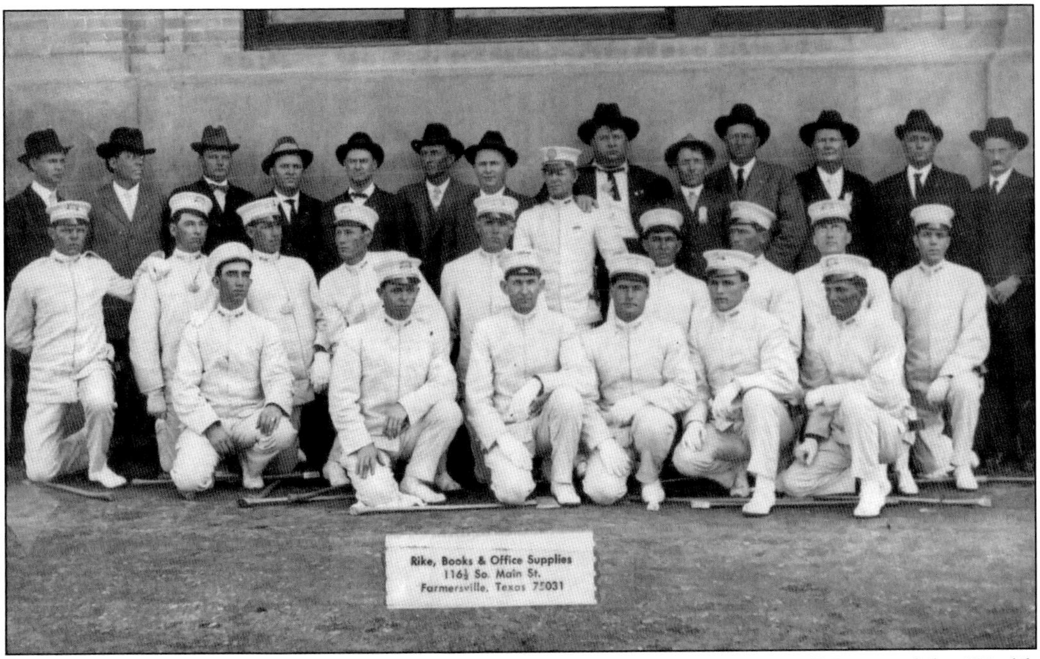

Pictured is the Farmersville Woodman of the World Team, Champion Drill Team of the World, 1914. Pictured are, from left to right, (first row) Dave Yeary, Tom Gibbs, J. H. McDonald, Will Petty, Will Aycock, and Henry Dillion; (second row) Jim Bowden, Tom Johnson, George Howard, Shellie Shaw, Tom Riddle, C. T. Click, English Shannon, and Bob Holsonbake; (third row) Will Chapman, T. L. Bailey, Eugene Worden, Dr. J. J. Rogers, Dan Neathery, R. C. McLeod, Pat Rutherford, captain Harve Nickles, mascot Sam Harris, R. C. Vicars, Bud Pendleton, Jack Taylor, and Ed Carmack.

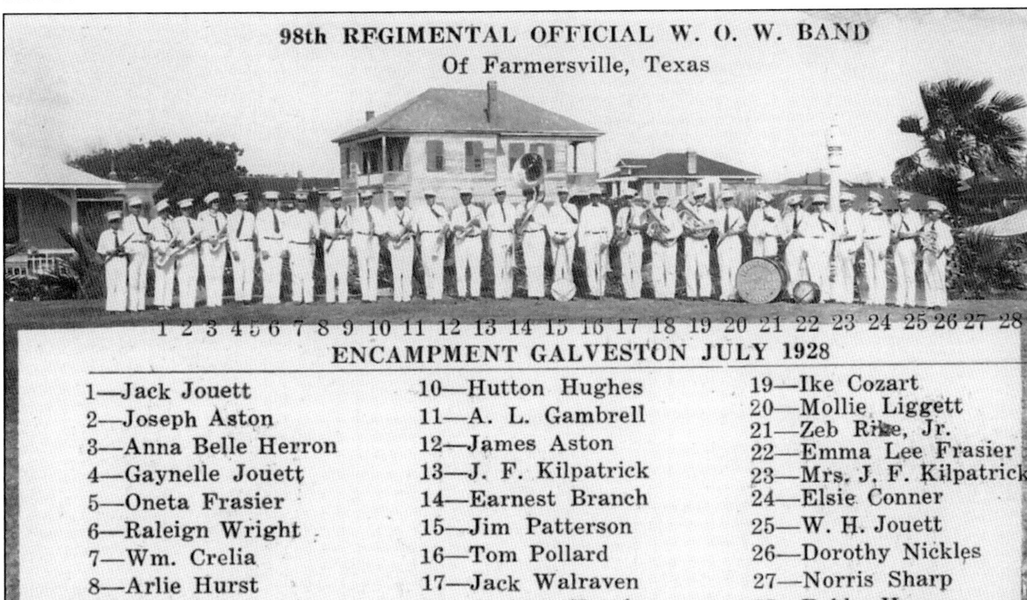

This postcard is of the 98th Regimental Official Woodman of the World Band of Farmersville pictured here in 1928.

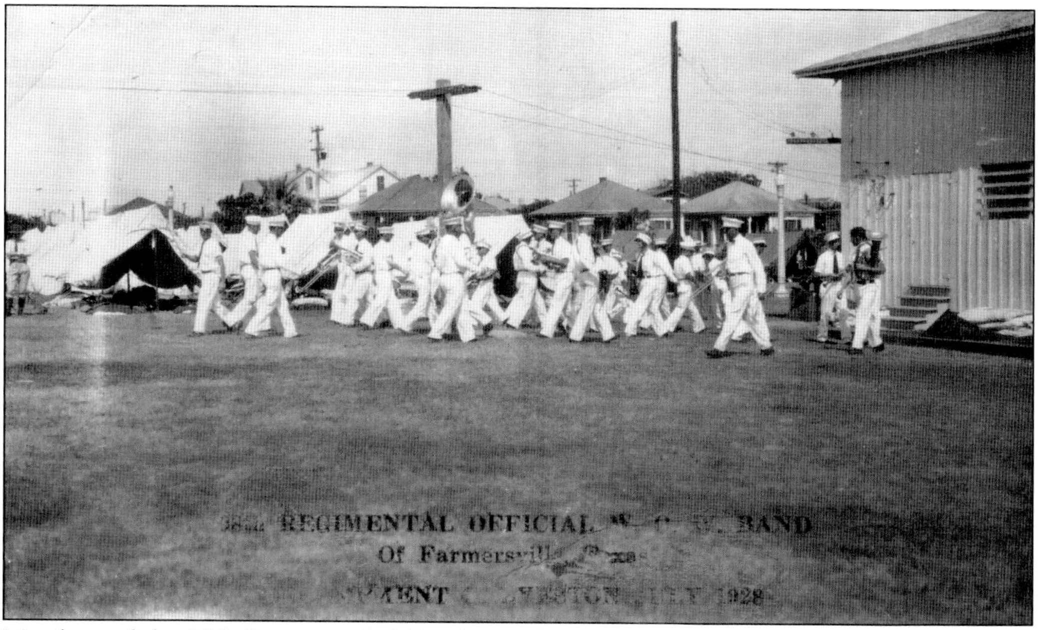

Members of the 98th Regimental Official Woodman of the World Band of Farmersville are shown on the bottom portion of the postcard. The band was at the Encampment in Galveston in July 1928.

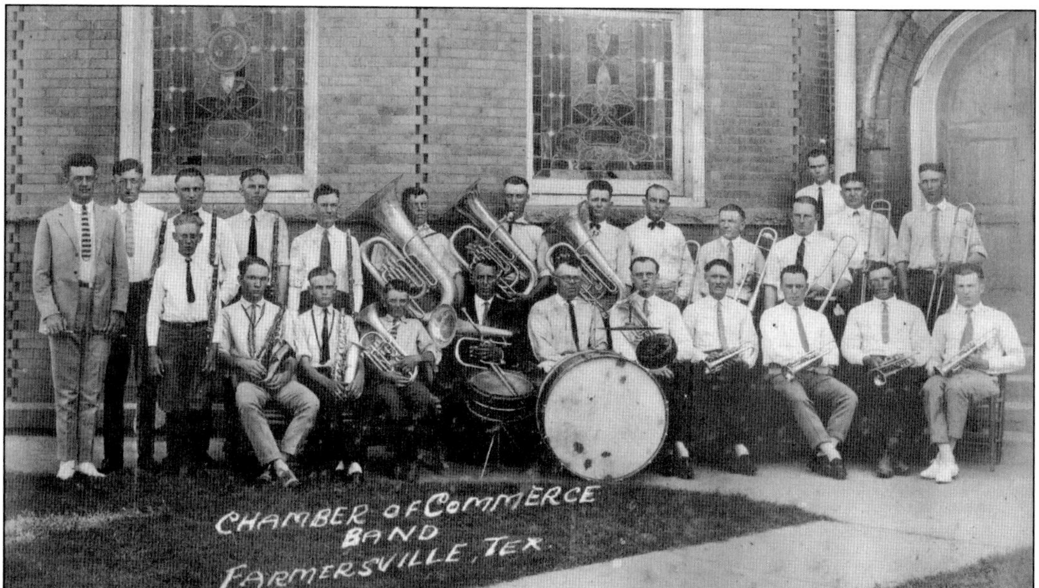

This Farmersville Chamber of Commerce Band represents the town well, both because of the number in the band and the instruments shown. This photograph was most likely taken in the 1920s. Pictured from left to right are (first row) E. Henslee, John Rogers, Cecil Leonard, Joe Wilcoxson, Charles Cobb, John Hale, Wallace Mason, Jesse Johnson, Douglas Shine, Lee Johnson, and Sam Redwine; (second row) Cecil Phillips, Arrington West, L. Craft, Clyde Baker, Jesse Dodderer, T. A. Bailey, Alton Roberts, John Redwine, Jack Walraven, Ernest Hall, Oniel Evans, Milos Stewart, W. M. Ball, and Hugo Simon.

Pictured in centennial finery is local pharmacist Bill Harrison. Harrison does not normally sport a mustache, but he grew one to keep himself out of jail.

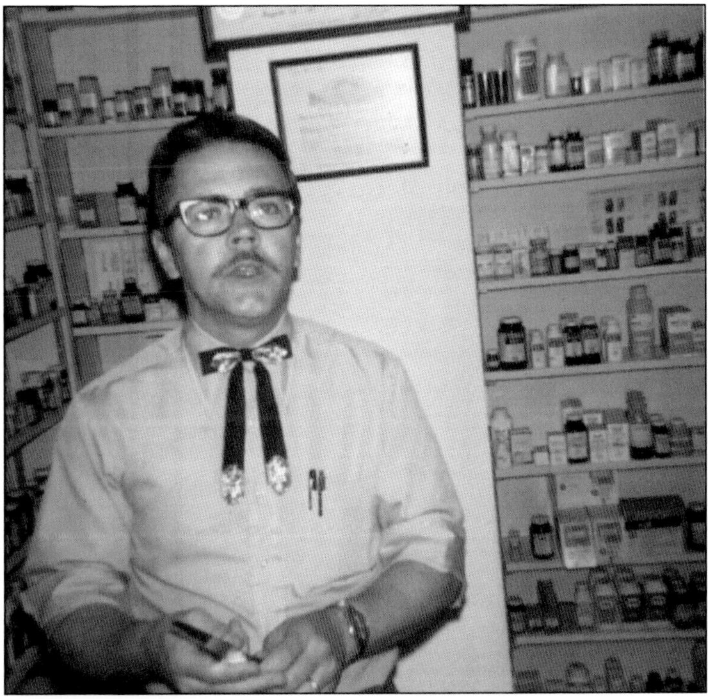

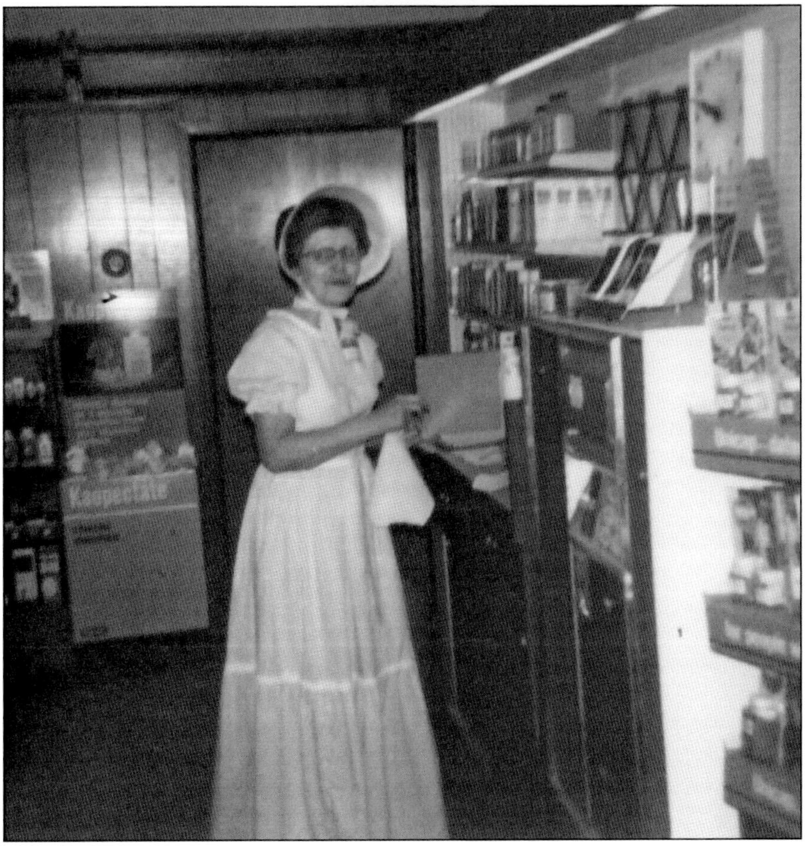

Robbie Wright is decked out in her bonnet, her long dress of the time period she represents, and her hankie hanging discreetly from her hand.

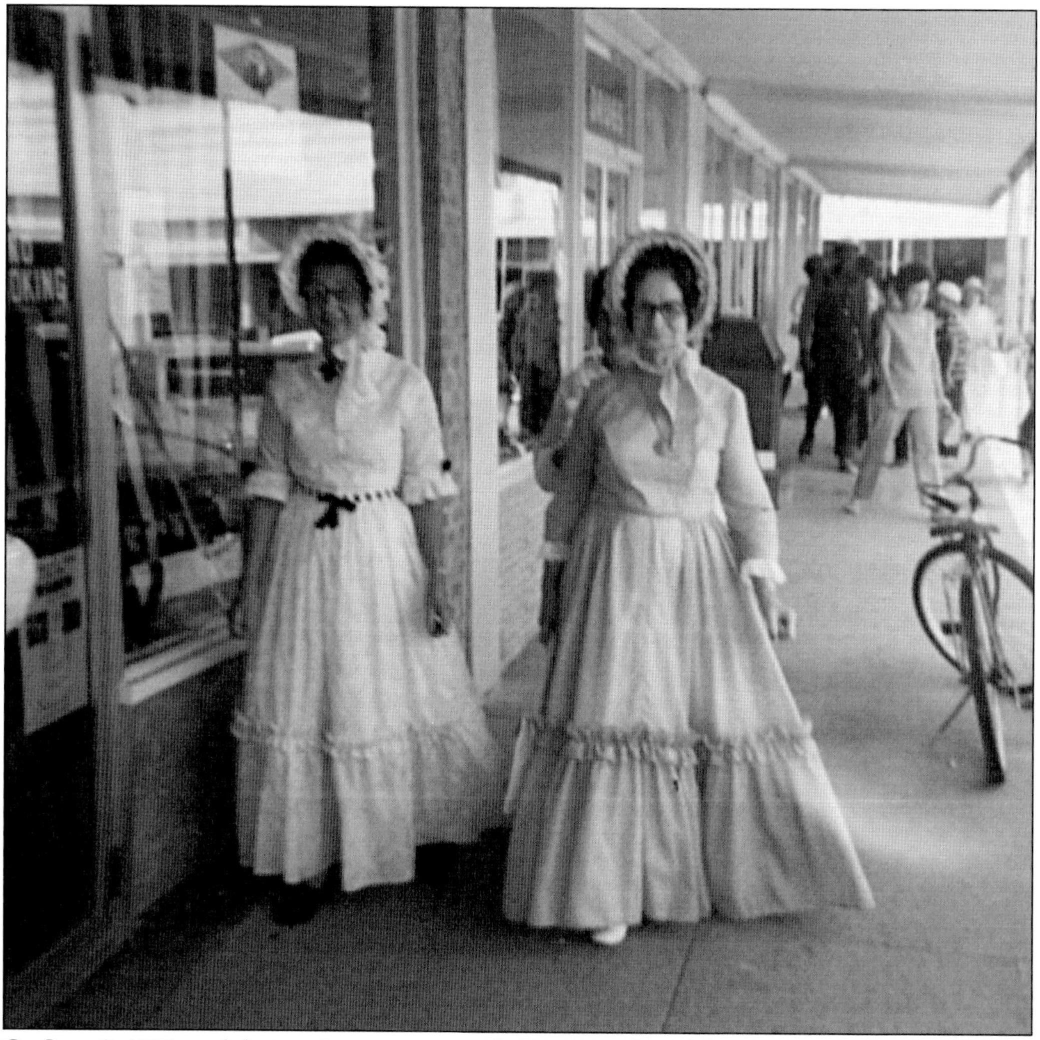

On June 2, 1973, and during the previous week, Farmersville celebrated its 100th birthday. The Farmersville Centennial Committee was established to head the festivities and eventually received a tax-free status. A Recipe Committee was formed, headed by Jeanette McCraw, to gather recipes for a centennial cookbook to sell. Men began to sprout beards and mustaches in order not to be fined for not having one. Little tiny combs were being sought to keep beards orderly. A $100 reward was offered for the best beard. Toby Hickman got a ball and chain around his ankle when he came to town with no mustache or shaving permit. The dedication of the Audie Murphy Memorial was on May 28. That memorial was paid for by donations from merchants. Gov. David Hall from Oklahoma flew in to make the dedicatory address for the historical marker. A centennial queen was chosen, and a pageant was written to be performed that would tell Farmersville's history.

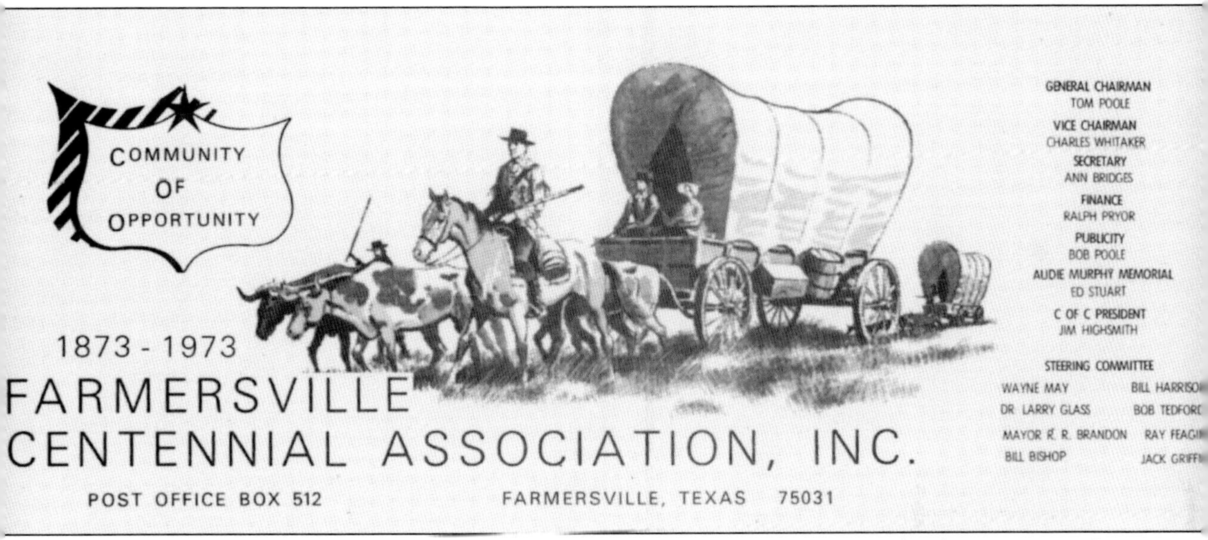

This stationery was printed for the Farmersville Centennial Association to use for their centennial celebrations in 1973. This stationery was used to invite dignitaries from Austin to attend the celebrations.

–PROGRAM–
of

COMMUNITY OF OPPORTUNITY

1873 1973
FARMERSVILLE
CENTENNIAL ASSOCIATION, INC.

CENTENNIAL PAGEANT

JUNE 2, 1973

"Our Place In History"

Written By
Patsy Johnson and Josalyn Poole

Adapted From A
History of Farmersville
By Charles J. Rike

Directed By
Josalyn Poole

Pageant Coordinator, Nella Trisdale

Publicity & Tickets, Jackie Phife

Music, Glenda Hart

Lighting, Bill Bishop

Stage Properties, Sharon Shinn

Concession, Larry Wisdom

Narrator, Bill Wilcoxson

Pageant Chorus
Directed By Ron Waggoner

Organist, Glenda Hart

Pianist, Kathy Waggoner

Sets by
Bennie Cook, Bud Weston and FHS Ag Boys

Recorded Sound
By Jeannine Langley

Lighting and Stage Technicians
Bill Bishop, Mont Hendricks, Wayne Johnson, Otis Wilder, Pete Vamvakas, Kelly Hardin, Gary Tarrant, Mark Anderson, and Randal and Kevin Shinn

**Program Compliments Of
The Farmersville Times**

–81–

The centennial pageant titled "Our Place in History" was written, directed, produced, and performed by local talent. The entire week of the centennial celebration concluded with the performance of the pageant in the high school football stadium on Saturday. The chairman of the Pageant Committee estimated the crowd at nearly 1,000 people. Both stands of the stadium were filled, and scores of visitors lined the fences or set up lawn chairs.

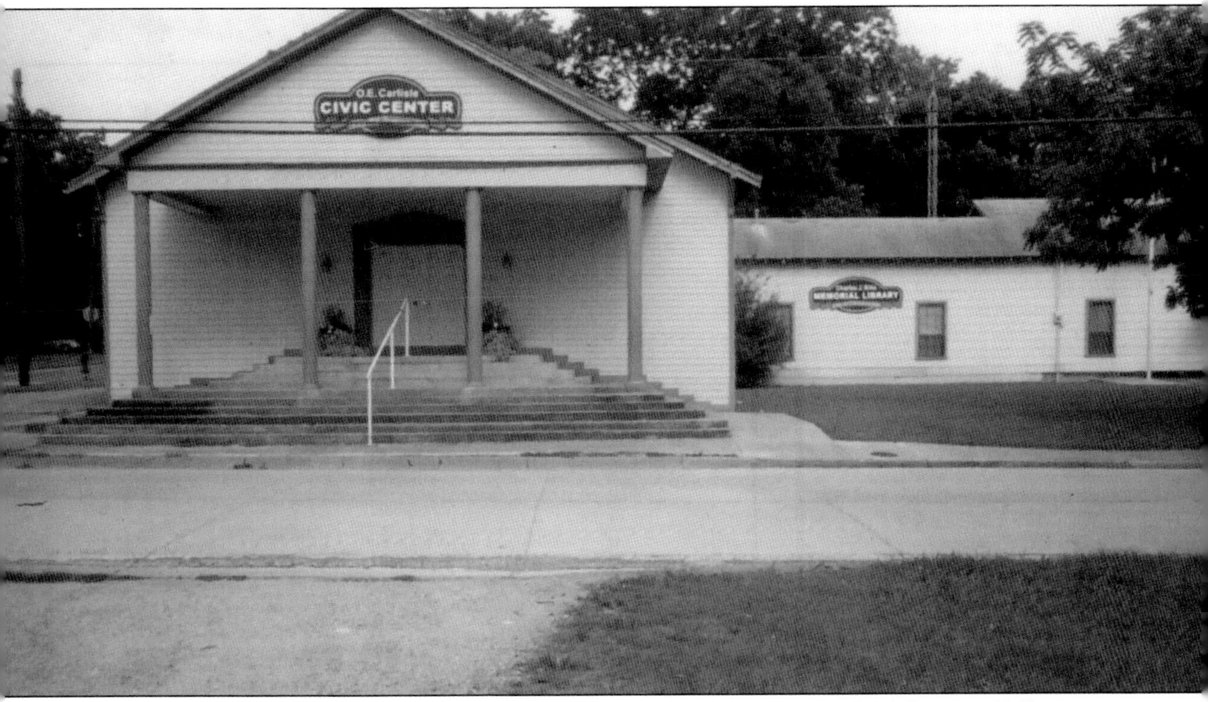

Farmersville Centennial, Inc., was organized in 1973 to stage the centennial celebration. Following that, the same group of concerned citizens began planning to secure, primarily at that time, a community center for the use of citizens and local clubs. Out of that group came the idea for a fund-raiser that has continued each year since that time. "Old Time Saturday" was born, a throwback to the days of old, when everyone came to town on Saturday night. That first "Saturday" netted $10,000 in 1980. An unused church building was purchased, with money coming from many different places. David McCall, a man from the neighboring Snow Hill community, contributed $20,000, with the stipulation that the center be named for O. E. Carlisle, who had given him a bank loan early in his business career that enabled him to be very successful in later years. That building was remodeled, eventually paid for, and became, as envisioned, a meeting place for local clubs and for citizens having family reunions, dinners, showers, and the like.

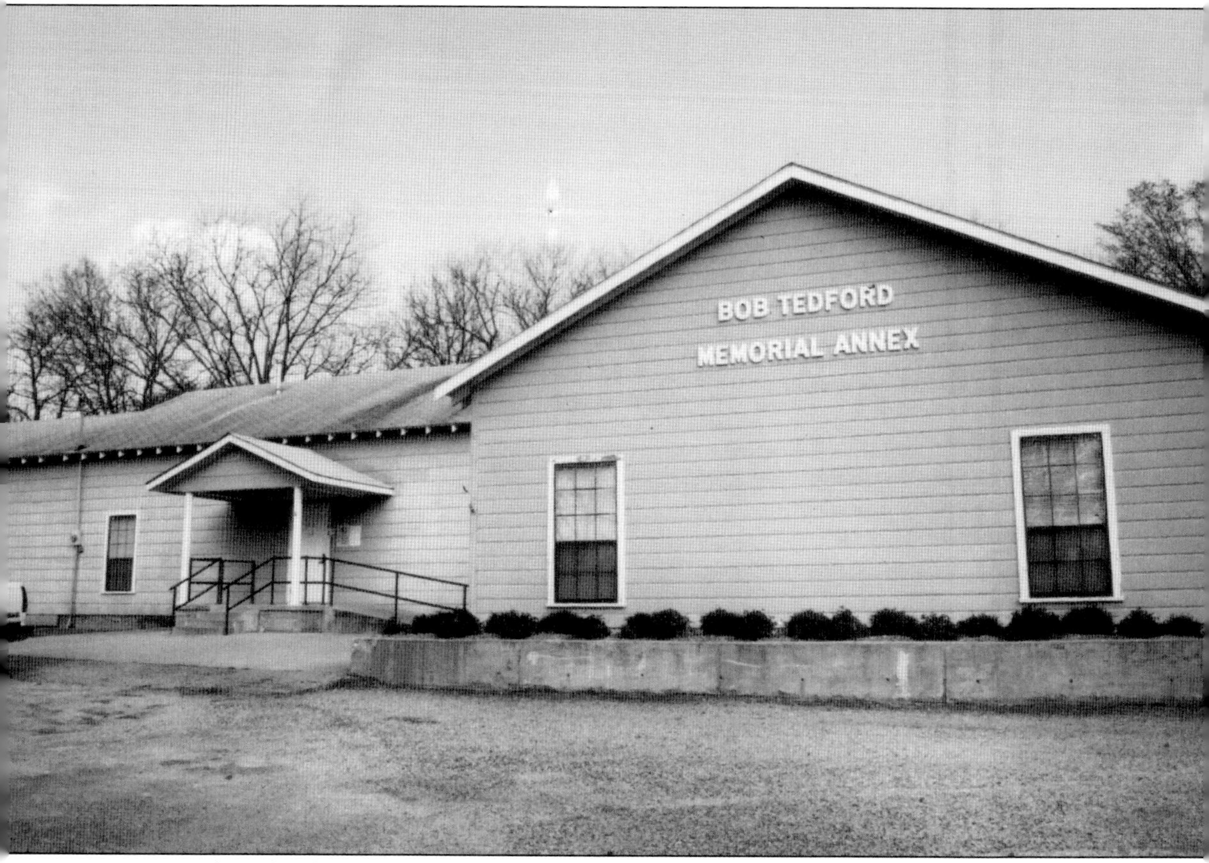

In 1979, when the plans were successful and money had begun to be raised for a community center, the vacant Church of Christ building located at Hill and Orange Streets was purchased. The church had erected a new building on Highway 78. On the side of the building was an 800-square-foot room that some ladies in town decided would make a place for a library. The men agreed and four ladies, Sandra Tedford, Zan Stuart, Rita Roose, and Walterine Sharp, began learning how to set up a library. For several months, these four, plus other volunteer ladies, processed books and did all things necessary to get a library operating. That library opened its doors on January 13, 1981. It has had two expansions, has entered the computer age, is very well used, and is appreciated by the majority of the people in the area.

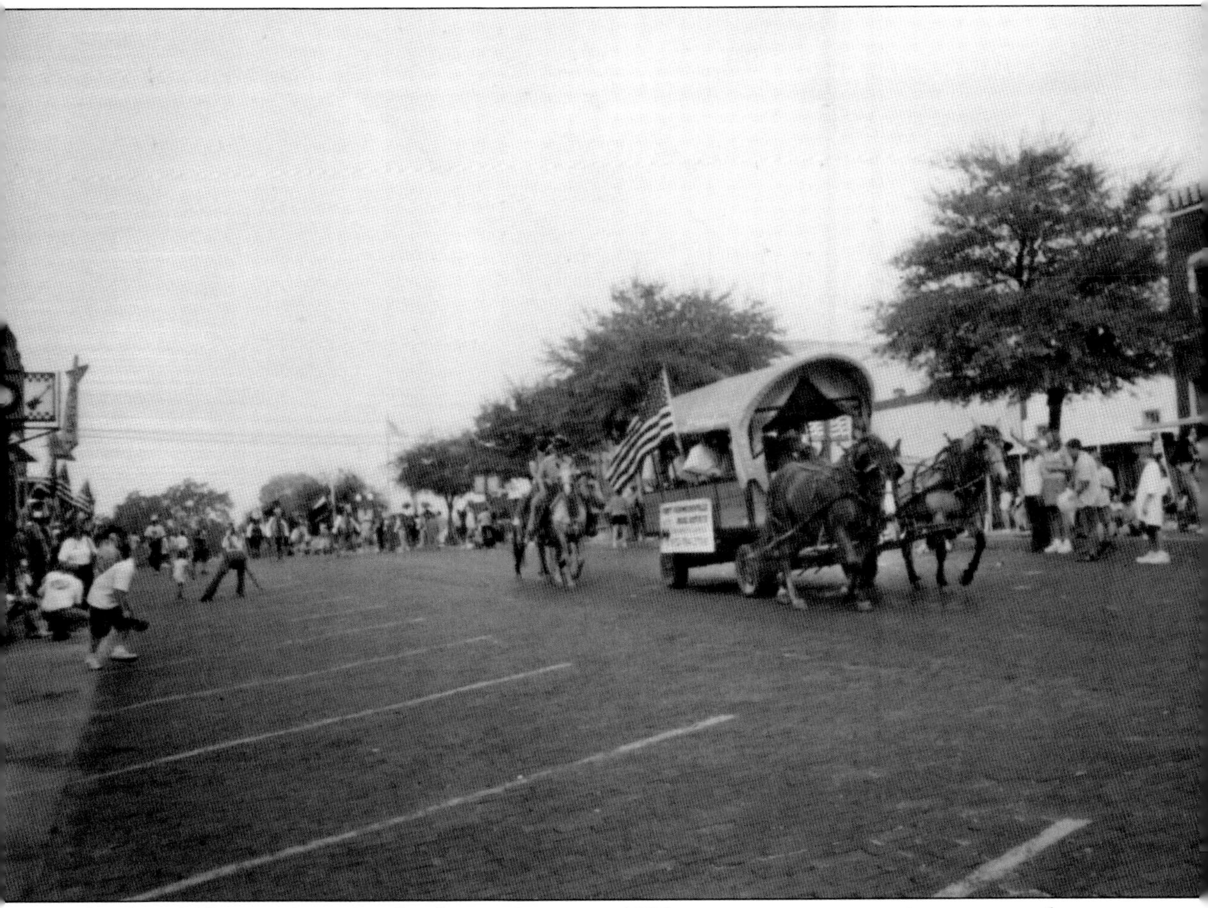

The first Old Time Saturday fund-raiser began in 1980 to secure a community center and was so successful that it has been held every year since. Held in the fall, from the first year through 2004, the event has raised a net profit of $365,628. The money has done many things to benefit the town. It paid the remainder of debt on the community center in 1981. It totally supported the library for 10 years, as well as expanded it twice. It paid for the construction of a senior citizen's center and helped with remodeling of the Boy Scouts center. Many other things have been done over the years to benefit the town and its citizens, who are the ones that have worked to make the fund-raiser a success by volunteering many hours. They have run booths and games, cooked, sold items, judged contests, and done numerous jobs every "Saturday" to help the event be successful.

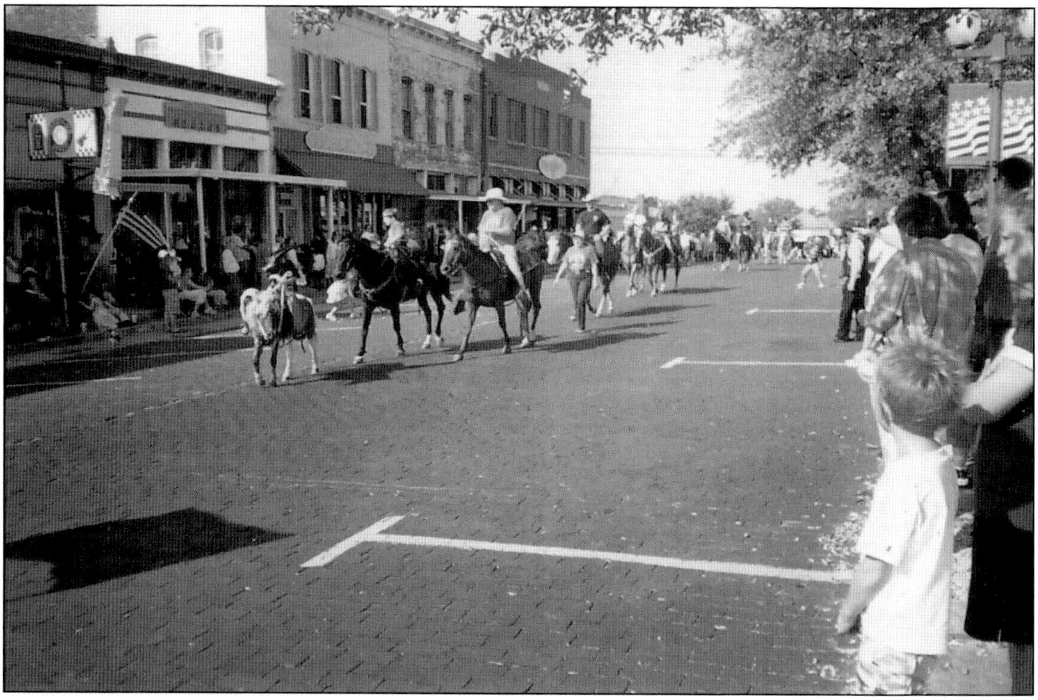

From covered wagons to horses, and everything in between, the Old Time Saturday parade gets under way, as pictured here. Slowly riding through downtown, a long parade meanders through the brick streets on the first Saturday in October. This parade kicks off yet another fund-raiser that has done, and continues to do, so much good for the town.

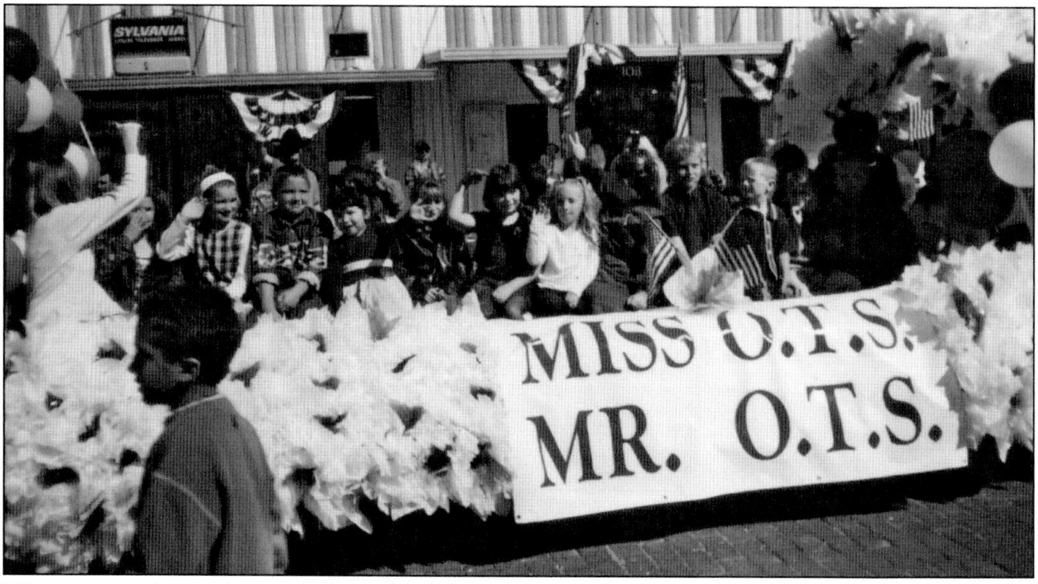

This picture shows the candidates for the Little Miss/Mister Old Time Saturday event. These contestants sell raffle tickets to residents for a chance to win a local handmade quilt and other prizes. The raffle winner is announced at the Old Time Saturday event. The young girl and young boy that sell the most tickets are crowned Little Miss and Little Mister and each child wins prizes.

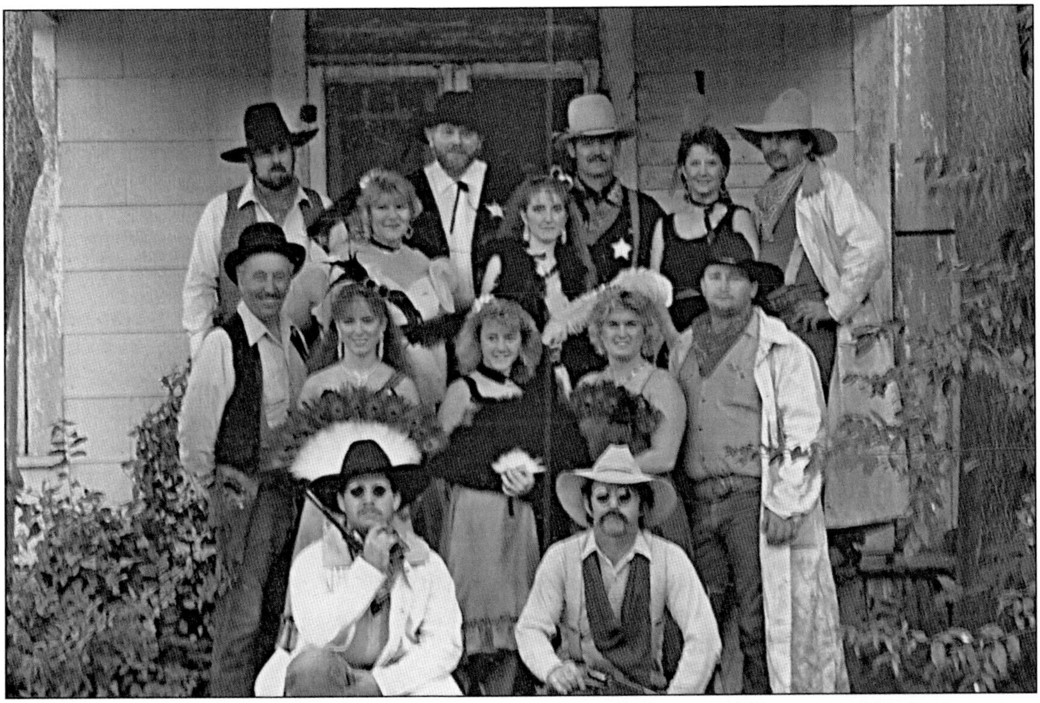

Pictured are gunfighters and saloon girls from the 1987 Old Time Saturday. From left to right are (first row) Don Neal and Danny Stinson; (second row) Charles Curington, Sharon Hayes, Randi Hall, Shella Hall, and Neal Howard; (third row) Christi Cheshier and Diane Yoro (fourth row) Richard Smith, Roger Alexander, Bob Bean, Judy Horton, and Steve Horton.

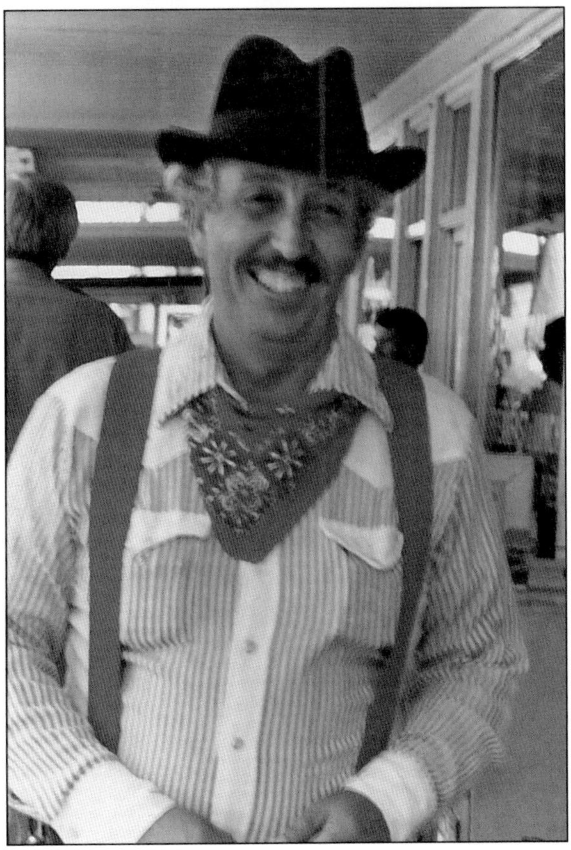

Charles Curington is pictured as a gunfighter. He has been in charge of lining up gunfighters, securing blank ammunition, and helping write a script for the show. Charles has seen to everything necessary for the shoot-outs since they began in 1987. He is very concerned with safety and always ensures that the gunfights do not endanger anyone. He has been a gunfighter himself each year.

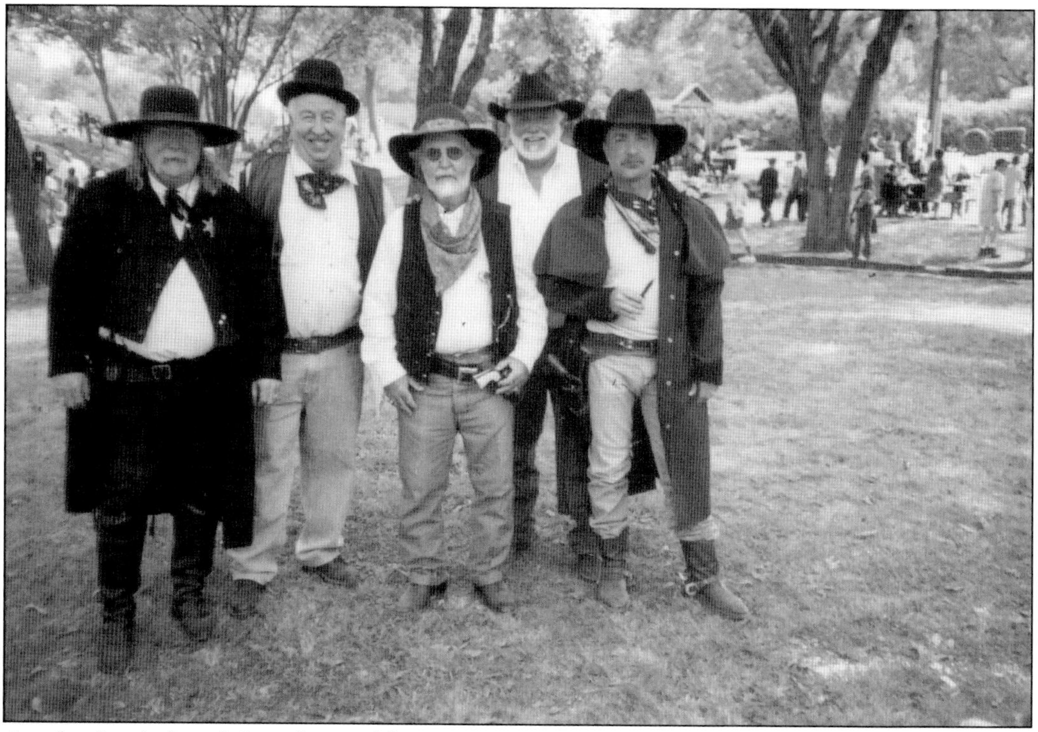

Another band of gunfighters have ridden into town to stir up trouble. They are identified as, from left to right, Glenn Helm, Charles Curington, George Key, Roger Alexander, and Mark O'Neal.

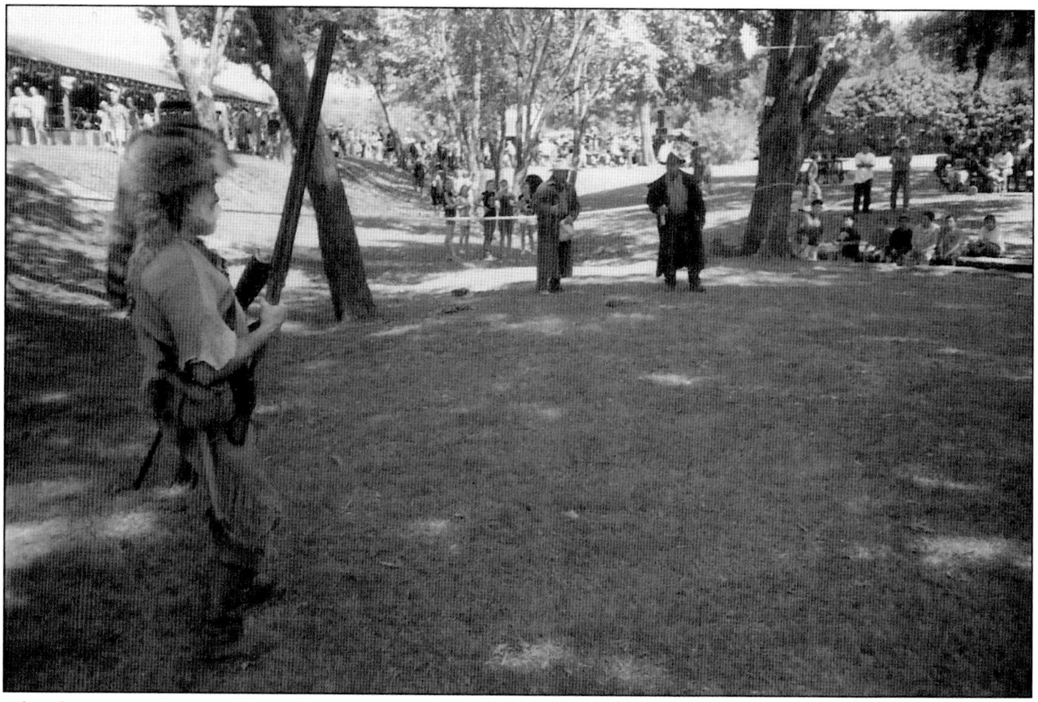

This lone man here, rifle in hand, is surely looking for trouble. "Woolley" Dave Brandt has come to town.

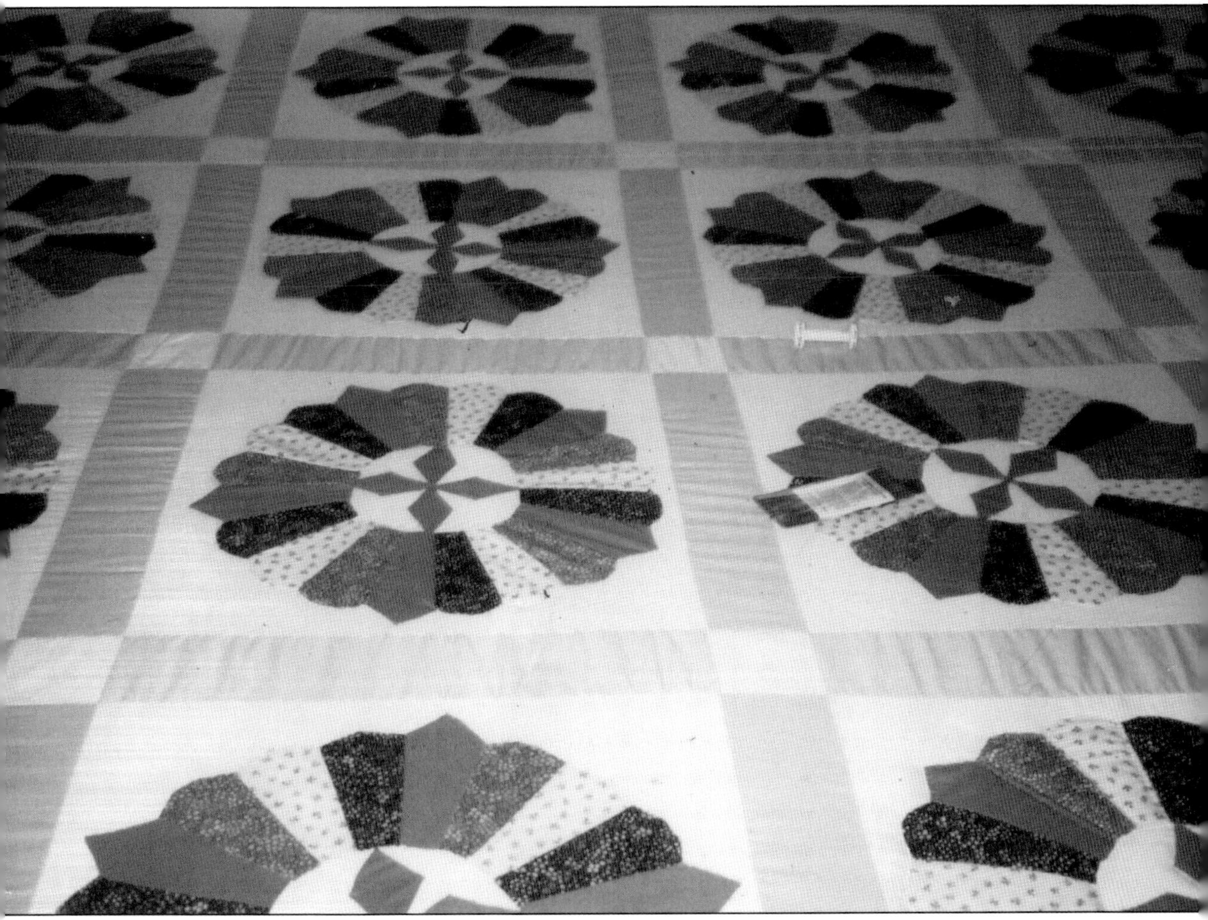

This quilt, named Dresden Plate, sold for $400 at an auction in 1994 at Old Time Saturday. Over the years, many quilts have been hand-quilted by several senior citizens to be sold at auction or won by people who bought tickets for the popular Little Miss/Mr. Old Time Saturday contestants. Some of the talented hand quilters who have contributed so much time and talent are Daphne Nordgaard, Oneta Barnett, Reba Mercer, Louise Hunt, and others have donated blocks or fabric. In 1993, five quilts were sold at an auction, bringing a total price of $1,150. In 1994, eleven quilts, with such names as Dresden Plate Quilt, Bow Tie Quilt, Nine Patch Quilt, and Christmas Log Cabin Quilt sold auctioned for $3,115. Most of these quilts were made in the senior citizens center where the ladies had collected quilting materials and had room for their quilting frames. Old Time Saturday funded construction of the senior citizens center, and the ladies have certainly done their part in helping to repay that.

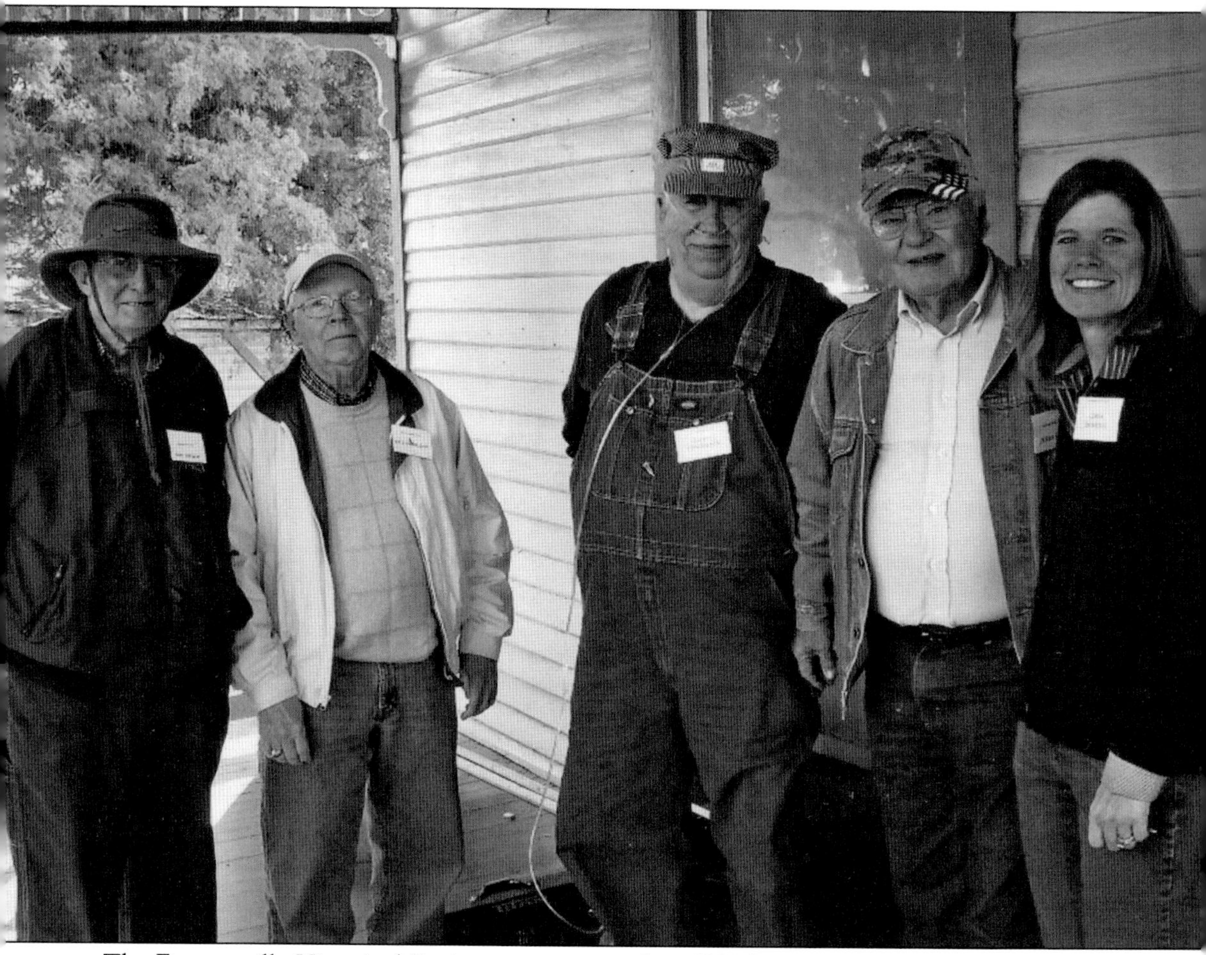

The Farmersville Historical Society was organized in 1989 by a group interested in preserving Farmersville history. In addition to restoration of the historical Bain-Honaker House, it secured a historical marker from the Texas Historical Commission in 1996 that stands in the front yard of the house. Inmates from the Collin County jail have worked numerous hours in restoration of the house, scraping and painting it, returning it to its original color, and doing other projects as needed. Many retired men in the community have volunteered their time in building a picket fence surrounding the yard, as there was originally. They spend many hours mowing the yards and trimming trees. Various fund-raisers have been held over the years to help with the restoration costs. These fund-raisers have included a style show/spring luncheon held each year with a silent auction for items donated by local and area merchants and friends. A tour of homes and a country store are held in the fall as well.

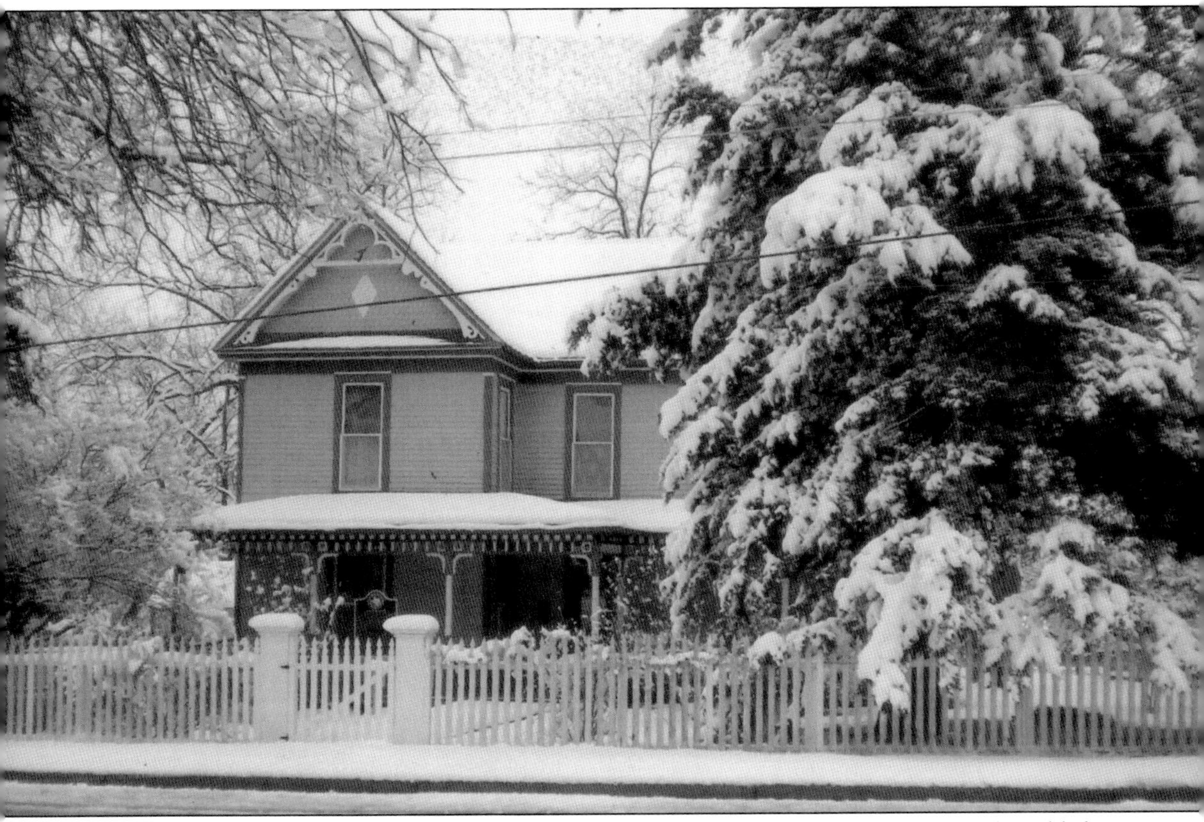

The Bain-Honaker House was given to the Farmersville Historical Society to restore and establish as a museum by Margaret Wienberger and Cassie Hagar, who inherited the house in 1928 from their grandmother. In 1865, Anna Hicks Bain, a widow, left the farm on Indian Creek and moved to Farmersville with her five daughters. One daughter, Mary Catherine, lived with her mother while her husband, Andrew Jackson Honaker, went to Kentucky to finish his medical studies. He died there and Cassie reared her son, Bain, there and never owned a home. She later married J. E. Jones, known as "Tarheel." He planted the pecan grove behind the house, which is still there. Bain was killed in 1927, leaving three children, Billy Bain, Margaret Lee, and Mary Catherine. Three generations of fatherless children have lived in the house. The Farmersville Historical Society has been very active in restoring the house and grounds to its original look. All of the work is done on a voluntary basis, in order to preserve this part of Farmersville's history.

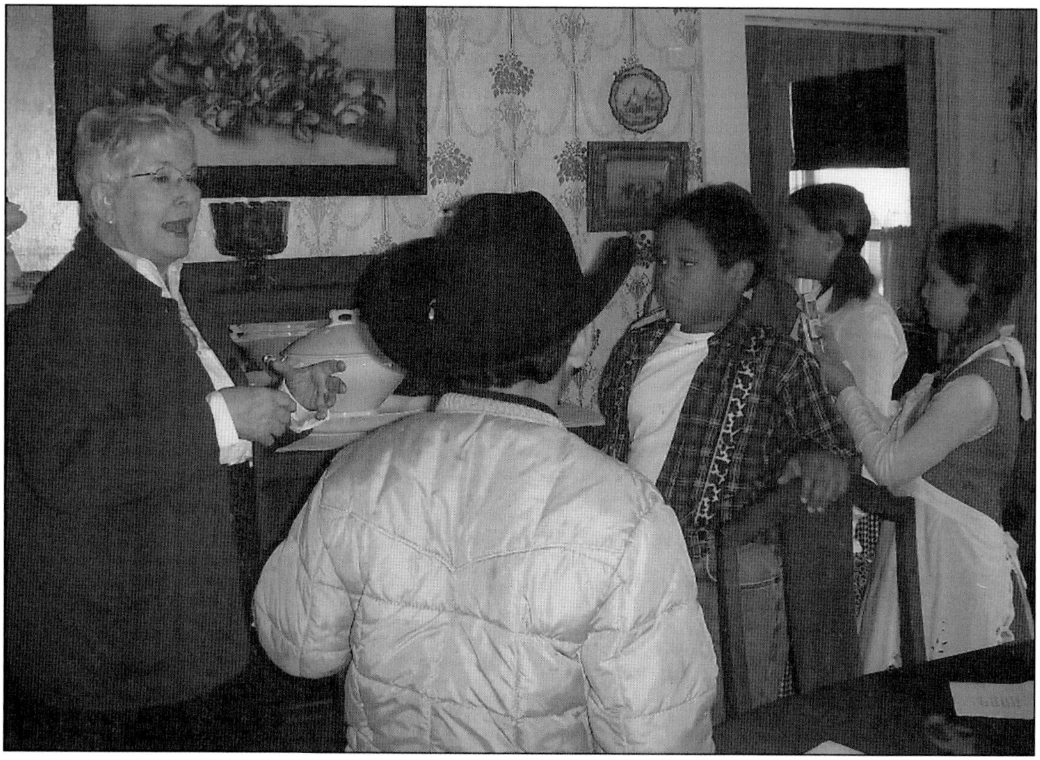

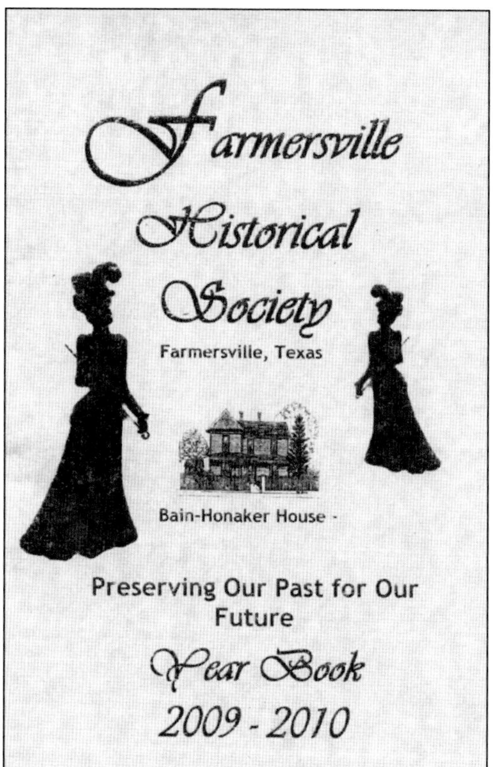

Above, retired teacher Ann Curington explains one of the many things that were necessary in the 1800s and early 1900s that have been improved or have been done away with since that time. The Farmersville Historical Society yearbook for 2009–2010 is shown at left.

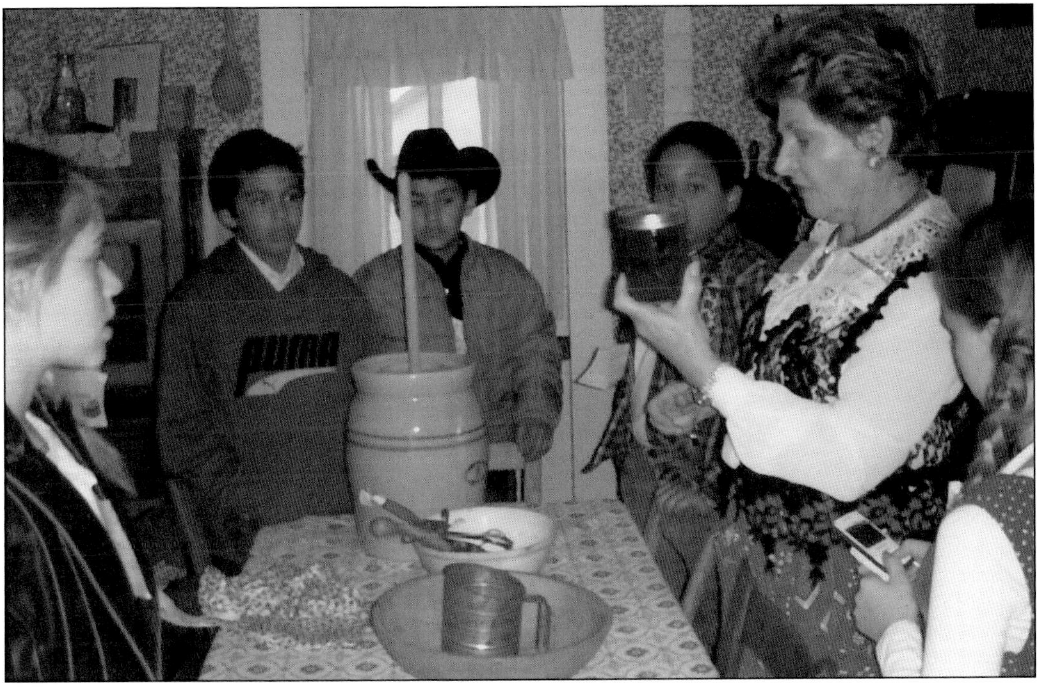

The Farmersville Historical Society, endeavoring to instill in the younger generation an awareness and appreciation of the history of the area, came up with a program to do just that. They call it the "Farmersville 1900 Program." The society has been presented the Margaret Hughston Educational Award during the first Preservation Celebration, organized by the Collin County Historical Commission. Billie Goldstein, pictured above, is speaking to a group of children in the kitchen.

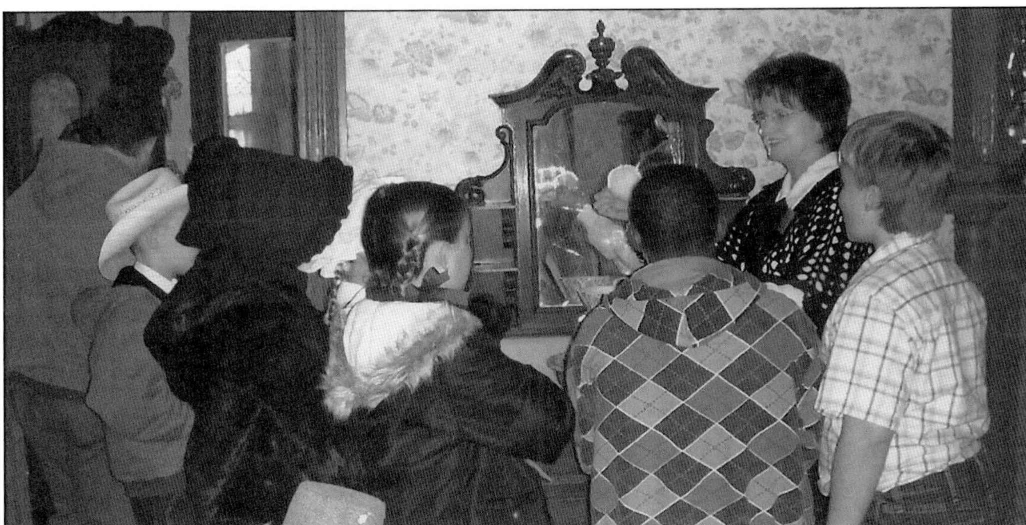

In a joint venture between the Farmersville Intermediate School and the Farmersville Historical Society, each year the fifth grade social studies class is bussed to the Bain-Honaker House for a day's activities. Using names researched from the 1900 census, each student takes an identity and dresses to fit the time period. Girls learn how to embroider and make quilts and cornhusk dolls. Boys help construct a henhouse, outdoor toilet, or perhaps a pigpen.

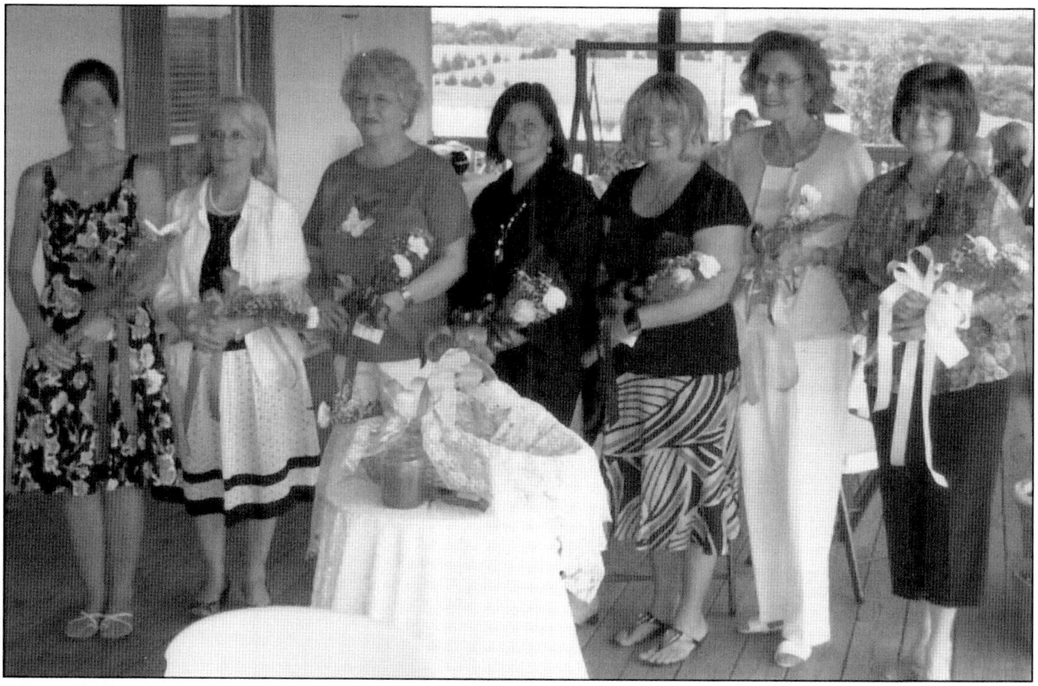

These ladies are officers of the Farmersville Historical Society. Standing, from left to right, are president Linda Dawkins, vice president Bettye Petree, recording secretary LoEtta Reavis, treasurer Diane Piwko, reporter Sheila Slaughter, historian Ann Rose, and parliamentarian Winnetta Morrow.

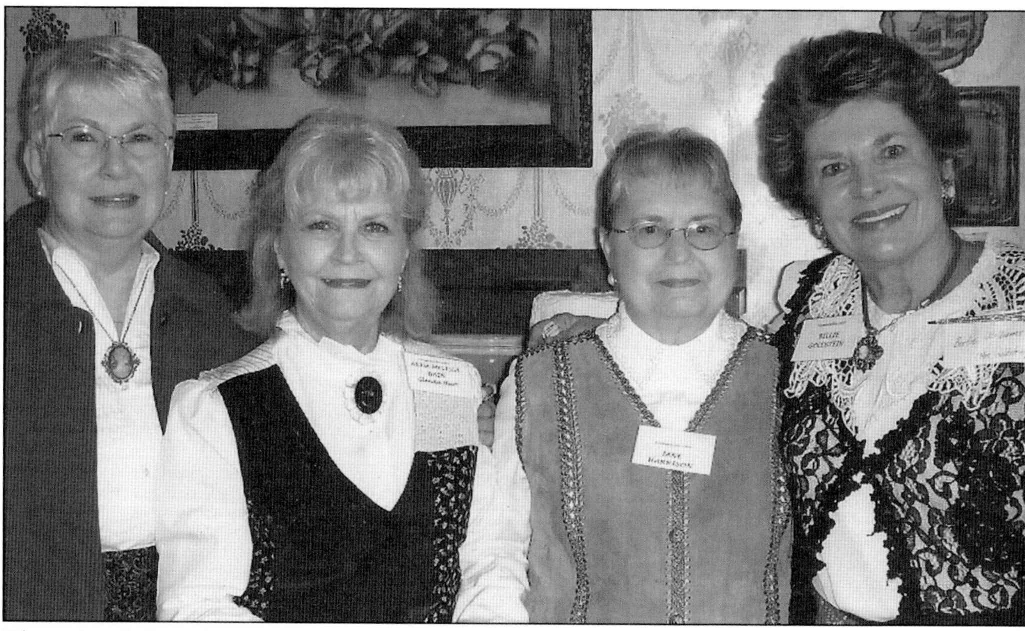

These four ladies, dressed in period dresses, pose during the "Farmersville 1900 Program," which teaches fifth-grade students various things that ancestors did daily back in the early 1900s. Standing, from left to right, are retired teacher Ann Curington, retired teacher Glenda Hart, retired pharmacy assistant Jane Harrison, and wife and mother Billie Goldstein.

Six

This 'n' That

In most categories of nearly anything, there are usually some things that do not fit into a particular slot. Such miscellaneous things are included in this chapter.

Gussie Nell Davis fits here, because there was no one quite like her. She was the lady who organized, trained, and traveled with the Kilgore Rangerettes. Born and raised in Farmersville, she brought those high-kicking girls to Farmersville in 1970 to perform at halftime for the enjoyment of everyone, probably most of all for herself. Her school, her town, her Rangerettes—she must have loved it.

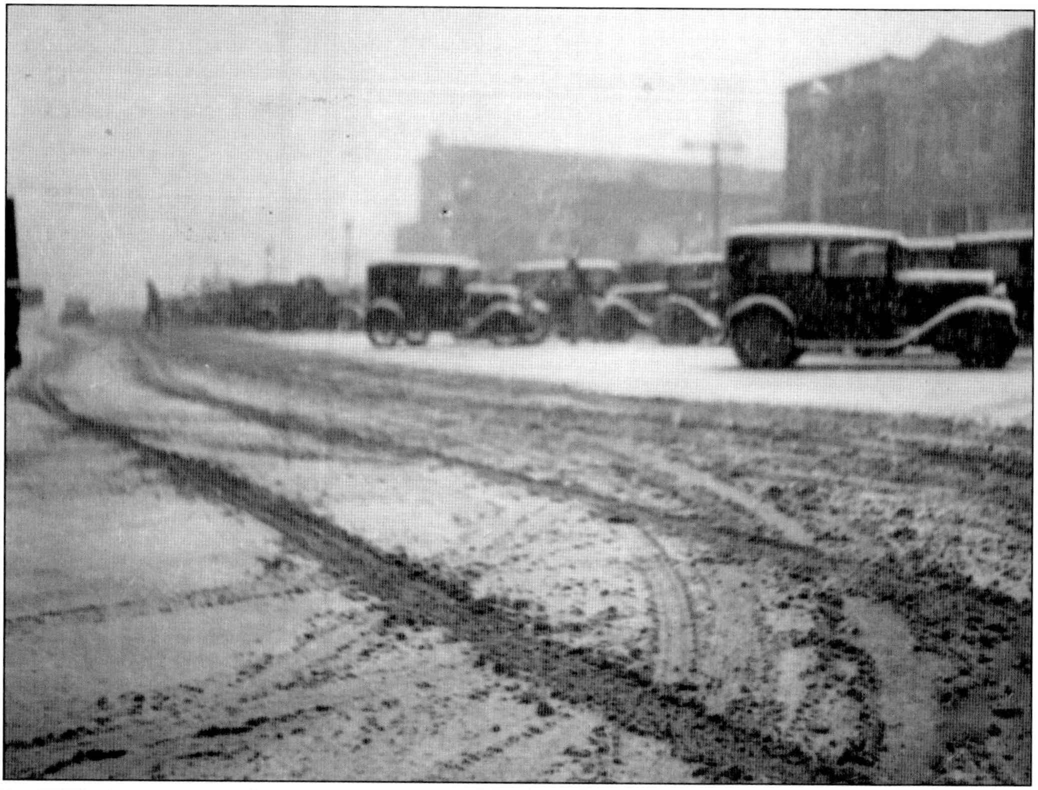

In 1900, the street on the square was so muddy that the wagons bogged down and stayed there for weeks. The streets were either muddy in wet weather or dry and dusty in dry weather.

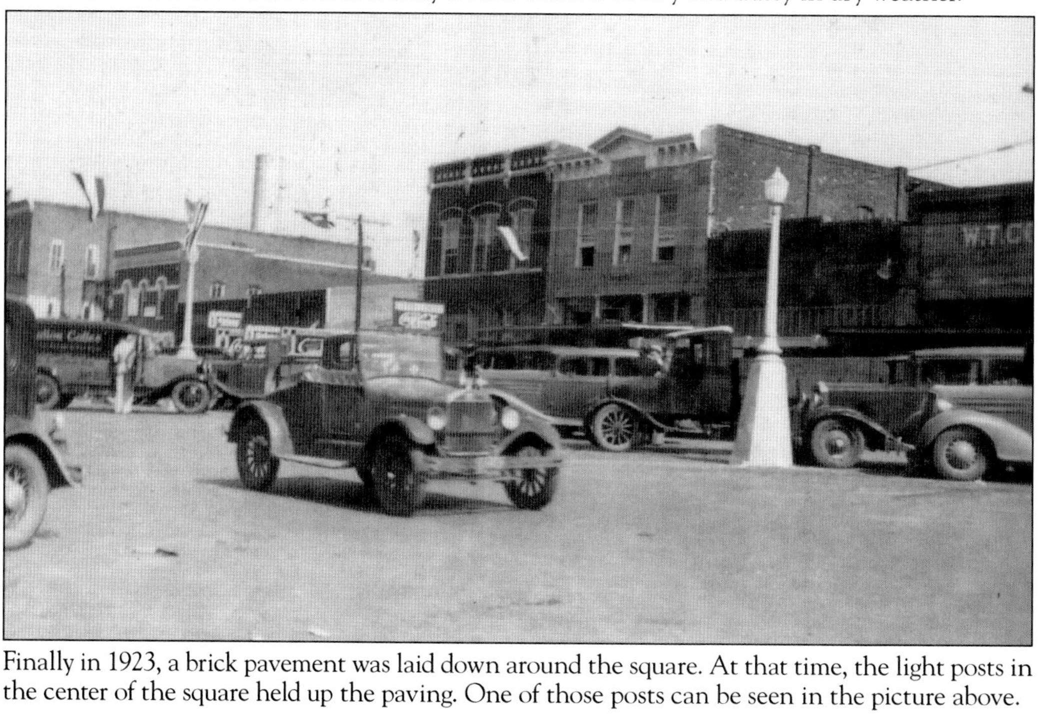

Finally in 1923, a brick pavement was laid down around the square. At that time, the light posts in the center of the square held up the paving. One of those posts can be seen in the picture above.

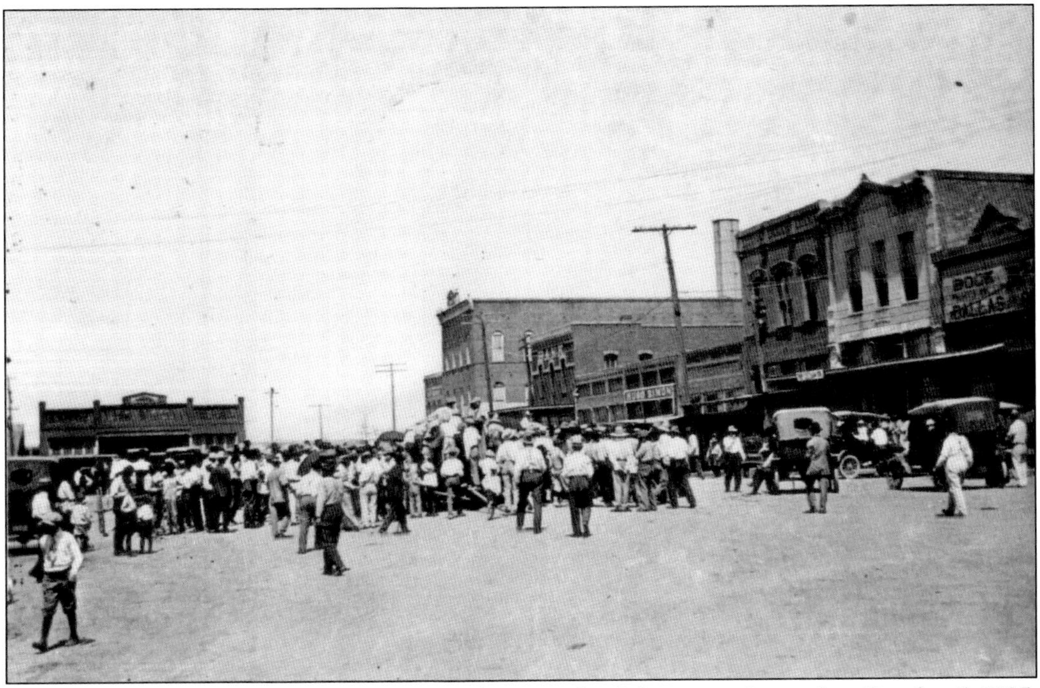

The above street scene was taken in 1918. The east side of the square burned on October 5, 1905, from the Aston Building on South Main Street to the Masonic building on North Main Street. The fire started around 8 p.m. in the Neathery Hardware building and lasted through the night. Among the buildings destroyed were the First National Bank, DeShields Dry Goods, Neathery Hardware, Neathery Dry Goods, Hope Drug Store, Bob Russell Jewelry, Norwood's Notions and Dry Goods, and Jim Glendenning's Café.

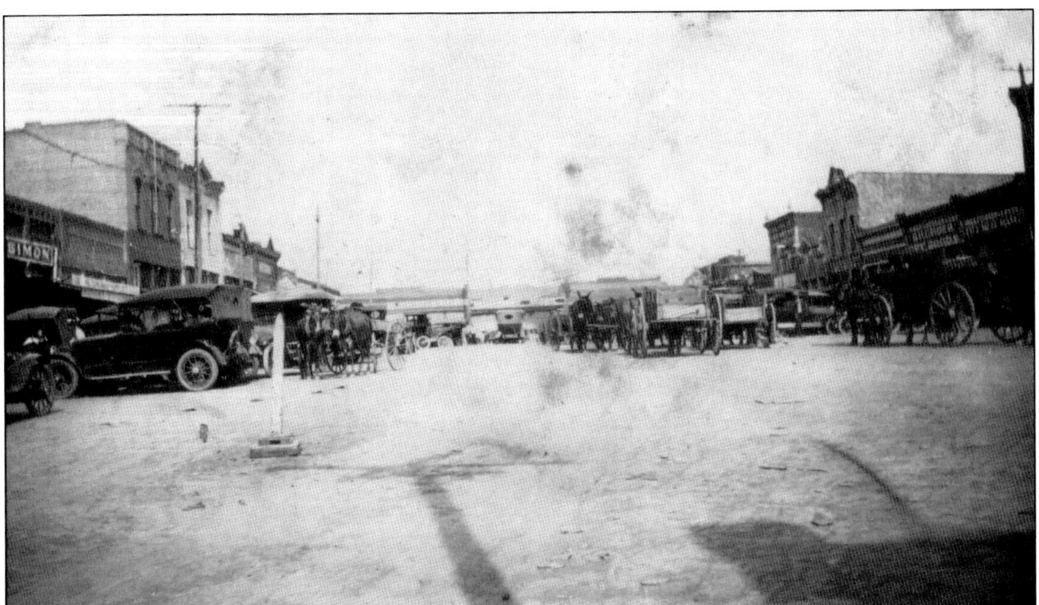

The view in this photograph shows the north and south sides of the square in 1920.

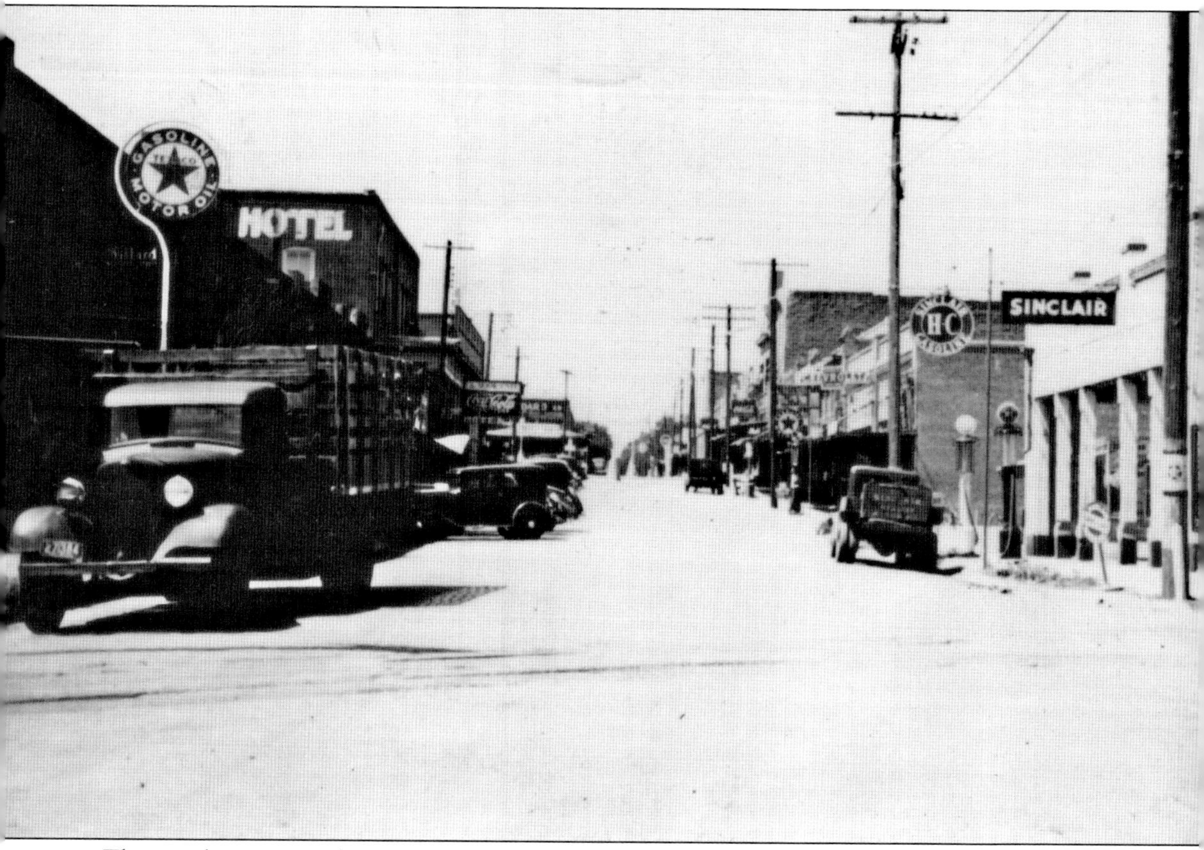

This article was printed in the *Farmersville Times* in 1909. It was a report from the civic improvement committee to the commercial clubs. "Farmersville People, Please Read" was the title. It continued as follows:

> After a careful inspection of the town, we find barbed wire fences standing along some of our main streets, which we consider a nuisance and believe the people owning the property on which they stand would gladly remove them if their attention was called to the matter in the proper way . . . The old rotten wood walks afford a place for the accumulation of filth of every description and a breeding place for fever and every other sort of disease germs. We would further suggest that every member of the club ask their wives and daughters to cooperate in the agitation for needed improvements and the beautifying of Farmersville. Respectfully Submitted: H. D. Honaker, J. W. Neathery, H. W. Rike, M. T. Harden, D. M. Yeary, Committee. April, 1909.

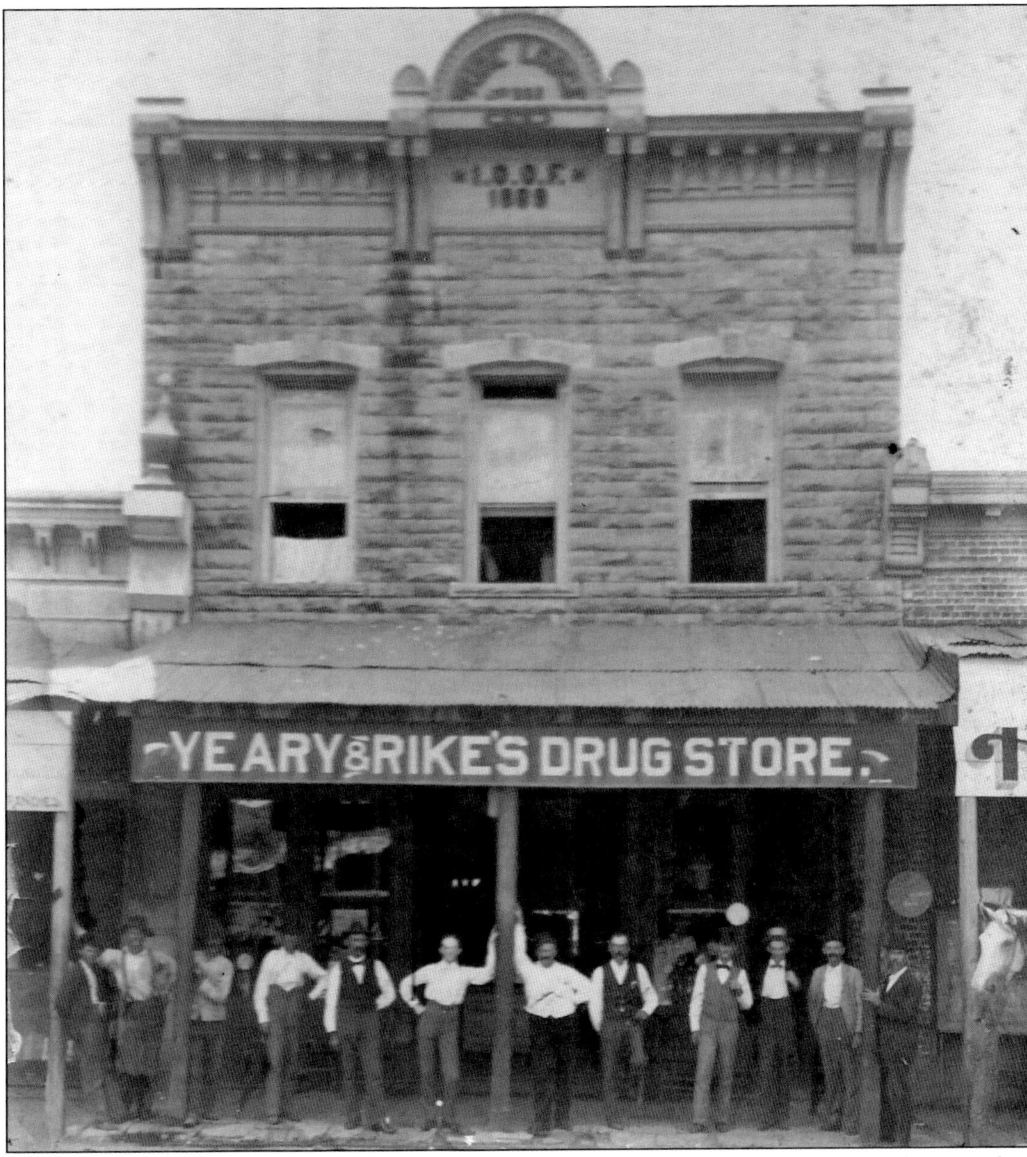

The Masonic Lodge has been active for many years in Farmersville. The building that stands at the corner of Main and College Streets was constructed in 1888. It was built of rock and stone mined from a rock pit owned by R. A. Rike, at a cost of $4,375. The chisel marks can still be seen in the rock on the building. It and the Aston Building are the only two original structures on the square. Many of Farmersville's prominent citizens have been affiliated with Masonic Lodge No. 214. But perhaps Sam Hamilton was the most famous. In 1898, he achieved the rank of "Worshipful Grand Master." He was the postmaster in Farmersville in 1870 and 1883. Hamilton also revised, corrected, and rearranged *The Taylor-Hamilton Monitor of Symbolic Masonry*. In 1903, when the ornate Methodist church was built, Hamilton wrote a history of the church. When that church building burned in 1924, that history was all that remained since all records had been destroyed. The Lodge Building was sold in 1956 to Bob Poole, editor of the *Farmersville Times*.

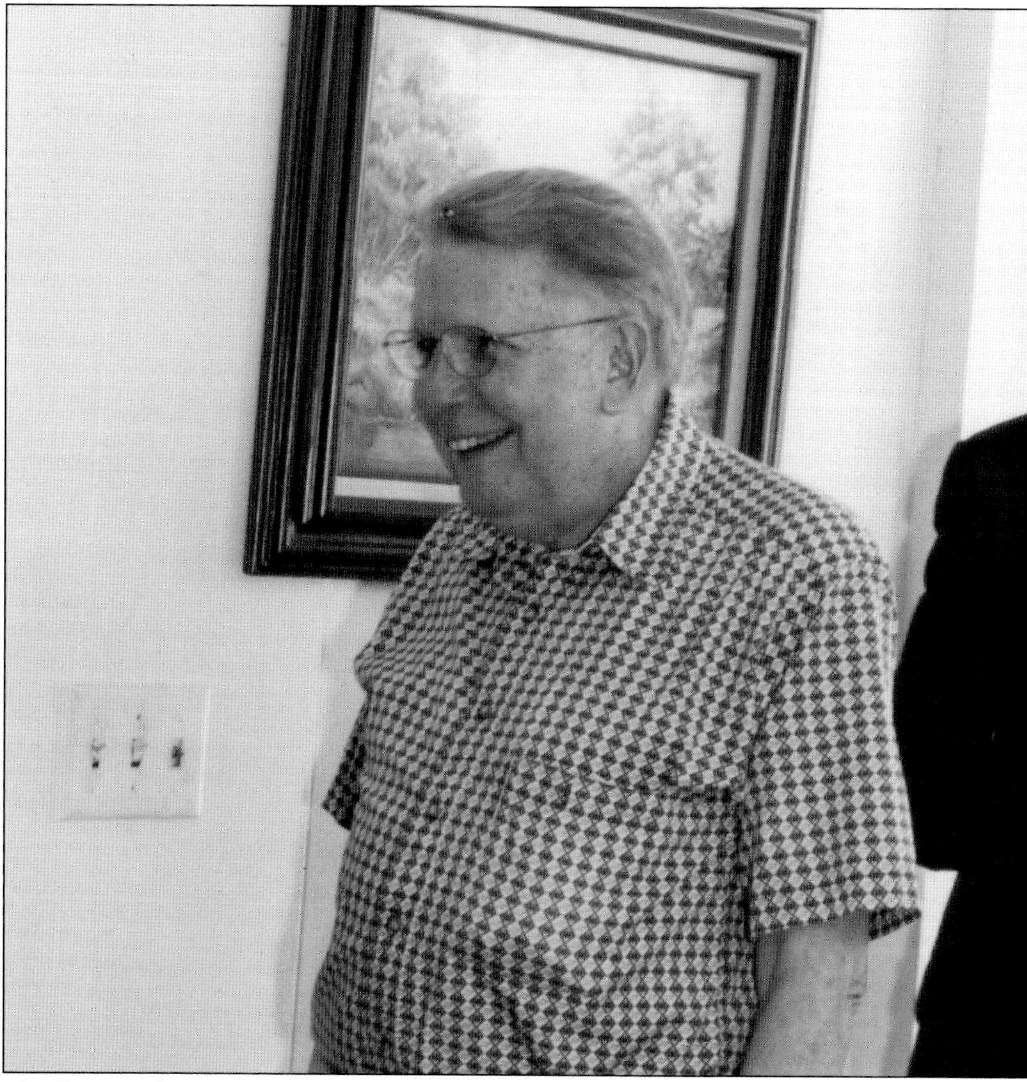

The *Farmersville Times* is the oldest newspaper in Collin County, retaining its original name. It was established in 1885, and the first issue was dated March 23, 1885. From 1904 until 1956, it was located in various buildings. In 1956, owner Burton Fielder moved into the location at 101 South Main Street. That building, the Masonic Lodge, was constructed in 1888 using lodge membership funds after the 1886 fire on the square that destroyed the previous Masonic Lodge. The *Farmersville Times* moved into the building in 1956. Then in 1959, Bob Poole bought the newspaper from Burton Fielder, the previous owner. Officials of the lodge approached Poole in 1965 about purchasing the building. Poole bought it and his late brother, Tom Poole Jr., joined him in the business. They formed a corporation in 1980 and operated the newspaper very successfully for many years. Bob retired in 2000, selling the newspaper to Chad Engbrock, who had the building restored. The Texas Historical Commission placed a marker at the building in 2009.

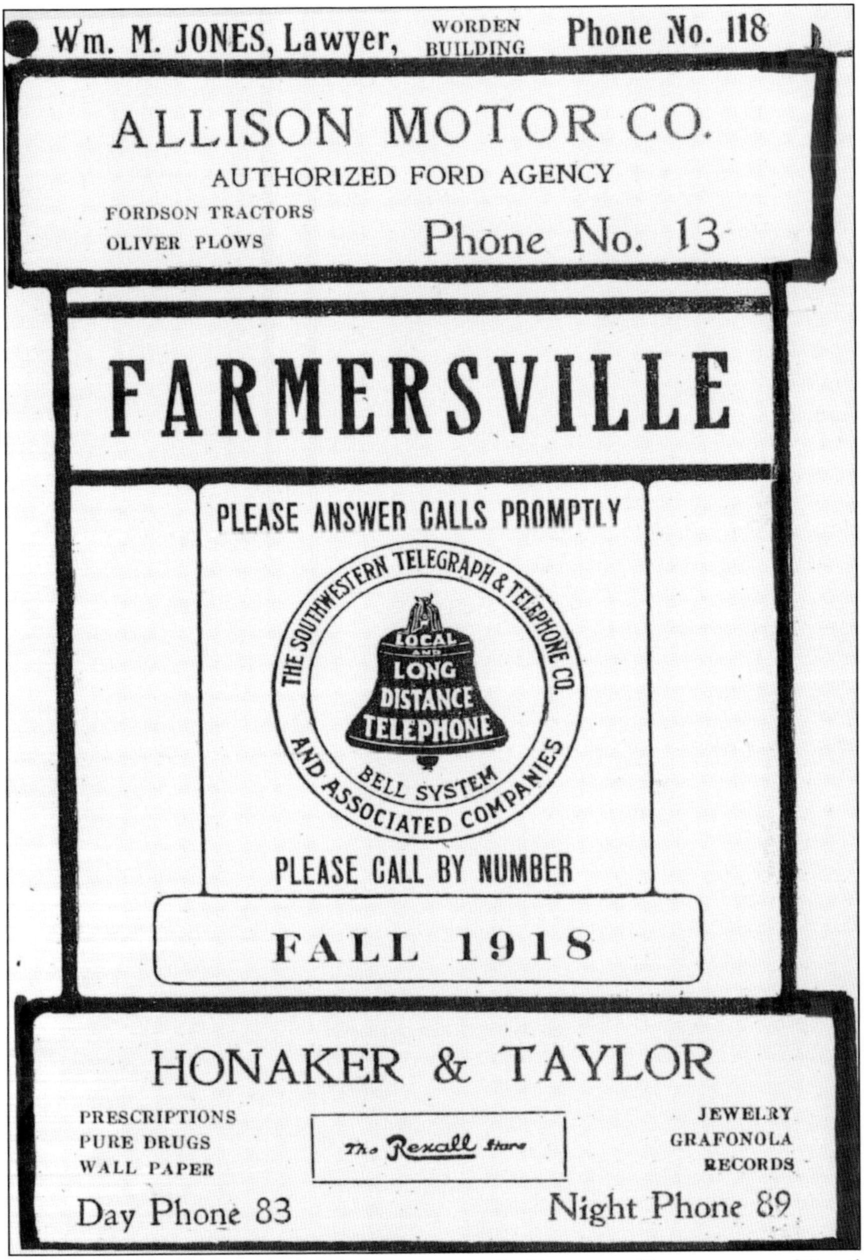

This is the front cover of a 1918 telephone directory for Farmersville, courtesy of Southwestern Telegraph and Telephone Company. The first use of telephones came to Farmersville in 1899, and Southwestern Telegraph and Telephone Company installed them. In January 1901, there were 69 telephones in use. The first local farmer lines were installed in 1905. Farmers and other users on those lines paid a 5¢ per call charge. The early day "party line" telephones were community affairs. They were used as a sort of exchange information bureau, with 10 to 20 subscribers on each line. Those early telephone lines were strung along the fence, with the poles in the fence line from house to house. The lines were sometimes strung on barbed wire posts, which were usually bois d'arc poles, sticking out of the ground about 20 feet. Dial telephones came to town in 1940, the first in Collin County.

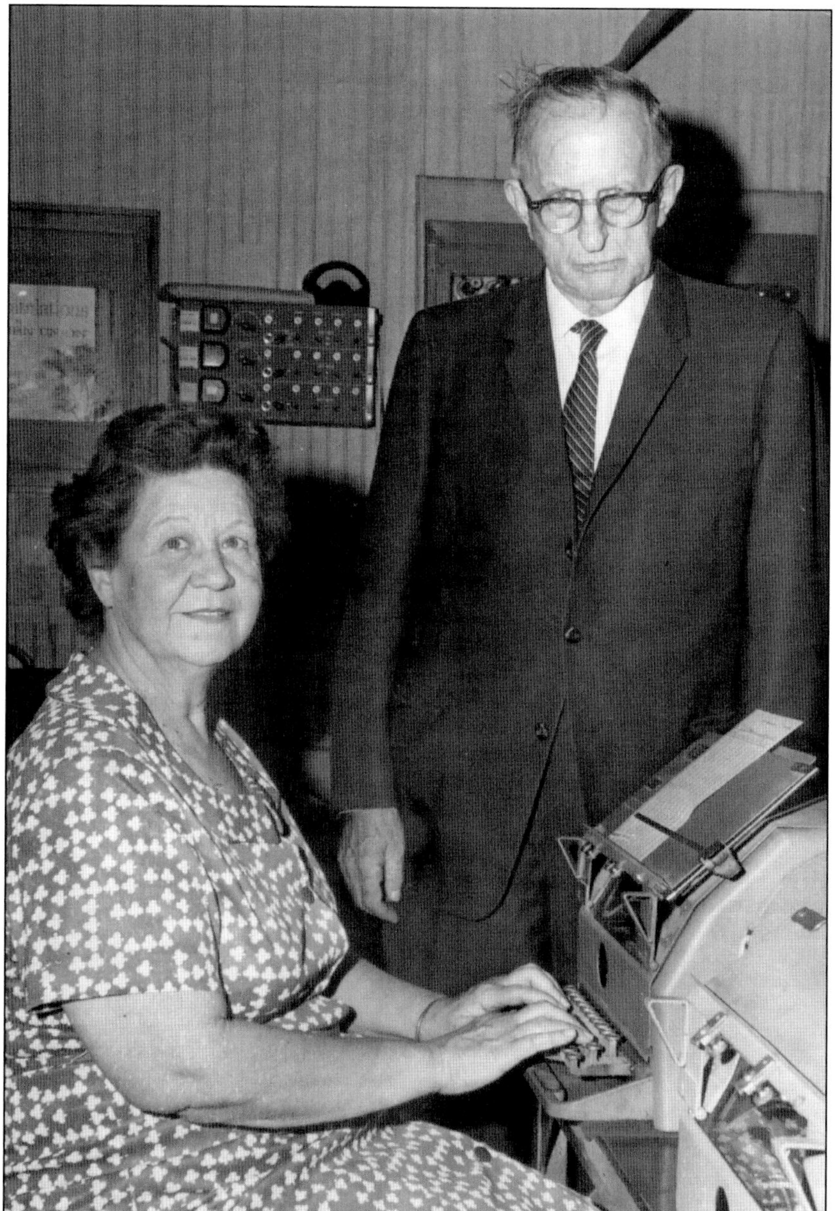

Elizabeth Bumpass, born in Farmersville, descended from a very long line of Bumpasses. That surname has been in Farmersville history since the very early days of its existence. Bumpass graduated from Farmersville High School in 1928. She recalls that her Sunday school teacher operated the one-man Western Union office there. She became interested in telegraph work through him. After attending three months at a Western Union operator's school in Tyler, Bumpass (as she's known by many) reported to Denison for her first job in December 1928. Her career with the company lasted for 43 years and ended in 1971 when the office closed. Pictured with Bumpass, as her job ends, is the first customer she served at Western Union, F. H. Kohfeldt. She's not sure how she'll spend leisure time now that she has been "retired," because she has worked since her graduation from high school. She has never had time for hobbies—or boyfriends, but quickly snapped, "I'm not about to start looking now!" referring to boyfriends, not hobbies!

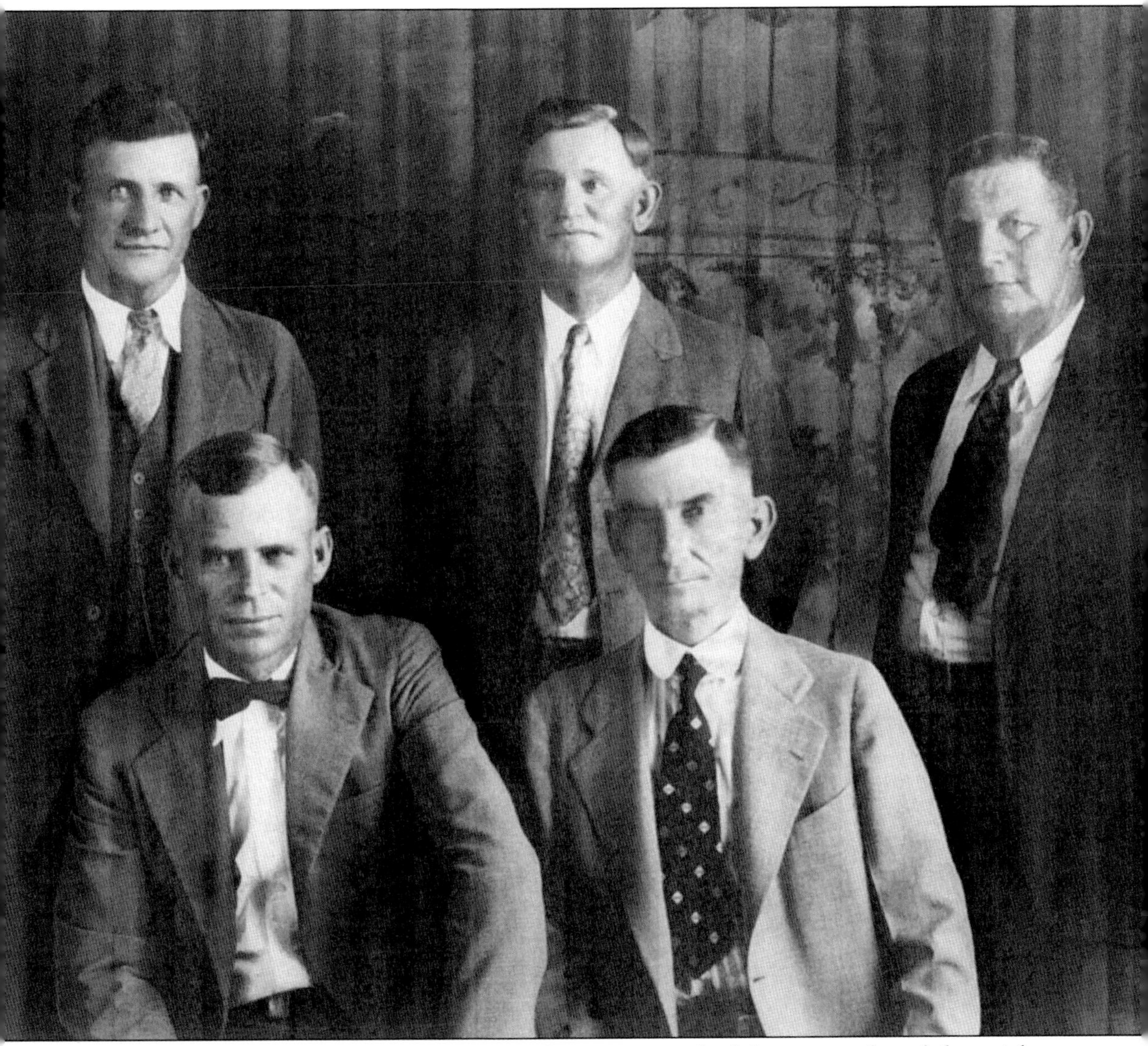
In 1929, the Collin County Commissioners' Court consisted of these men, from left to right: (first row) Don Davis and Judge E. W. Merritt; (second row) Lee Cook, C. C. Whitt, and Wilson Spain, who was a Farmersville resident.

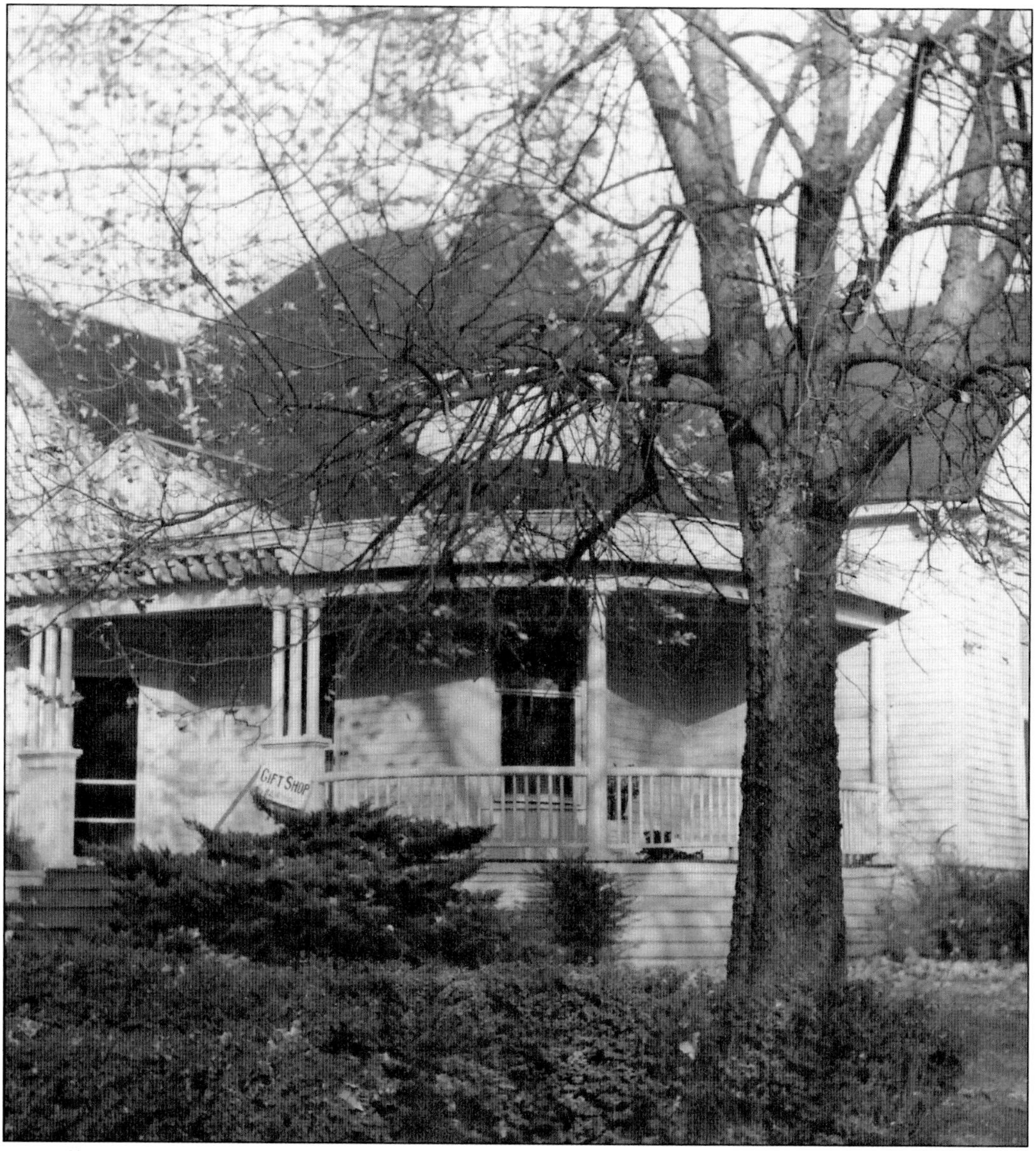

Dr. Allen Neathery, one of the first doctors in Farmersville, came to Texas in 1886. His son Seymour married Laura Lindsay. They and their children lived in this house at the time of his death in 1922. Laura and the children, Hattie, Alice, Lynn, John, and Phoebe acquired title to the house in 1929 from Fred Pendleton. Laura provided room and board for teachers and others. Hattie and Jess Aycock were married in the house in 1923. Mrs. Bob Russell bought the house in 1946, though it burned in 1948. Russell built a small house there a year later. The house was located on the east side of Main Street, the second house south of Houston Street.

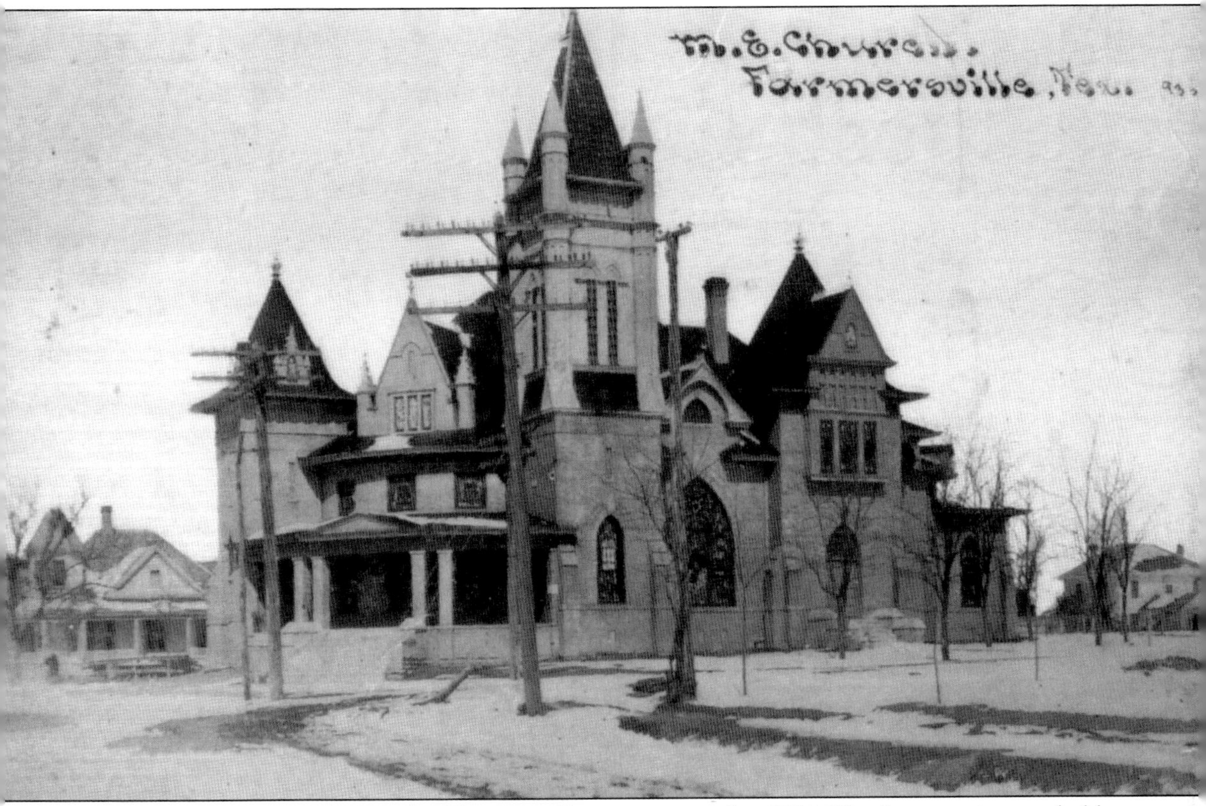

The Methodist Episcopal Church of Farmersville was organized in 1856. The first meeting was held in a schoolhouse west of town, possibly located on the farm of R. A. Rike and his wife, Mariah Seitz (Sides) Rike. In 1875, an acre of land was bought on North Main Street and a wooden building was constructed at a cost of $4,000. An acre of adjoining land was also purchased, and a parsonage was built that was later destroyed by fire in 1892. In 1902, that wooden building was demolished to make way for a new, larger building. A very ornate brick building was erected; the first services were conducted on May 3, 1903. On December 28, 1924, the building was destroyed by a fire of unknown origin, following Sunday morning services. A third brick building, less ornate, replaced the burned one, and initial services were held there in March 1926. The Methodist church has been meeting at its present location for 135 years. Since 1856, a member of the Honaker family has been a member at this church.

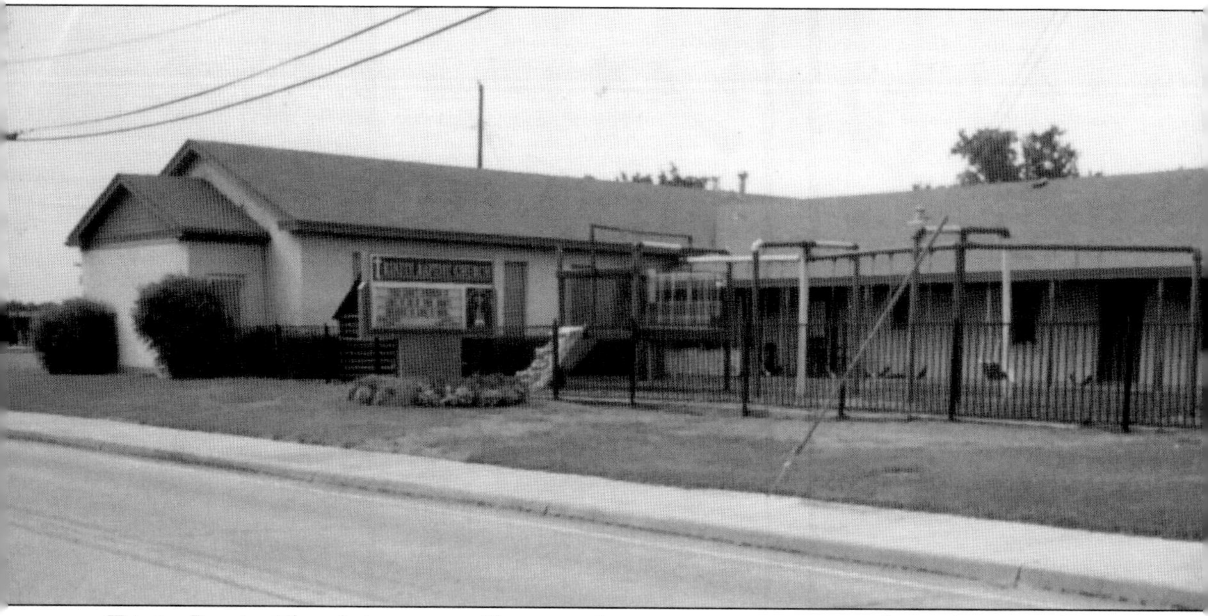

Trinity Baptist Church is so named because three congregations merged together to make one. Prairie Grove Baptist was located at Aleo, a few miles from Farmersville. The church began in 1896 on land donated by W. Y. and Florindo Carver. Church members gathered twice a year—with the ladies bringing lunch and the men furnishing a barrel of water—in order to clean the cemetery located east of the church building. (Audie Murphy's mother and grandparents are buried in that Aleo Cemetery). The church declined in the 1950s, and in 1958 it joined with Midway Baptist, which had been in existence since 1915, and Brushy Baptist, to form a combination of the three, named Trinity Baptist. Mrs. Roy Carpenter donated the lot at McKinney and Hamilton Streets. The church building was constructed within seven months and was dedicated in October 1958. After the New Mesquite Baptist Church was destroyed by a tornado, many of its members began to attend Trinity Baptist Church.

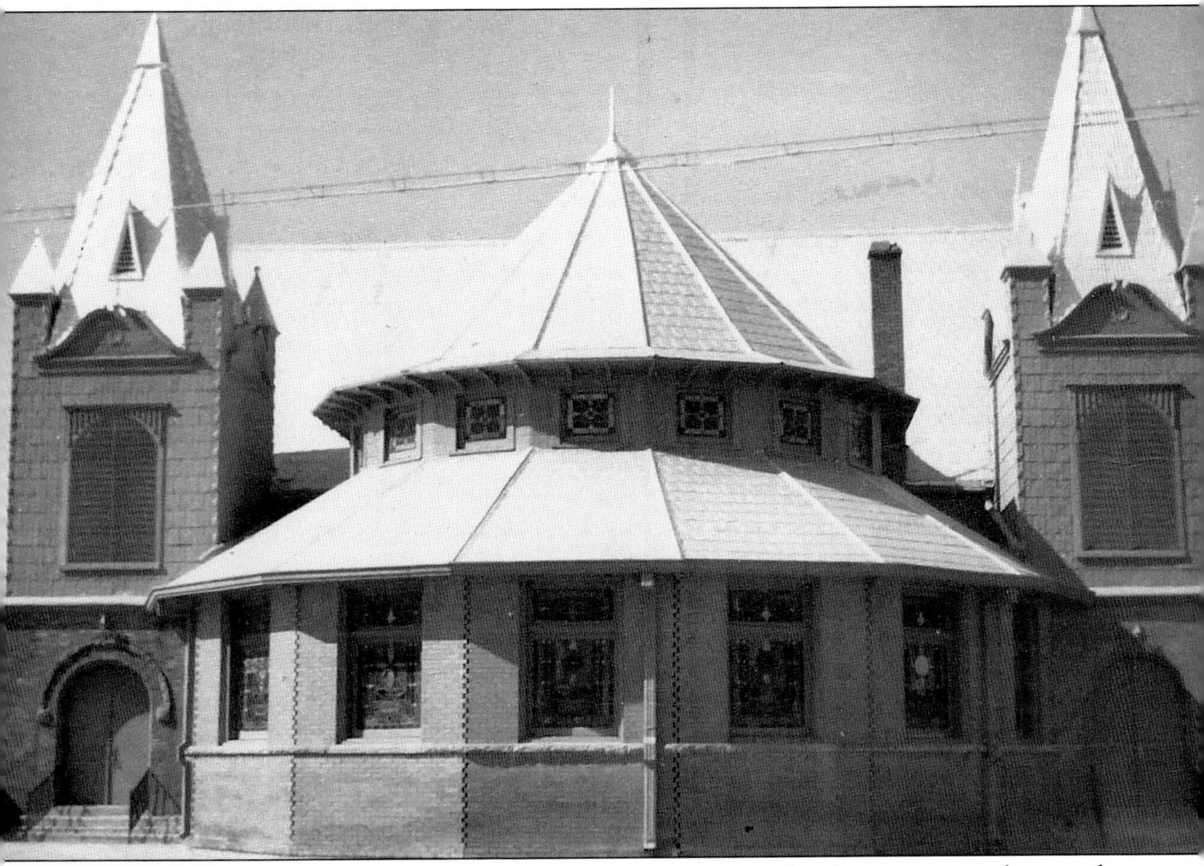

First Baptist Church was organized in 1865. It was formed at a brush arbor meeting at the site of the present church located just off the square on Washington Street. The church had no building so services were held in the lower room of the old Masonic Building until 1877. Then church members had a frame structure built that was later replaced by the building in the photograph above in 1900.

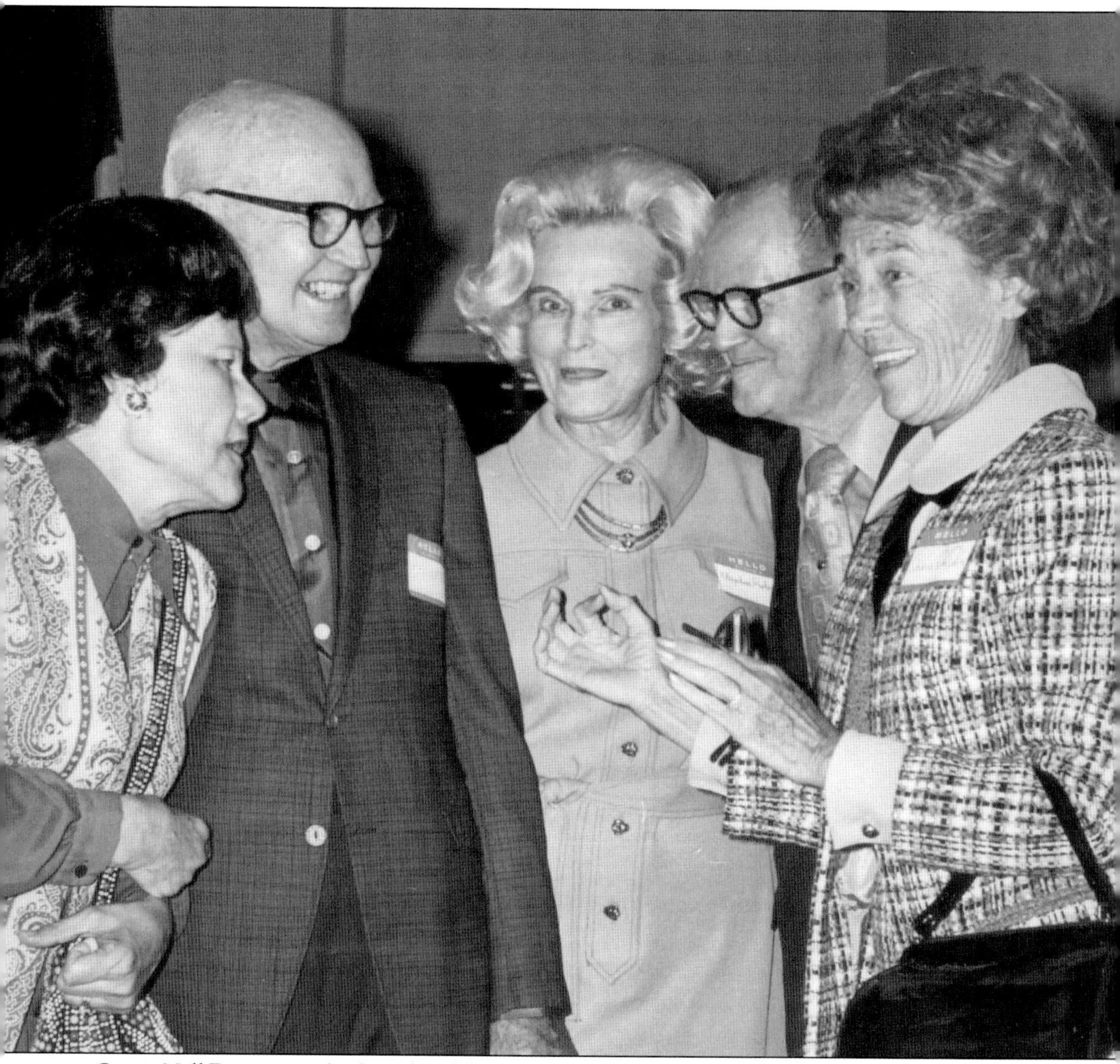

Gussie Nell Davis is on the far right of this picture with old classmates. She was born in Farmersville in 1906 and graduated from high school in 1921 at the age of 15. In an interview, she stated, "All I ever really wanted was to dance on the stage. But I grew up in Farmersville and in Farmersville, if you danced, you were thrown out of the church—any church." Her first job was at Greenville High School, where she invented the girls drill team, "The Flaming Flashes." In 1939, hired by Kilgore College, she was asked to keep fans in their seats at halftime. The Kilgore Rangerettes certainly did that. Under her training, they became the first dance drill team in the world. They march in the Macy's Thanksgiving Day Parade and have performed in Cotton Bowl festivities for 43 years. In 1970, Davis and the Rangerettes came to Farmersville and performed at halftime. Davis received numerous awards before retiring in 1979. At age 87, she passed away and returned to Farmersville for the last time for burial.

Seven

Audie Murphy, American Hero

Audie Murphy was the most decorated soldier of World War II. He grew up with nothing and was faced with great responsibility at a young age. After his mother, Josie, died, Murphy's two younger sisters and one younger brother were placed in the Boles Orphans Home, some miles from Farmersville. One of the first things he did, as soon as he was able to after the war, was make arrangements to get his siblings out of that orphanage.

Murphy was the kind of person who saw what needed to be done and just did it. He saw that burning tank in France, saw the enemy coming, and heroically jumped on the tank to defend their position.

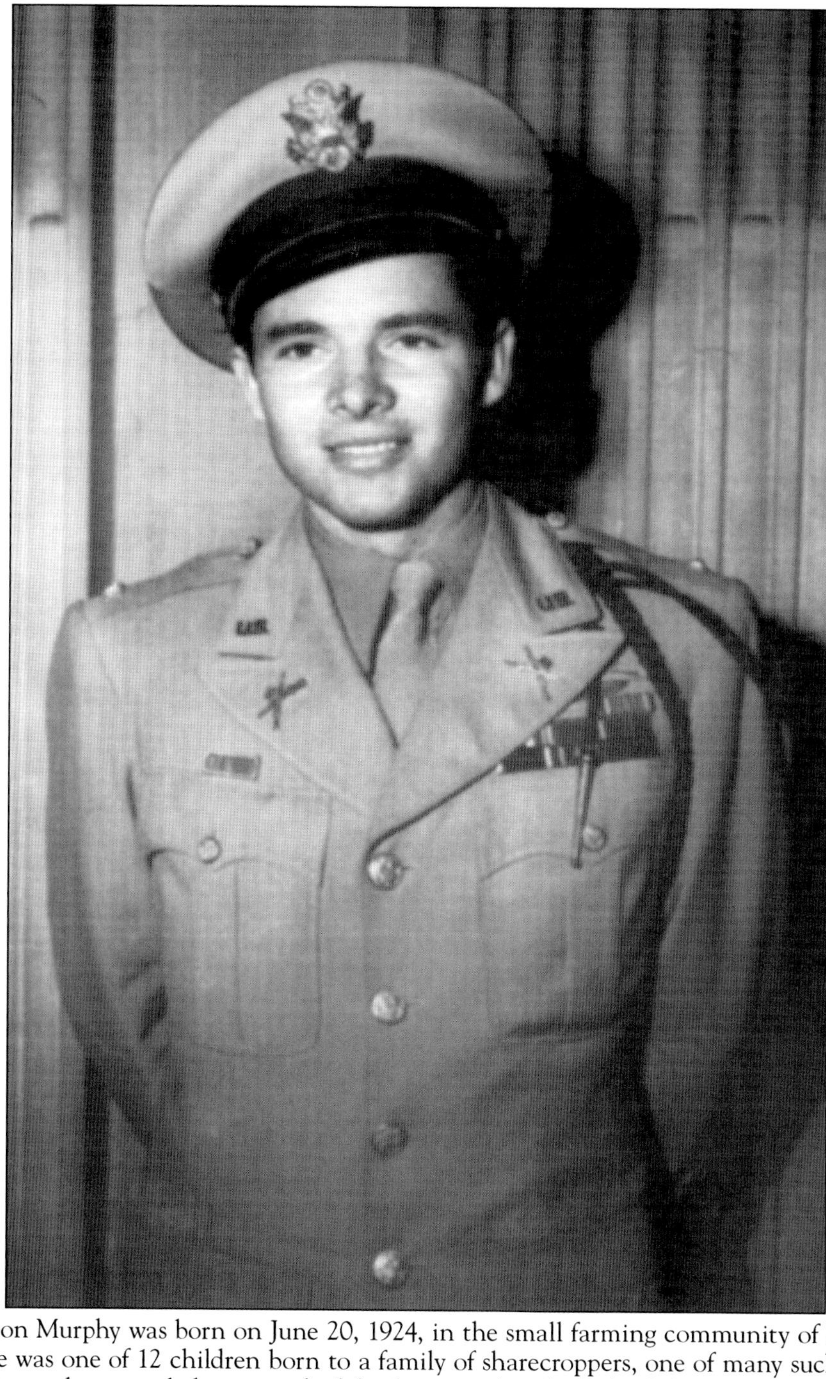

Audie Leon Murphy was born on June 20, 1924, in the small farming community of Kingston, Texas. He was one of 12 children born to a family of sharecroppers, one of many such families of that time, who struggled to even find food to eat. An alcoholic father deserted the family when Audie was 16 years old. At an early age, Audie became a good marksman hunting game such as squirrels and rabbits to help feed his family. Not long after his father left the family in May 1941, Josie Killian Murphy, Audie's mother, died of a serious heart condition complicated by pneumonia. She died five days before her 50th birthday. (Courtesy of the Audie Murphy National Fan Club.)

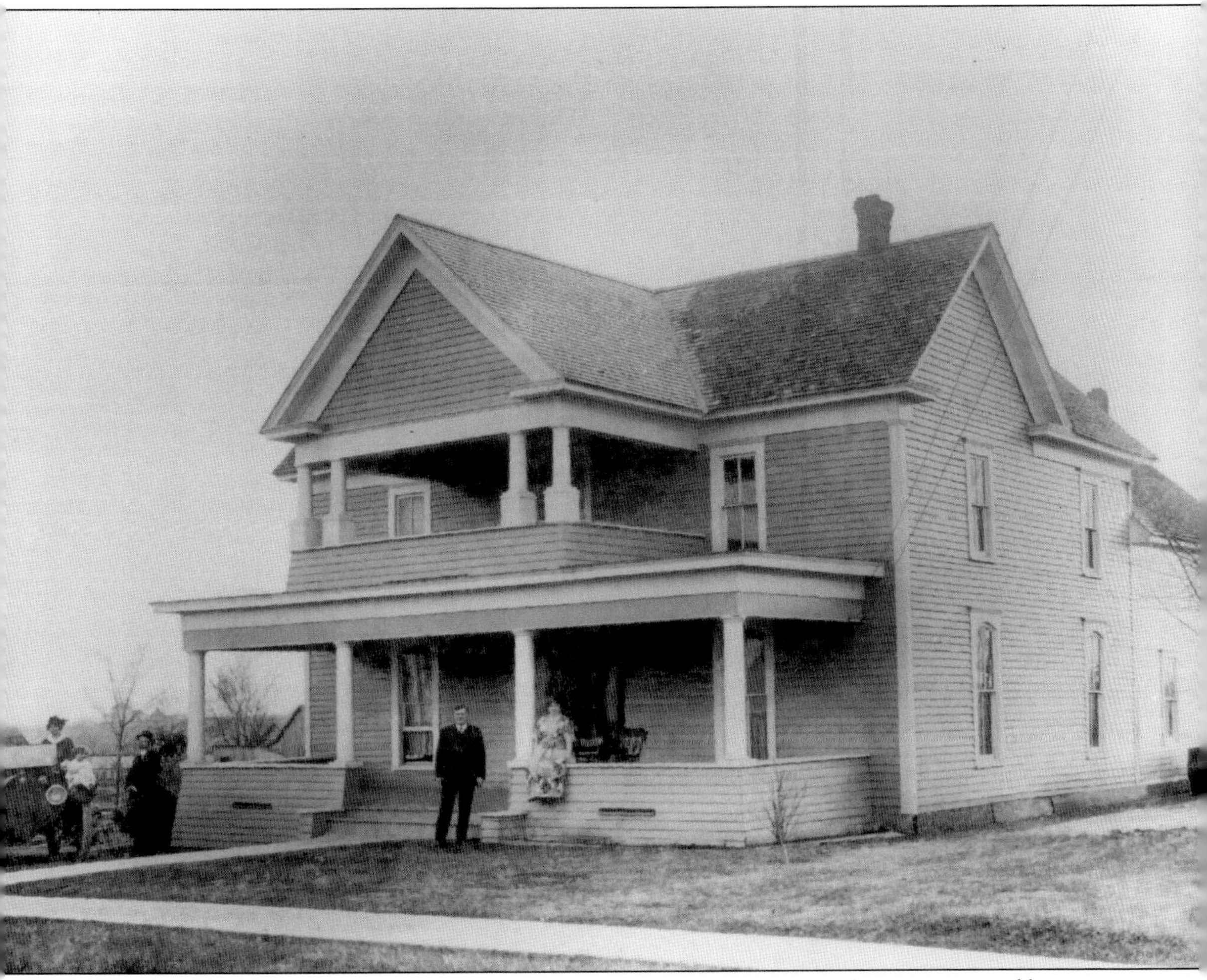

R. L. Russell and Lula May Wisenbaker were married on May 28, 1913. They are pictured here in front of their home on South Washington Street. R. L. was a jeweler, watchmaker, and optician until his death in this house in 1944. Two years later, Lula May sold the house to Audie Murphy. Murphy bought the house for his sister Corinne, her husband, Poland Burns, and their children. He wanted a house large enough that he could bring his younger sisters and brother, Nadine, Billie, and Joe from the orphan's home to live there with his sister. The house is not standing; it burned at a later time.

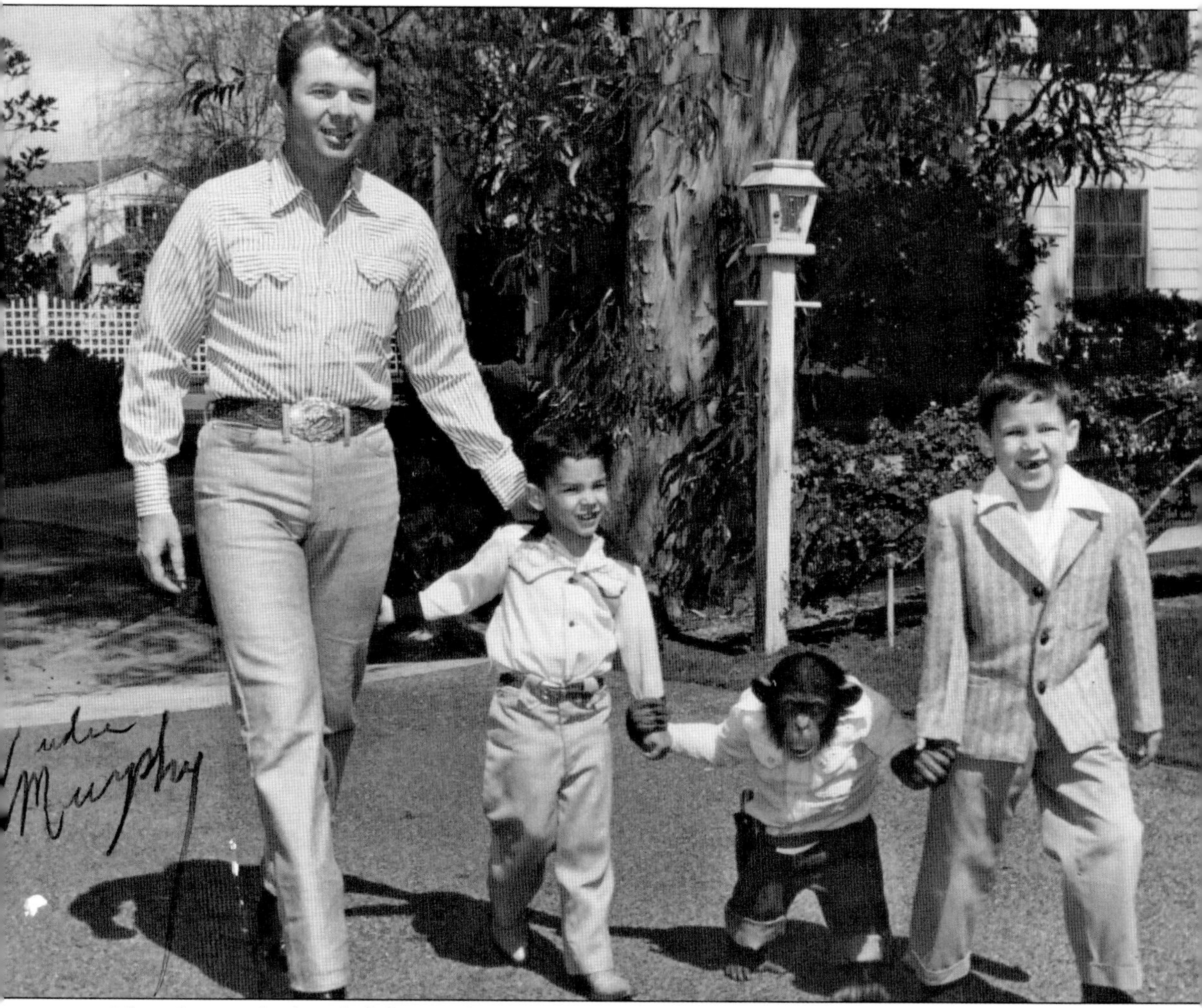

After the war had ended, James Cagney invited Audie Murphy to come to Hollywood. Audie accepted and pursued a career in motion pictures. He was a supporting actor in 1948 and starred in many films during the 1950s and 1960s. His first marriage to Wanda Hendrex failed. He later married Pamela, an airline stewardess flying out of Dallas. Audie is pictured here with his two sons, Terry and Skipper, and a friend. Audie always suffered from memories and nightmares of the war, and slept with a gun under his pillow for some years. His resulting condition from the war would today more than likely be called post-traumatic stress disorder.

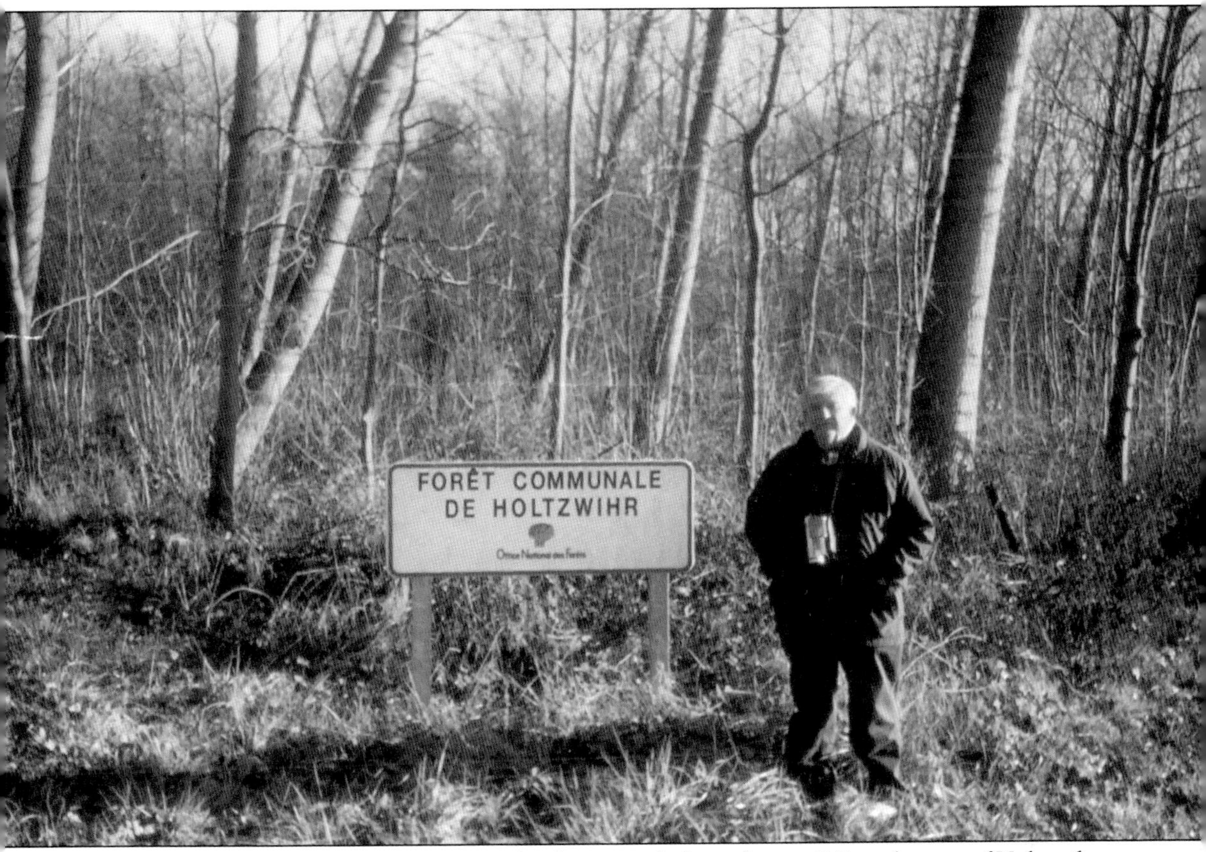

In the midst of a battle with the Germans, fought one mile from the small French town of Holtzwihr, two American tanks were disabled and one was on fire. Audie Murphy ordered his remaining company back into the woods. He leaped on the burning tank, which was loaded with fuel and ammunition, and used its .50 caliber machine gun to hold off the Germans. He held that position for more than an hour, killing or wounding more than 50 Germans until they began to retreat. He suffered a leg wound. This act earned Audie the Congressional Medal of Honor. Pictured here is the spot where Audie commandeered the burning tank, which sat until 1949, four years after the war had ended. Henry Bodden, from Owasso, Oklahoma, visited the site in France and presented these pictures to the Charles Rike Library to add to its collection.

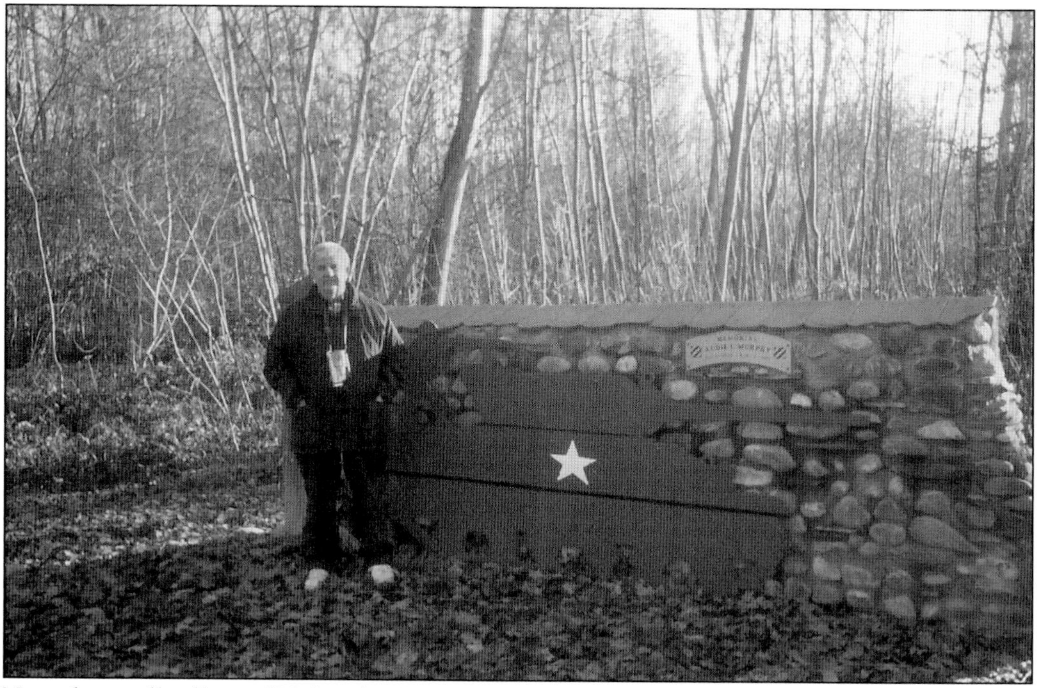

Near the small village of Holtzwihr, France, very close to the German border along the Rhine River and the last stronghold of the Germans in France in World War II, stands a monument that was erected by the townspeople in honor of Audie Murphy for their liberation. The plaque seen at the top reads "Memorial Audie L. Murphy."

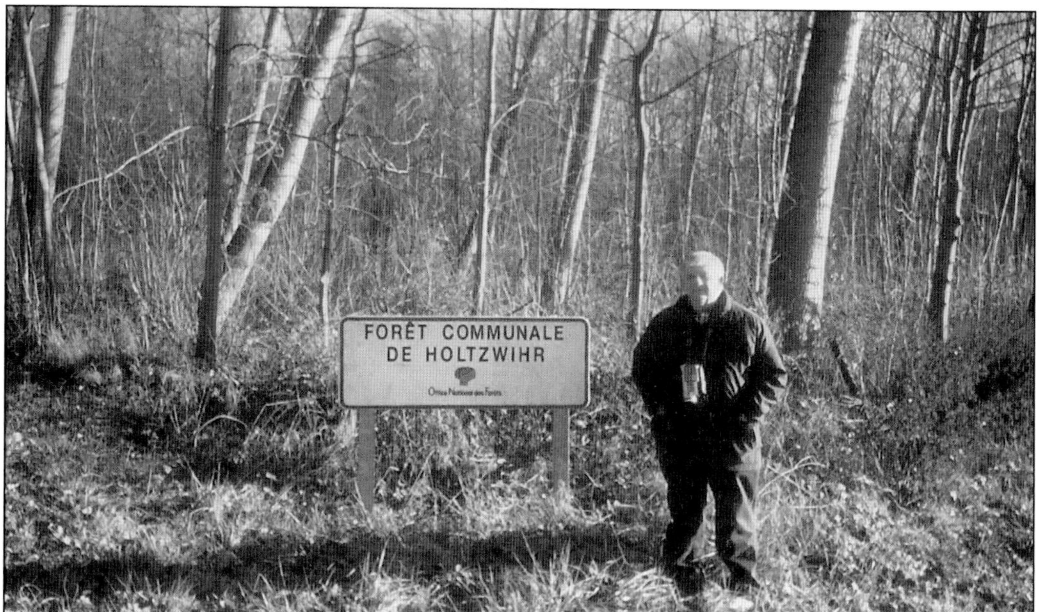

This is the village one mile from where Audie Murphy stood on the burning tank, manning the machine gun. The fact that the monument specially honors Audie Murphy rather than the U.S. Army or the company and soldiers in the area at that time, makes it very apparent as to whom they thank for their freedom.

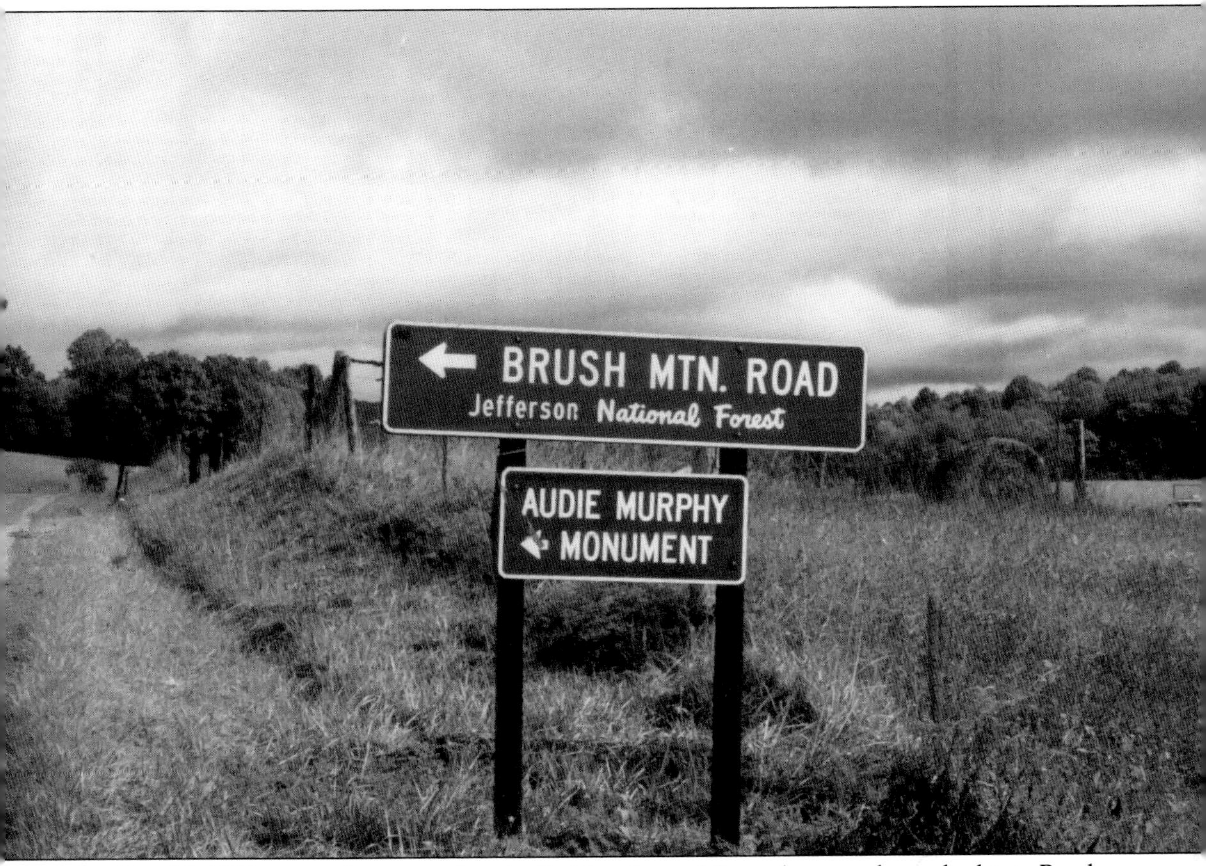

On May 28, 1971, an airplane carrying Audie Murphy and five other people crashed into Brush Mountain, several miles west of Roanoke, Virginia. The airplane was 300 feet from the top of that mountain. All six people aboard were killed. Bad weather had developed, the pilot was not trained in instrument flying, and the mountain was not visible. Audie and the others were on a business trip. Audie was 46 years old. That date, May 28, would have been the 80th birthday of Audie's mother, Josie Murphy, who passed away in 1941. This crash ended the life of the most decorated soldier of World War II. He had fought in nine major campaigns across the European Theater. Audie was credited with killing 240 Germans and wounding and capturing many more. A monument was erected at the crash site by the Veterans of Foreign Wars in 1974.

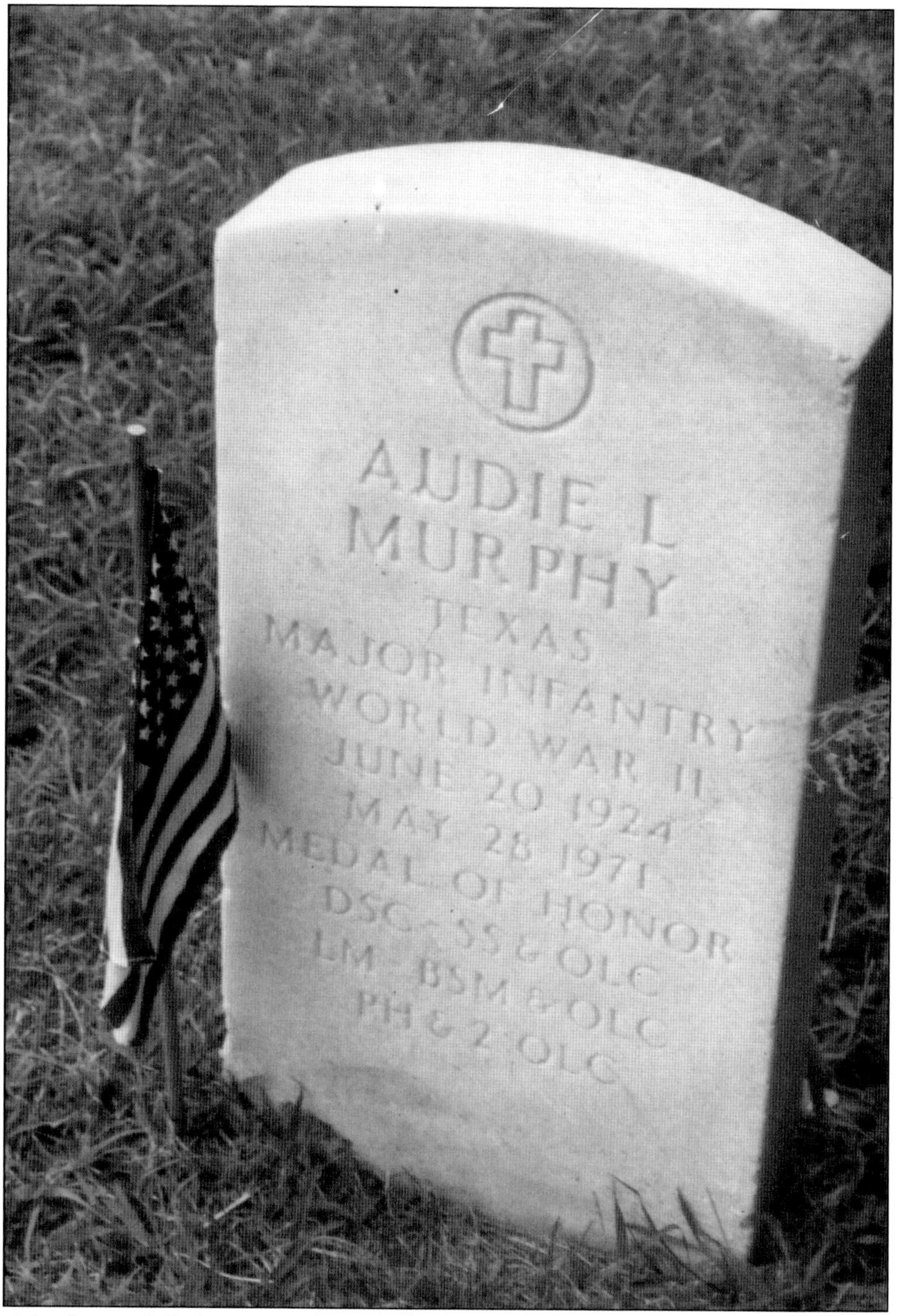

Audie Murphy was killed in an airplane crash near Roanoke, Virginia, leaving his wife, Pamela, and two sons to survive him. On June 7, 1971, this most decorated soldier of World War II was buried in Arlington National Cemetery with full military honors. He lies among all those comrades who fought and fell in so many wars over the years. Audie's grave is the second most visited grave in Arlington National Cemetery, second only to John F. Kennedy's. At the time of his funeral in Washington, a service was also held in Farmersville with five of his brothers and sisters attending.

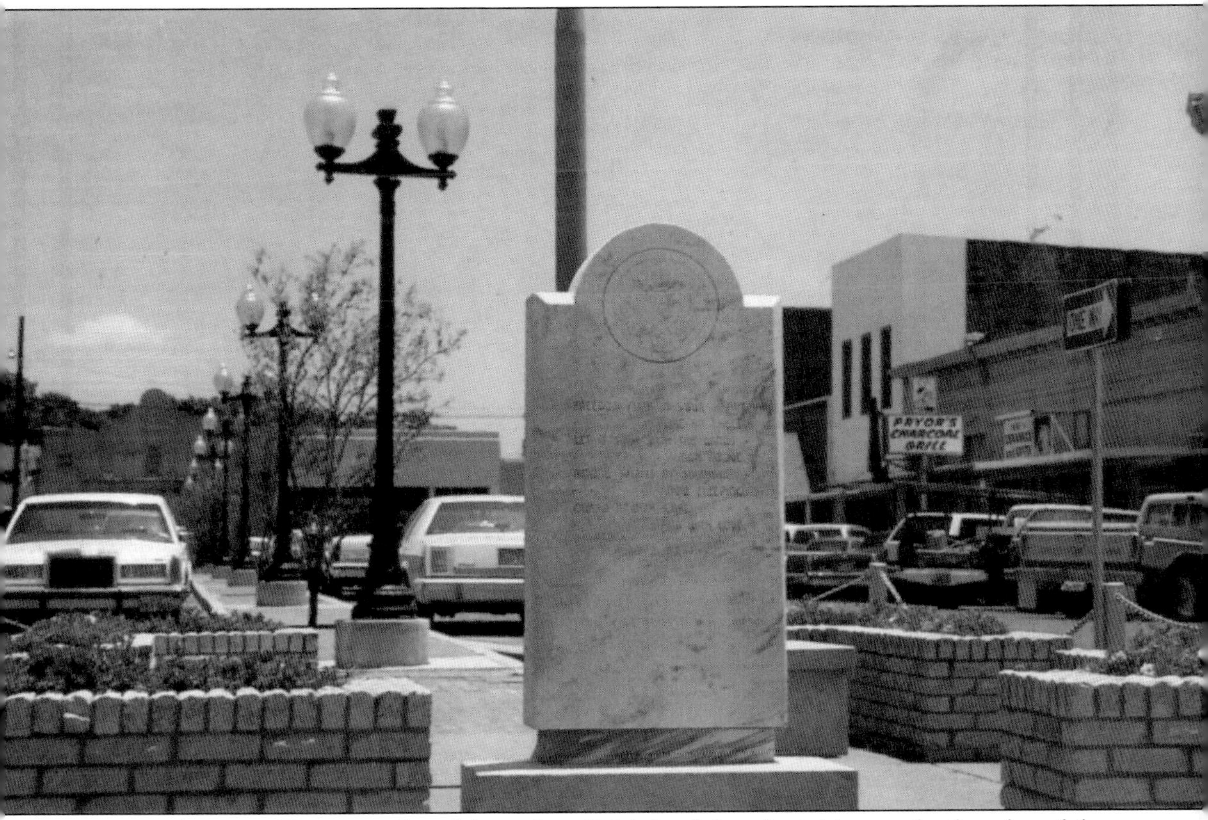

In 1973, the city of Farmersville celebrated its 100th birthday. Activities on the first day of the weeklong celebration were centered around the dedication of the Audie Murphy Memorial, which had been placed in the center of the square. Former U.S. senator Ralph Yarborough of Austin was the dedicating speaker. The memorial was financed by Farmersville businessmen. On one side of the monument is a tribute to Murphy and all other Americans who have served their country in war and peace. The reverse side quotes one of Murphy's poems, "Dusty Old Helmet," written in 1968: "Freedom flies in your heart like an eagle. Let it soar with the wind high above. Among spirits of soldiers now sleeping, guard it with care and with love."

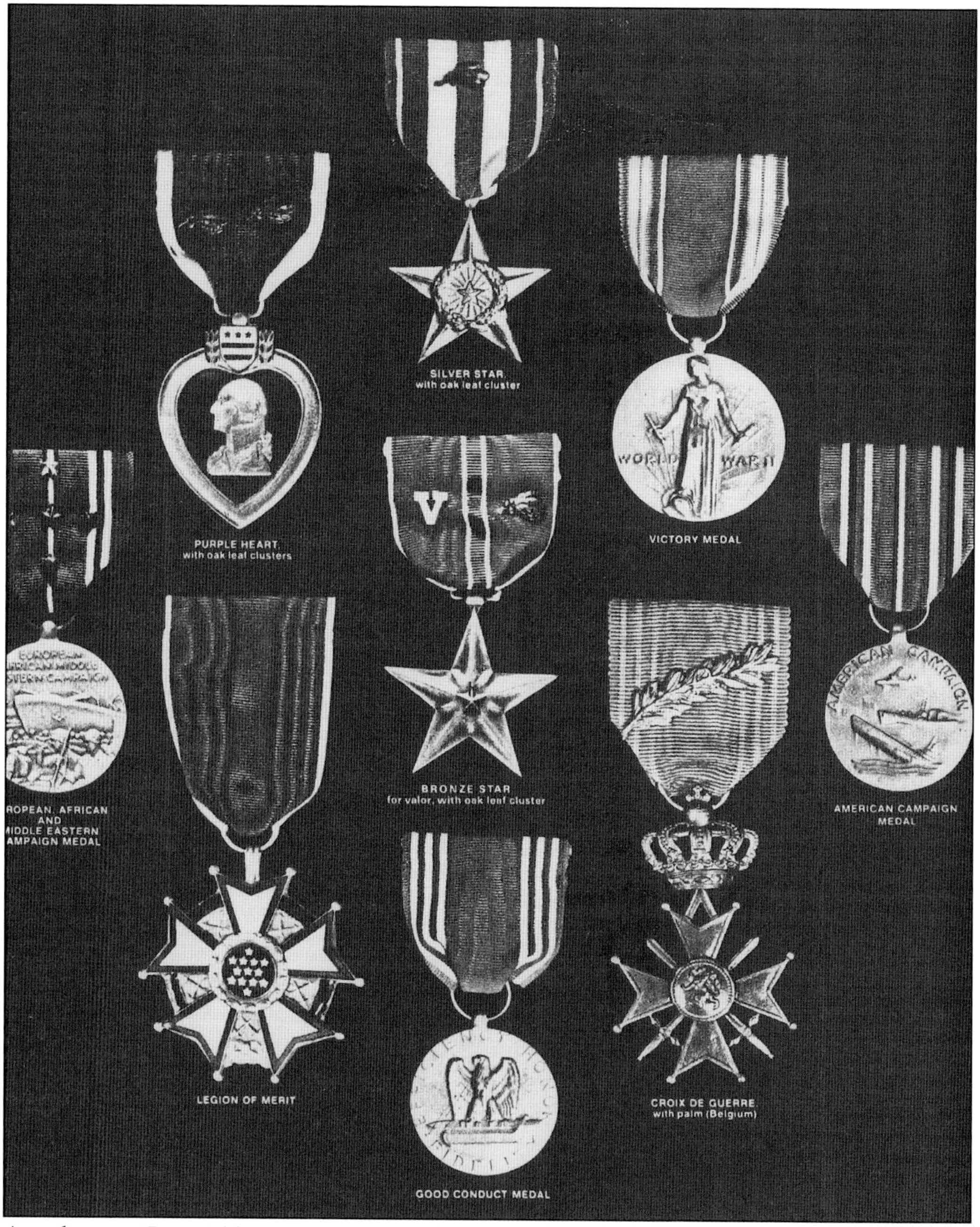

At either age 17 or 18 (there is some dispute), Audie enlisted in the U.S. Army after being denied enlistment in other branches of the armed services, probably due to his small stature and youthful appearance. Audie quickly excelled in military service and was soon promoted to sergeant. Later he earned a battlefield commission to second lieutenant. During the course of the war, Audie earned 33 awards and decorations from the United States and five awards from Belgium and France. He was wounded three times.

Index